THE NATURE AND VALUE OF VAGUENESS IN THE LAW

Lawmaking is – paradigmatically – a type of speech act: people make law by saying things. It is natural to think, therefore, that the content of the law is determined by what lawmakers communicate. However, what they communicate is sometimes vague and, even when it is clear, the content itself is sometimes vague.

This monograph examines the nature and consequences of these two linguistic sources of indeterminacy in the law. The aim is to give plausible answers to three related questions: In virtue of what is the law vague? What might be good about vague law? How should courts resolve cases of vagueness? It argues that vagueness in the law is sometimes a good thing, although its value should not be overestimated. It also proposes a strategy for resolving borderline cases, arguing that textualism and intentionalism – two leading theories of legal interpretation – often complement rather than compete with each other.

Volume 10 in the series Law and Practical Reason

Law and Practical Reason

The intention of this series is that it should encompass monographs and collections of essays that address the fundamental issues in legal philosophy. The foci are conceptual and normative in character, not empirical. Studies addressing the idea of law as a species of practical reason are especially welcome. Recognising that there is no occasion sharply to distinguish analytic and systematic work in the field from historico-critical research, the editors also welcome studies in the history of legal philosophy. Contributions to the series, inevitably crossing disciplinary lines, will be of interest to students and professionals in moral, political, and legal philosophy.

Recent titles in the series

Volume 6: Law and Authority under the Guise of the Good
Veronica Rodriguez-Blanco

Volume 7: Shared Authority
Dimitrios Kyritsis

Volume 8: Private Law and the Value of Choice
Emmanuel Voyiakis

Volume 9: Freedom and Force: Essays on Kant's Legal Philosophy
Edited by Sari Kisilevsky and Martin J Stone

The Nature and Value of Vagueness in the Law

Hrafn Asgeirsson

•HART•
OXFORD • LONDON • NEW YORK • NEW DELHI • SYDNEY

HART PUBLISHING

Bloomsbury Publishing Plc

Kemp House, Chawley Park, Cumnor Hill, Oxford, OX2 9PH, UK

1385 Broadway, New York, NY 10018, USA

HART PUBLISHING, the Hart/Stag logo, BLOOMSBURY and the Diana logo are trademarks of Bloomsbury Publishing Plc

First published in Great Britain 2020

A catalogue record for this book is available from the British Library.

Library of Congress Cataloging-in-Publication data

Names: Hrafn Asgeirsson, 1978- author.

Title: The nature and value of vagueness in the law / Hrafn Asgeirsson.

Description: Oxford ; New York : Hart, 2020. | Series: Law and practical reason; vol 10 | Includes bibliographical references and index.

Identifiers: LCCN 2019053935 (print) | LCCN 2019053936 (ebook) | ISBN 9781849466066 (hardcover) | ISBN 9781509904457 (Epub)

Subjects: LCSH: Law—Interpretation and construction. | Law—Philosophy. | Vagueness (Philosophy)

Classification: LCC K290 .H73 2020 (print) | LCC K290 (ebook) | DDC 340/.1—dc23

LC record available at https://lccn.loc.gov/2019053935

LC ebook record available at https://lccn.loc.gov/2019053936

ISBN: HB: 978-1-84946-606-6
ePDF: 978-1-50990-444-0
ePub: 978-1-50990-445-7

Typeset by Compuscript Ltd, Shannon
Printed and bound in Great Britain

To find out more about our authors and books visit www.hartpublishing.co.uk. Here you will find extracts, author information, details of forthcoming events and the option to sign up for our newsletters.

ACKNOWLEDGEMENTS

This book has benefited from an incredible variety of interactions with a huge number of people – colleagues, friends, and family – each of which I am incredibly grateful for. Much of it is based on a doctoral thesis submitted at the University of Southern California, although the bulk of the material has subsequently been worked into stand-alone publications, often with significant additions. It is presented here in its published version, along with a significant amount of new material as well.

It is hard to overestimate my debt to Andrei Marmor, whose work and patient advice has helped improve all aspects of the book. I considered myself particularly lucky to be able to work with him during my time at USC and I'm grateful for continued conversations and advice over the past several years.

Gideon Yaffe also provided me with excellent advice on countless occasions – many of the ideas in this book are there in large part because of him. I would also like to thank Scott Altman and Gary Watson for their input. Several of their comments have helped me frame the issues in the book better, particularly in chapter seven. As a general matter, my work also owes a lot to Scott Soames and Mark Schroeder.

I would also like to thank the Australian Research Council for their support during my postdoctoral time at Monash University, School of Law, as well as my excellent colleagues during that time – Jeff Goldsworthy, Dale Smith, and Patrick Emerton. Thanks also to the Icelandic Research Fund and the University of Iceland for their support during my subsequent postdoctoral position, and in particular to my colleagues Elmar Unnsteinsson, Finnur Dellsén, and Eiríkur Smári Sigurðarson. I should also thank the University of Oxford Centre for Ethics and Philosophy of Law, along with University College and the late John Gardner, for their support during my time as HLA Hart Visiting Fellow. Last, but certainly not least, I am grateful for my tremendous colleagues at the University of Surrey, School of Law and the Surrey Centre for Law and Philosophy. In addition, I would like to extend specific thanks to Kory DeClark, George Pavlakos, Lawrence Solum, Alex Sarch, Ólafur Páll Jónsson, Timothy Endicott, Brian Bix, Barbara Baum Levenbook, and Nicos Stavropoulos.

Finally, my greatest debt is to my wonderful wife, Anna Thorvaldsdottir. I'd like to thank her, well, for *everything*, and dedicate this book to her.

I am grateful to the editors and publishers of the following prior publications for the permission to incorporate them into the book:

"On the Possibility of Non-Literal Legislative Speech," in A. Capone & F. Poggi (eds.), *Pragmatics and Law: Theoretical and Practical Perspectives* (Dordrecht: Springer, 2017), pp. 67–101

"Can Legal Practice Adjudicate Between Theories of Vagueness?" in R. Poscher and G. Keil (eds.), *Vagueness and Law: Philosophical and Legal Perspectives* (Oxford: Oxford University Press, 2016), pp. 95–126

"Expected Applications, Contextual Enrichment, and Objective Communicative Content: The Linguistic Case for Conception-Textualism," *Legal Theory* 21 (2015): 115–135; © Cambridge University Press 2017

"On the Instrumental Value of Vagueness in the Law," *Ethics* 125:2 (2015): 425–448; © 2015 by the University of Chicago

"Vagueness and Power-Delegation in Law: A Reply to Sorensen," in M. Freeman and F. Smith (eds.), *Current Legal Issues: Law and Language* (Oxford University Press, 2013), pp. 344–355

"Vagueness, Comparative Value, and the "Lawmakers' Challenge","*Archiv für Rechts- & Sozialphilosophie* 98:3 (2012): 299–316

CONTENTS

Introduction

Lawmaking is – paradigmatically – a type of speech act: people make law by saying things. It is natural to think, therefore, that the content of the law is determined by what lawmakers communicate. However, it is sometimes vague what content they communicate, and even when it is clear, the content itself is sometimes vague. As a result, the law is to some extent vague. In this book, I examine the nature and consequences of these two linguistic sources of indeterminacy in the law. The aim is to give plausible answers to – or at least to help address – three related questions: In virtue of what is the law vague? What might be good about vague law? How should courts resolve cases of vagueness?

Many laws not only contain vague expressions, but contain expressions that are likely to generate deep disagreements over how to appropriately apply the relevant norms. These expressions – such as 'neglect', 'reasonable', and 'with all deliberate speed' – are typically associated with multiple attributes that cannot be measured in common units, which entails that for many cases there will be no answer to the question whether the relevant law applies to them. As a result, the content of these laws is to a considerable extent vague.

The second type of vagueness in the law is primarily due to the fact that lawmakers and their audience rarely share much information regarding legislative intent. As a result, interpreters are often not in a position to determine whether or not the legislature intended the relevant law to be construed literally. Consequently, it is sometimes vague whether the content of a law is its literal content or some non-literal pragmatic enrichment of that content.

Legal indeterminacy of these two types, I argue, is sometimes a good thing. First, lawmakers sometimes do better to enact law with vague content, and to let interpreters handle borderline cases if and when they arise, than to try to work out a more determinate alternative. Second, lawmakers sometimes do better to make it vague what the content of a law is than to not legislate at all.

However, we also have at least three good reasons not to overestimate the value of vague law. First, some of the value associated with the use of vague terms in the law is wrongly attributed to vagueness. Second, due to the highly contingent nature of behavioural incentives, we should not overestimate the extent to which vague law incentivises people to take desirable courses of action. Third, because there is reason to doubt that courts generally have any special expertise with respect to underlying purposes of many of the 'affected' areas of law, such as tort and contract, we should not overestimate the extent to which they are able to maximise fidelity to law in deciding borderline cases.

Nevertheless, I argue, courts can often appropriately decide borderline cases by consulting reliable statements about legislative purpose made by lawmakers at key points in the legislative process. In particular, if lawmakers can be expected to possess relative expertise with respect to the relevant domain of conduct or if there is sufficient need to respect the legislative bargains that facilitated the relevant legislation, then judges should – other things being equal – resolve vagueness in the law by deference to such statements of intent.

The Structure of the Book

There is an overarching theme that binds the chapters of the book together, of course, but the aim is not to present a specific argumentative thread running from beginning to end. Instead, the chapters are connected by a particular focus – on vagueness and law, specifically, but also on law and language, more broadly. However, although the book is not intended to provide a complete statement on the topic, I do hope it helps make piecemeal progress on a variety of closely connected issues.

Since most of the arguments in the book presuppose an account on which the legal content of a (valid) statute or constitutional clause directly corresponds to its communicative content, I begin – in chapter one – by presenting the main components of such an account, grounded in claims about the nature of authority and about how individual legal contents interact to produce the overall legal content of a given system. Such an account is of course bound to be controversial, so for those who do not feel inclined to go along when I move from claims about language to claims about legal content, it is perhaps worth pointing out that – as even Greenberg (2011) notes – it is still the case that, on any plausible jurisprudential theory, the meaning of a legislative text will be 'highly relevant to the statute's contribution to the content of the law'.[1]

While chapter one concerns the general relationship between law and language, chapter two narrows the focus down to vagueness, focusing on arguments by Timothy Endicott and Jeremy Waldron. Endicott has argued that vagueness in the law is sometimes valuable because some forms of human conduct simply cannot be regulated by precise norms.[2] In these cases, he thinks, vagueness is valuable in virtue of being a necessary means to valuable legislative ends. I argue that vagueness is actually not a means to the relevant legislative ends. Rather, vague law is a necessary consequence of an even more important feature of the law, which I call *incommensurate multidimensionality*. Value, however, only 'transmits' from ends to means, but not to necessary consequences of those means. This critique

[1] See Greenberg (2011) 219.
[2] Endicott (2011).

also applies to many versions of the popular view – marshalled, for example, by Waldron – that vagueness is valuable because it is necessary for securing valuable flexibility in the law.

In chapter three, I turn to a thoroughly sceptical view regarding the value of vagueness in the law. Roy Sorensen has argued that it is a mistake to think that vagueness has a constructive function in law, such as delegating limited lawmaking power to officials.[3] It merely *appears* to be functional, he says, due to 'a cluster of logical and linguistic errors' about its nature.[4] In response to Sorensen's argument, which threatens to take away what is traditionally thought to be the main reason for thinking that vagueness in the law can be a good thing, I argue that lawmakers sometimes do better to enact vague law – and thus to delegate limited lawmaking power to agencies and courts – than to set simple bright-line rules or to work out complex precise alternatives.

In chapter four, I continue to examine the power-delegating value of vagueness in the law, but my primary concern will be the relationship between vagueness, uncertainty and (desirable) behaviour, focusing on arguments by Endicott, Sorensen and Gillian Hadfield. Endicott argues, for example, that vague law allows the courts to work out the details of the law, which may be preferable in domains where the courts satisfy certain competence conditions, and that vague law can give people incentive to avoid creating risk to others or to contract out of liabilities in cost-effective ways.[5] Although I agree with certain aspects of Endicott's view, I argue that due attention to issues like the highly contingent nature of behavioural incentive and the limits of judicial competence shows that the value of vagueness in the law should not be overestimated. I also address Sorensen's concerns about whether uncertainty about liability in fact gives people a valuable behavioural incentive, since his argument raises important general worries about one of the main grounds on which vagueness has been taken to be valuable to law, especially by scholars influenced by law and economics, including Hadfield (and, to some extent, Endicott).

Chapters two to four concern the value of using vague terms in legislation. We can call this vagueness *of* content. In chapter five, I turn to another – somewhat neglected – form of vagueness: vagueness *about* content. As I aim to show, not only is the content of a legislative utterance often vague, it is often vague what the content of such an utterance is. The starting point for this discussion is the simple observation that in ordinary conversational settings it frequently happens that speakers assert something other than what they literally say. Given the ubiquity of this phenomenon, it makes sense to ask whether it also frequently happens that *legislatures* assert something other than what they literally say.

Andrei Marmor has argued that non-literal legislative speech is rare.[6] According to Marmor, a speaker succeeds in asserting something other than what she literally

[3] Sorensen (2001a).
[4] Sorensen (2001a).
[5] Endicott (2011).
[6] Marmor (2008).

says only if it is obvious that she cannot be intending to assert the literal content of her remark. And that rarely happens in law, he says. I argue that the epistemic constraint on non-literal assertion is often lower than Marmor holds – although its exact 'height' may (like standards of proof) vary between legal domains. I also argue, however, that Marmor's argument can be fruitfully revised: the content of a statutory directive is rarely determinately different from its literal content, due to the fact that legislative contexts generally contain little unequivocal information about legislative intent.

The fact that the conversational background in the legislative speech context generally isn't rich enough to warrant a reinterpretation, however, does not entail that the content of the law is – by default – its literal content. I argue that once we analyse all the relevant pragmatic aspects of legislative utterances, we see that there is plenty of room for indeterminacy about utterance content on the framework I adopt. The basic idea is that in certain cases in which the audience is warranted in withholding belief regarding the speaker's communicative intention, the primary content of the relevant utterance is indeterminate between the literal content of the sentence uttered and some non-literal enrichment thereof. This has significant consequences for the analysis of a number of important but controversial legal cases, which I discuss in some detail.

Given what I say in chapters one and five, in particular, my view may seem to imply a version of textualism. And, as I discuss in chapter six, in one sense it does, at least insofar as textualism is taken to be a theory of legal *content* rather than legal *interpretation* (on the understanding that legal interpretation is the act of developing the law in the face of indeterminate/inconsistent legal content or a particularly problematic result). Textualism, however, is more than just a theory about legal content – it is primarily a normative theory of adjudication of which such a theory is a part. And as I explain, my view differs significantly from full-fledged textualism. Part of the reason is that I think that legal content is often less determinate than textualist rhetoric suggests. Mainly, however, the difference is that I don't think that the standard textualist considerations support their limited view of the judge's role in all cases in which interpretation is called for.

In chapter seven, I conclude my main discussion by arguing that interpreters can use similar strategies to resolve the two types of vagueness that I have discussed: sometimes, the law's background purpose(s) will dictate a decision. However, I also argue that there are significant restrictions on the sort of background rationale that courts can legitimately appeal to, at least insofar as the aim is to maximise fidelity to law. I propose that such appeal is restricted to what I call the *operative rationale* of the law: roughly, justification that lawmakers are willing to offer publicly under sincerity-inducing conditions.

It is one thing, however, to say that borderline cases *can* be settled by reference to legislative purposes and another to say that they *should*, and so we need to consider what normative reasons judges might have to resolve cases of vagueness on the basis of the relevant statute's background justification. I think that there are at least two types of reason for such deference. First, judges can have authority-based reasons to defer to legislative intentions, if the legislature can be expected to possess expertise regarding the relevant domain of conduct. Second, however, judges may also have non-expertise-based reasons to defer to the legislature's intentions in borderline cases. I argue that one of the strongest reasons in favour of resolving borderline cases by reference to legislative rationale is that doing so respects legislative bargaining and thereby helps preserve a fundamental feature of the legislative institution.

Thus, although the book is primarily about specific questions regarding the nature and value of vagueness in the law, the discussion hopefully also sheds significant light on other important issues in jurisprudence. It will emerge – in particular from chapters one, six and seven – that two of the leading theories of legal interpretation in a significant sense often complement – rather than compete with – each other. If what I say in these chapters is correct, a sophisticated version of textualism is the best theory of legal content – the content of the law is determined by what the legislature can reasonably be taken to have said – while a constrained version of intentionalism is often the best theory of legal interpretation in borderline cases – in cases of vagueness, the law should sometimes be precisified in accordance with the justification that lawmakers are willing to offer publicly under sincerity-inducing conditions.

Chapter eight, meant to be read in tandem with chapter one, is perhaps a bit more like an appendix than a chapter, but I have decided to include it here due to the way it connects the specific topic of the main discussion (vagueness) back to the more general topic of law and language. In the chapter, I focus on an argument by Scott Soames for the claim that facts about legal practice can in an important sense adjudicate between rival theories of vagueness.[7] If he is right, that's exciting both from the point of view of philosophy of law and philosophy of language. The argument is also likely to generate considerable optimism about what else we might expect to learn about language by looking at the law.

The purpose of the chapter is to significantly temper any such expectations, by arguing that – for reasons explained in chapter one – we have to give up the one premise of Soames's argument that he seems to take to be uncontroversial: that the legal content of a statute or constitutional clause is *identical* with its communicative content. I argue that due to the need for a fairly complex account of the relationship between communicative content and legal content, we should – as a general matter – be quite cautious about drawing general conclusions about language on the basis of facts about legal practice.

[7] See Soames (2012).

1

Authority, Communication and Legal Content

As I mentioned in the Introduction, the majority of the arguments in this book presuppose an account of legal content on which the legal content of a (valid) statute or constitutional clause directly corresponds to its communicative content. Following Mark Greenberg, let's call any view that embraces such an account a version of the *communicative-content theory of law*.[1] In this chapter, I develop a specific version of this theory – first sketched in Asgeirsson (2016) – grounded in claims about the nature of authority and about how individual legal contents interact to produce the overall legal content of a given system.

Recently, the communicative-content theory has come under serious pressure from several philosophers of law and legal scholars – including Greenberg, Lawrence Solum, and Dale Smith – who point out that legal textbooks are full of examples in which there appears to be some clear difference between the communicative content of a statute or constitutional clause and its legal content; a 'gap', if you will. We can call this the *Gappiness Problem* for the communicative-content theory of law (keeping in mind that the apparent gaps here are gaps in the theory's explanation of legal content and not gaps in the law itself). I argue that the problem raised by these examples gives us good reason to reject certain versions of the communicative-content theory, but hope to show that the account of legal content I provide – the *Pro Tanto view*, as I call it – manages to avoid the problem by allowing us to explain away the apparent gaps in a principled and unified way.

I also hope to show how the Pro Tanto account fits into a wider jurisprudential picture, both by noting its consequences for the individuation of legal obligations, powers, permissions, etc and, more foundationally, by linking it up with a conception of authority on which one of the central functions of law is to help subjects better comply with the reasons that apply to them. Given that, in so doing, I will be moving through several of the most prominent jurisprudential issues of the past century or so (authority, semantics and pragmatics of legal statements, legal content, legal normativity, legislative intention), a full defence of the resulting jurisprudential framework will require a book of its own, but I can at least take a chapter here to provide a robust and fairly comprehensive overview of its main components.

[1] See Greenberg (2011b) 217 ff.

I should emphasise, though, that although I hope to make some modest contributions along the way, the aim in this chapter is not to produce a philosophically newsworthy, wholesale account of the nature and normativity of law, but rather to show, as transparently as possible, the way in which the communicative-content theory is supposed to get its force. What this means, in part, is that many interesting issues, closely connected to what I discuss here, will have to be left for another occasion, or addressed only very briefly and/or at a fairly high level of abstraction. But, hopefully, we will at least have a plausible picture on which it is true – and in some significant sense necessarily so – that the legal content of a statute or constitutional clause directly corresponds to its communicative content.[2]

I. The Communicative-Content Theory of Law and Its (Recent) Critics

Before I go on to discuss the problems for the communicative-content theory raised by Greenberg, Solum, and Smith, I should note that it is not always clear exactly what relation proponents of the theory take to obtain between the two types of content. It might be a metaphysically 'tight' relation like identity or constitution, or it might be a slightly 'looser' relation like grounding or supervenience.[3] What they share, however, is the view that the legal content of a statute or constitutional clause in some relevant sense *directly corresponds* to its communicative content.

It is also not always clear what people mean when they talk about the legal content of a statute or constitutional clause. Sometimes, it seems to refer simply to the legally relevant propositional content of the authoritative utterance in question, which makes sense if the relation between communicative content and legal content is taken to be one of identity or constitution. Legally authoritative utterances, however, do more than simply represent what legal obligations, powers, permissions, etc we have in virtue of the law being what it is; they also create them, which is why we can speak about the 'effect' that the enactment of a statute or constitutional clause has on the law. It seems appropriate, therefore, to identify the legal content of a statute or constitutional clause with the contribution that it makes to our legal obligations, powers, permissions, etc.

[2] As I'm sure will become obvious to some readers, the positive view developed and partially defended here owes a great deal to a constellation of contributions to the general jurisprudence debate made by Joseph Raz and Andrei Marmor, and to work by Scott Shapiro and John Gardner. I should also note that my thinking here has been particularly influenced, in one way or another, by recent work by Marmor, Mitch Berman, David Plunkett, Daniel Wodak, Richard Ekins, Samuele Chilovi and George Pavlakos. In addition, Barbara Baum Levenbook's thoughtful engagement with the ideas presented here has also been important for their development.

[3] Here, I set aside the complication that on some views, constitution *is* identity, and on others, constitution is a type of grounding.

Already, this presents a *prima facie* problem for certain versions of the communicative-content theory. The communicative content of a statute or constitutional clause is – depending on one's view about linguistic content – a set of possible worlds, an abstract information-carrying object (typically, an *n*-tuple of objects and properties, or – more recently – objects and properties bound together by some structure-providing relation), or a representational cognitive act-type. But the legal content of such a provision, I have said, is its contribution to the law – ie a legal obligation, power, permission, etc (or set thereof). Metaphysically, therefore, these two types of content appear to be quite distinct. If that is correct, it cannot be the case that the legal content of such a provision is identical with, or constituted by, its communicative content. Or so the worry goes.

This is an important worry, to be sure. But it is neither novel nor necessarily fatal. The most promising way to respond to this charge of 'category mistake', it seems to me, is to try to parallel replies to a similar objection in metaethics, to the effect that reasons can't be propositions because 'they are the wrong sort of beast'.[4] As many authors have pointed out, there are – *contra* critics' appeal to intuition – several refined ways to make fairly palatable the idea that reasons can be propositions.[5] We might therefore be able to make equally palatable the idea that legal obligations, powers, permissions, etc are propositions, too. For one, it would be rather odd if propositions could constitute one type of normative phenomenon but not another, unless we have some special, yet-to-be-identified reason to believe that reasons are somehow importantly different from obligations, powers, permissions, etc or that specifically legal-normative phenomena are somehow importantly different from 'ordinary' normative phenomena.

We may, of course, not be persuaded by this response, and still be inclined to believe that, whatever they turn out to be, legal-normative phenomena definitely aren't propositions. I will return to this issue further below, but for our more immediate purposes here, we do not need to settle this particular matter, since there are other, more decisive reasons to believe that legal content is not identical with, or constituted by, communicative content. As I argue below, all-in-all, the Gappiness Problem is persuasive against identity-based versions of the communicative-content theory and provides a strong case against constitution-based versions (although a lot depends here on what we take the constitution relation to require; more on this below). This leaves grounding- and supervenience-based views. Since supervenience claims suffer from known explanatory shortcomings, I propose a version of the communicative-content theory on which the fact that the legal content of a statute or constitutional clause directly corresponds to its communicative content is grounded in facts about the nature of authoritative expression and the constitutive rules of legal systems. If successful, the Pro Tanto view about legal content both avoids the category-mistake problem and allows us to provide

[4] Dancy (2000) 115.

[5] See eg Schroeder (2007), Lord (2008) and Morganti and Tanyi (ms); but see also Mantel (2015) for a recent critique of propositional accounts of reasons.

a principled and unified response to the Gappiness Problem, while preserving a robust version of the communicative-content theory.

A. Some Apparent 'Gaps' between Communicative Content and Legal Content

As I have indicated, what recent critics of the communicative-content theory have in common is that they direct our attention to run-of-the-mill examples in which legal practice indicates that there is some clear difference between the communicative content of the relevant legal provisions and their legal content. Insofar as the actual practice of skilled practitioners is good evidence of the relation between legal texts and the content of law, this means trouble for the communicative-content theory.[6]

Greenberg (2011a) points out, among other things, that in the United States, the requirement of *mens rea* is presumed to be part of any rule specifying a criminal offence, even if the language of the provision contains no such requirement. 'It would be a strain', he says, 'to argue that *mens rea* requirements are somehow part of the linguistic content of criminal statutes, whatever their wording and whatever the circumstances of their enactment.'[7] Rather, in Greenberg's view, the common law presumption modifies the legal content of statutes whose language does not contain the relevant requirement, and does so without thereby modifying their communicative content. Thus, if Greenberg is right, there is a gap between the communicative content of such criminal law statutes and their legal content.

At the constitutional level, Solum (2013a; 2013b) has pointed out that the legal content of the First Amendment of the U.S. Constitution appears to be considerably richer than its communicative content, due to the development of associated doctrines of constitutional law. For example, constitutional doctrine surrounding the First Amendment provides the legal landscape with rules concerning expression via billboards and notions such as *prior restraint*, neither of which can be said to be part of the communicative content of the relevant constitutional text – ie that 'Congress shall make no law … abridging the freedom of speech'.[8] Nevertheless, both are typically taken to be part of the legal content of the First Amendment; the relevant doctrines, Solum says, 'provide the "legal content" of the First Amendment freedom of speech'.[9] According to Solum, it is therefore 'clear that [communicative content and legal content] are not identical', since the former 'does not contain the elaborate structure of free-speech doctrine'.[10]

[6] Greenberg (2011a) 72.
[7] ibid, 76.
[8] US Const Am 1.
[9] See Solum (2013b) 20; see also Solum (2013a).
[10] Solum (2013b) 20.

Adding to the examples supplied by Greenberg and Solum, Smith (ms) delivers what is perhaps the most direct blow to identity- and constitution-based versions of the communicative-content theory. First, Smith – elaborating on a point made by Solum (2008) – points out that mistaken precedents seem to change the legal content of the relevant statutes in such a way that there is – necessarily and by definition – a difference between their communicative content and their legal content.[11] He invites us to consider, for example, an appellate decision resulting from a court's mistaken identification of statute's communicative content. 'If the court's mistake is central to its decision', he says, 'that error becomes part of the law', by which he means that the decision modifies the legal content of the statute, without thereby modifying its communicative content.[12] Consequently, a gap has been created between the two types of content. Or so it seems.

Second, Smith argues, some statutes specify that other already enacted statutes should be interpreted in a particular way – perhaps in accordance with their remedial purpose or in accordance with human rights – and thereby seem to change the legal content of the relevant pre-existing statutes without any change in their communicative content. Victoria's Charter of Human Rights and Responsibilities Act, for example, specifies – among other things – that '[s]o far as it is possible to do so consistently with their purpose, all statutory provisions must be interpreted in a way that is compatible with human rights'.[13] In doing so, the Act modifies the contribution that some pre-existing provisions made to the content of the law, Smith argues.[14]

Note that it doesn't seem to make sense to argue that the Act also modified the communicative content of the statutes whose legal content was affected. How could it? As Smith points out, the Act cannot reasonably be taken to affect what the legislators intended to communicate by enacting the pre-existing, now modified, provisions. And the Act certainly does not constitute new evidence of their original communicative intentions. Thus, like mistaken precedents, interpretive provisions that affect pre-existing legal provisions appear to create a gap between communicative content and legal content, which – according to the communicative-content theory – should not exist.

The examples provided by Greenberg, Solum and Smith all put serious pressure on the communicative-content theory of law. To be sure, one could argue that the communicative-content theorist might be able to account for the *mens rea* requirement as contextually implied, since criminal statutes are enacted in a context containing information about firmly established common law doctrines.[15]

[11] See Solum (2008) 7.

[12] Smith (ms) 21.

[13] *Charter of Human Rights and Responsibilities Act 2006* (Vic), s 32(1).

[14] Similar reasoning, I think, applies in the case of the Canadian Federal Interpretation Act, which specifies that '[e]very enactment is deemed remedial, and shall be given such fair, large and liberal construction and interpretation as best ensures the attainment of its objects'. See the Canadian Federal Interpretation Act, RS, c I-23, s 11.

[15] See eg Manning (2003) 2467. See also Ekins and Goldsworthy (2014) 56.

But this requires getting rather – and perhaps unjustifiably – creative with the resources available to the communicative-content theorist in order to get around the problem posed by Greenberg's example. Arguably, for example, a great deal of criminal law is addressed to ordinary citizens, who are by no means conversant with legal conventions, however firmly established. As a result, knowledge of substantive legal doctrines – such as *mens rea* – on behalf of the audience cannot always be assumed, which has significant consequences for this 'contextual enrichment' strategy.[16] Further, even if this could somehow be made to work, it is hard – if not impossible – to see how this approach could be used to tackle the examples provided by Solum and Smith.

In response to Solum's example, one could perhaps argue that it is a mistake to take at face value the apparent intuition of legal practitioners that doctrine surrounding constitutional provisions *modifies* their legal content. Maybe doctrine just *adds* content to constitutional law, supplementary to the legal content contributed by the relevant provision. Supplementation is rather different from modification. Or so the response goes.

On this 'supplemental content' approach, the communicative content of the free speech clause would have to be some kind of general and abstract principle, which doctrine then 'implements' or adds more definite content to, rather than an unrestricted prohibition. Or else we are stuck with the appearance of modification – ie, of constitutional doctrine limiting the unrestricted scope of the free speech clause. This approach, then, requires the legal content added by constitutional doctrine to be *consistent* with the communicative content of the First Amendment.

[16] Consider, eg, the majority's reasoning in *Staples v United States* (Scalia joining) (511 US 600 (1994)). In *Staples*, the question was whether or not Mr Staples had – by possessing an unregistered machine gun – violated the National Firearms Act, 26 USC § 5861(d), which states that 'It shall be unlawful for any person … to receive or possess a firearm which is not registered to him in the National Firearms Registration and Transfer Record.' It was an undisputed fact that Mr Staples *did not know* that the firearm he possessed required registration, due to the fact that the weapon was a semi-automatic model inconspicuously modified to operate as an automatic one.

Now, the Act does not explicitly contain any requirements regarding the epistemic state of the 'possessor', and the district court therefore concluded that the Act *did* cover Staples's situation and he was sentenced to probation and a fine; the court of appeals affirmed. The Supreme Court majority, however, argued that the relevant part of the Act had to be construed 'in light of the background rules of the common law … in which the requirement of some *mens rea* for a crime is firmly embedded' (511 US 600, 605 (1994)). For Justices Thomas and Scalia, this meant that the communicative content of the legislative utterance was something roughly equivalent to the following: it shall be unlawful for any person … to receive or possess a firearm which is not registered to him in the National Firearms Registration and Transfer Record, *unless the person does not know that the object in question belongs to a type of firearm that requires such registration*. In other words, due crucially to the background assumptions shared by the legislature and its intended audience, the actual communicative content of §5861(d) is a *pragmatic enrichment* of its literal content. Or so they argued.

The problem with this line of reasoning, however, is that if ordinary citizens are generally the intended audience of criminal law, then the doctrine of *mens rea* cannot reasonably be taken to form part of the actual common ground and, consequently, there is no linguistic basis for claiming that the communicative content of §5861(d) is a corresponding pragmatic enrichment of its literal content. Thus, if the Act's legal content includes a *mens rea* requirement, as legal practice says it does, then its legal content is different from its communicative content.

I think we find the ingredients for something like the supplemental content approach in Solum's own work on originalism. As he points out, an originalist might say that while the Supreme Court does not have authority to change the legal content of the Constitution, it does – under certain conditions – have authority to adopt further rules of constitutional law, so long as they are consistent with that content.[17] I don't think we are forced, however, to say that these rules become part of the legal content of the First Amendment itself, as Solum's example assumes – it seems possible to hold instead that they constitute additional legal content, contributed by the development of constitutional doctrine. Such content is *associated* with the First Amendment, to be sure, but – on the view under consideration – doctrine does not actually contribute to the legal content of the Amendment itself.

As we will see, there is some kinship between this response and the Pro Tanto view introduced in section II. However, in contrast to the Pro Tanto view, which aspires to offer a unified response to the Gappiness Problem, the scope of the originalist response under consideration is significantly limited. Due to the consistency constraint, for example, the supplemental approach cannot explain away Greenberg's *mens rea* example, since the doctrine is inconsistent with the communicative content of criminal statutes whose language does not contain such a requirement (functioning, as it does, to limit their scope). Nor does it offer a way to handle Smith's examples.

I do not pretend to have examined every reasonable response to the Gappiness Problem, but do think it is resistant enough to give us good reason to reject identity-based versions of the communicative-content theory. Granted, we might – with some creative effort – be able to explain away some of the apparent gaps in one way or another, but no unified or comprehensive strategy seems available to proponents of this version of the theory. The 'contextual enrichment' strategy cannot explain away the apparent gap between the communicative content of the First Amendment and the legal content of free speech doctrine, just as the 'supplemental content' strategy cannot explain away the apparent gap between the communicative content of criminal statutes whose language does not contain a *mens rea* requirement and their legal content. And, more importantly, neither strategy can at all explain away the apparent gaps created by mistaken precedent and interpretive statutes.

The Gappiness Problem also puts very significant pressure on constitution-based versions of the communicative-content theory, but a bit more needs to be said since constitution – not being identity – allows for the constituted entity to have properties not shared by the constituting entity, which opens up the possibility that some such properties explain away the apparent gaps. I will return to this issue below (section III), but first, let me introduce the Pro Tanto account, which highlights nicely – I think – the properties that legal content must have in order to avoid the Gappiness Problem. Once we have a clearer idea of what is needed

[17] See eg Solum (2013b) 22.

in order to explain away the apparent gaps, we will be in a better position to see why the problem also provides a strong case against constitution-based versions of theory.

II. The Pro Tanto View about Legal Content

As I have indicated, the Pro Tanto view about legal content is meant to provide the ingredients for a principled and unified reply to the Gappiness Problem by allowing us to explain away the apparent gaps between the communicative content of the relevant statute or constitutional clause and its legal content. The key is to recognise that legal reasons – like 'ordinary' reasons – can be defeated by other reasons, either by rebutting or undercutting. A reason is subject to rebutting defeat if it is outweighed by another conflicting reason – consider, for example, a scenario in which a person's reason not to damage her new shoes is outweighed by a reason to help someone in need. Undercutting defeat, on the other hand, occurs when a reason is affected by another reason in such a way that its weight is reduced, either partially or completely – such as, perhaps, when the weight of a reason to help is to some extent reduced by the fact that the person is herself responsible for being in trouble.[18]

I should note that the framework that forms the basis of the proposed account is far from novel. Rather, I take it to be a broadly Razian view that relies on an independently attractive framework for explaining the nature of reasons generally, inspired in part by recent work in epistemology, metaethics, and deontic logic.[19]

The Pro Tanto view is intended as a contribution to the debate concerning the appropriate principles of individuation regarding legal content – ie, how legal obligations, powers, permissions, etc are individuated. Broadly following Raz (1972), the idea behind the proposed view is that it is theoretically beneficial to provide what we can call an 'atomistic' account of legal content, an account that elucidates the contribution that individual laws make to people's legal obligations, powers, permissions, etc by 'carving small and manageable units out of the total legal material in a way that will promote our understanding of the law by classifying laws into various types and by showing how these laws interrelate and interact with one another'.[20]

Critics of the communicative-content theory, on the other hand, tend to be sceptical about the value of such accounts and often emphasise what we might call the 'holistic' appearance of the law. Dworkin (1977), for example, plainly says that he pays 'no attention to [the general problem of the individuation of

[18] See Dancy (2004) 42.
[19] See eg Pollock and Cruz (1999), Dancy (2004), Schroeder (2011), Horty (2012) and Bader (2016); see also, eg, Prakken and Sartor (1996).
[20] Raz (1972) 831.

laws]', indicating that what matters is the normative status of people subject to law (ie their obligations, permissions, powers, etc), rather than the way in which their status is 'composed' – much like the significance of a book lies in the information it provides, rather than how the propositions it contains are individuated and how they combine to form the content of the book.[21] In a similar vein, Greenberg (2004) argues that the 'real' problem of legal content is how normative facts make certain aspects of legal practice relevant to people's normative status, rather than how law practices 'determine the content of the law by contributing propositions which then get amalgamated'.[22] 'The content of the law', he says, 'is not determined by any kind of summing procedure, however complicated.'[23] And it is a mistake, he thinks, to assume that there are 'discrete issues of what considerations are relevant to the content of the law and how the relevant considerations combine to determine the content of the law'.[24]

A. The Basic Notions, and 'Mechanics', of the Pro Tanto View

The basic idea of the Pro Tanto view is twofold and fundamentally fairly simple. (For ease of exposition, I will restrict the following explication to obligation-imposing statutes and constitutional clauses.) First, the legal content of an obligation-imposing statute or constitutional clause is neither identical with, constituted by, nor (merely) supervenes on its communicative content (more on constitution, grounding, supervenience in section III.B below); rather, its enactment grounds a defeasible legal reason to take or refrain from a specified course of action (if certain circumstances obtain), a reason that corresponds directly to its communicative content. Second, in much the same way that 'ordinary' *pro tanto* reasons interact with each other to determine what a person ought all-things-considered to do, the legal reasons provided by enactment often interact with other (antecedent or subsequent) legal content to determine the all-things-considered legal obligations that people subject to the relevant system have.

On the Pro Tanto view, then – contrary to what most authors seem to assume, including critics of the communicative-content theory – it is not the case that the considerations appealed to (precedent, doctrine, presumption, interpretive provision, etc) *modify* the content that the enactment of a legal provision contributes to the law (obligations, powers, permissions, etc). Rather, they *interact* with that content in a certain way, by either undercutting or outweighing the reasons provided by it.[25]

[21] Dworkin (1977) 74, 75–76.
[22] Greenberg (2004) 176.
[23] ibid, 177.
[24] ibid, 192.
[25] For now, I leave it open how best to analyse particular cases. Some cases may be better analysed in terms of outweighing, but generally I think it is more promising to analyse the relevant cases in

To fix these ideas, let us contrast, for example, the Pro Tanto account with the view that, unlike excuses and other affirmative defences, decisions on justifying circumstances actually modify the 'affected' rule, by altering the conditions under which people count as having committed an offence.[26] On the 'modification view', the rule has changed and no longer gives subjects a reason to take or refrain from the specified course of action in the circumstances decided upon; the court's decision (that the defendant's actions were justified in the relevant circumstances) has therefore altered the relevant statute's legal content, without affecting its communicative content. In contrast, on the Pro Tanto view the rule still provides the same reasons as before, but some of these reasons are now defeated by the court's decision.

We will get a better sense of the 'mechanics' of the Pro Tanto view when I explain how the view proposes to tackle the Gappiness Problem. As the example above illustrates, however, one of the core ideas behind this account is that a defeated reason is still a reason, which allows us to sensibly say that the (*pro tanto*) legal content of an 'affected' statute or constitutional clause remains intact.

The difference between modification and interaction is, of course, far from intuitive and it might be tempting to think that, say, decisions on justifying circumstances defeat some of the reasons provided by the relevant rule to such an extent that they no longer constitute any reasons at all.[27] In that case, the Pro Tanto view just collapses into a modification view. The usual way to counter this line of reasoning – due to Schroeder (2011) – involves a scenario in which someone's evidential reason is increasingly undermined by an iteration of the defeating condition, but we can illustrate the relevant point with an example that is closer to home.[28]

Let's stick with the criminal case in which a court decides on justifying circumstances and stipulate that the court in question is a trial court. By hypothesis, the decision of the trial court defeats some of the reasons provided by the statute (for subjects to take or refrain from the specified course of action, if certain circumstances obtain) to such an extent that they constitute no reasons at all. The set of reasons affected by the decision is determined by the scope of the justifying circumstances specified by the court. But let's then say that the decision is appealed and that the district court of appeal decides to uphold the trial court's judgment. As a result of the appellate court's decision, it seems that the statute in question now provides even *less* reason for subjects to take or refrain from the relevant

terms of undercutting defeat. It seems clearly odd, for example, to say that Virginia's Racial Integrity Act of 1924 – which was deemed unconstitutional – gave white and non-white citizens a reason not to intermarry, while the constitution gave them a reason *against not* – ie, *for* – intermarrying and that the constitutional reason outweighed the statutory reason. It seems clearly better to say that, in fact, the Equal Protection Clause *undercut* the reason provided by the statute in such a way that, in fact, the Act carried no genuine weight at all (but that – from a purely legal point of view – it *would have*, if it hadn't been for the 14th Amendment).

[26] See eg Fletcher (2000) 812.

[27] See eg Pollock and Cruz (1999) 37, Dancy (2004) 74 and Horty (2012) 228–29.

[28] See Schroeder (2011) 334–35.

course of action, vis-à-vis the specified circumstances. That is, the appellate court's decision adds some measure of practical 'oomph' to the trial court's decision on justifying circumstances, evidenced by the intuition that in deliberating about what to do, it is now appropriate for subjects to place more weight on the fact that any of the justifying circumstances obtain (if they do). This, however, makes sense only if – subsequent to the trial court's decision – the statute still provides reasons whose weight can be (further) reduced by the appellate court's decision, which contradicts the hypothesis.

We can iterate this scenario with increasing levels of judicial authority (for example, state supreme court, federal district court, federal circuit court, and the US Supreme Court). I want to be non-committal about what happens at the highest level, but at least until a decision has been made at that level, the statute in question still provides subjects with *some* reason to take or refrain from the specified action in the justifying circumstances specified by the trial court, although their weight may have been rendered 'inconsequential' already at that level.[29] And that is all we need to get the Pro Tanto view going.

The Pro Tanto view, then, relies crucially on the general idea that – just as with evidential reasons – many cases in which we are inclined to think that a practical reason has been completely defeated are actually cases of partial undercutting defeat. In these cases, the defeated reasons are still reasons, but their weight has been reduced below some threshold of relevance. Getting back to the Gappiness Problem, the strategy is to apply this line of reasoning to any alleged 'modification' of legal rules provided by the enactment of a statute or constitutional clause – unless this modification can reasonably be taken to have come about linguistically, by way of contextual enrichment. What is going on, according to the Pro Tanto view, when the contribution that a statute or constitutional clause makes to the body of law does not seem to correspond directly to its communicative content is that there is some interaction between it and other legally relevant considerations which explains this apparent difference. Thus, despite appearances, there is – on this view – no real gap between the communicative content of the relevant provision and its legal content. It's just that its *all-things-considered* legal 'effect', if you will, depends on the legal content of other legal-normative considerations.[30]

[29] Another way to illustrate this point in the context of practical reasons is to imagine a scenario in which your boss, Al, tells you to φ, but then his boss, Burt, comes along and tells you to ignore Al's orders, only to be followed by Burt's boss, Cecil, who also tells you to ignore Al's orders. Assuming that authority is transitive in this case, it seems that although Burt's orders to ignore Al's orders undercut the reason you had to φ (in virtue of Al's having ordered you to), you have even less reason to φ now that Cecil has also ordered you to ignore Al's orders. If that is correct, then some reason must have remained after Burt's orders to ignore Al's orders, although its weight may have been reduced below some threshold of relevance.

[30] I take the Pro Tanto account to have some distinct advantages over Baude & Sachs's (2017) account of the interaction between statutes and other rules (rules of interpretation). On their view, what I have called the *all-things-considered* content is attributed to the statute via a direct function from statutes and rules of interpretation. But it seems to me that this function is for the most part left a 'black box', in which case it merely models rather than explains – whereas the Pro Tanto account, if successful, explains why there is such a function.

B. How the Pro Tanto View Handles the Gappiness Problem

The Pro Tanto view, then, has a relatively straightforward way to handle the problems for the communicative-content theory of law raised by Greenberg, Solum and Smith. Starting with Greenberg's *mens rea* example, and assuming we are talking about cases in which contextual enrichment is an unreasonable stretch, the Pro Tanto view takes criminal statutes whose language does not contain a *mens rea* requirement to actually give officials a reason to apply those statutes to cases in which a 'guilty mind' is absent; this reason, however, is defeated by common law doctrine. This analysis may seem to raise issues about the distribution of the burden of proof in criminal cases involving the relevant statutes, since the Pro Tanto view might seem to predict that the absence of *mens rea* should be treated as an affirmative defence, which does not reflect legal practice. Issues about the burden of proof, however, do not and – I think – should not depend on the metaphysics of legal rules. It does raise issues, though, regarding what weight we should give to the intuitions of skilled legal practitioners when we evaluate philosophical theories of law. I address this issue further at the end of the present discussion.

Moving on to Solum's First Amendment example, the issue was that doctrine surrounding the First Amendment provides rules concerning prior restraint, expression via billboards, and other freedom-of-speech-related notions that cannot reasonably be said to be part of the communicative content of the constitutional text. This was considered a problem for the communicative-content theory because these rules are typically taken to modify the legal content of the First Amendment. Either the communicative content of the free speech clause is a general and abstract principle, the legal effect of which is made more definite by constitutional doctrine, or – compounding the problem – it is entirely unrestricted in character, but limited in its legal effect by the rules of implementation adopted by the Supreme Court. Either way, constitutional doctrine modifies the legal content of the First Amendment without modifying its communicative content and, hence, the former is neither identical with nor constituted by the latter.

The supplemental content approach, as we recall from the discussion in the previous section, requires the supplemented content to be consistent with the legal content provided by the free speech clause, which in turns requires us to take its communicative content to be a general and abstract principle, at least insofar as the aim is to save the communicative-content theory. (This consistency constraint was also the source of the limited scope of this approach.) On the Pro Tanto view, in contrast, there is no constraint of consistency, and so the communicative content of the First Amendment can readily be taken to be unrestricted, in which case its legal content is unrestricted, too. Absent other considerations, the First Amendment – on this view – gives officials a reason not to make *any* law abridging the freedom of speech, including, for example, law restricting expression via billboards, and to declare unconstitutional any law that does so.

The 'normative landscape' may change, however, once other relevant considerations are introduced. Consider, for example, the case of *Metromedia, Inc. v City of San Diego*, in which the Supreme Court recognised that 'at times, First Amendment values must yield to other societal interests' and ruled that a San Diego ordinance substantially limiting the erection of billboards in the interest of traffic safety (and city appearance) was not wholly unconstitutional.[31] Once issued, the Court's ruling – on the Pro Tanto view – defeats some of the reasons that officials, in virtue of the First Amendment, previously had. What explains the appearance of restricted legal content in the case of the First Amendment – ie its *all-things-considered* legal 'effect' – is the interaction between reasons provided by the Constitution and reasons provided by constitutional doctrine. But the latter does not *modify* the legal content itself; a defeated reason is still a reason.

The Pro Tanto account offers a similar solution to the two problems raised by Smith. The first issue was that mistaken precedents seem to change the legal content of the relevant statutes in such a way that there is – necessarily and by definition – a difference between their communicative content and their legal content. On the Pro Tanto view, however, such precedents do not modify their content. An appellate decision, for example, may result from a court's mistaken identification of a statute's communicative content and the mistake may indeed become part of the law, broadly speaking, but – *contra* Smith – the error does not become part of the statute itself. Accordingly, there is no gap between communicative content and (*pro tanto*) legal content, although there is, of course, a gap between communicative content and *all-things-considered* legal effect. This gap, however, is explained by the interaction between reasons provided by the relevant provision and the reasons provided by the court's ruling.

The second issue raised by Smith was that some statutes specify that other already enacted statutes should be interpreted in a particular way and thereby seem to be able to change the legal content of the relevant pre-existing statutes without changing their communicative content (which remains fixed). On the Pro Tanto view, however, provisions like Victoria's Charter of Human Rights and Responsibilities Act do not actually modify the legal content of already enacted statutes whose pre-2006 legal contents were not fully consistent with human rights. Rather, their legal content remains the same, but some of the reasons they give rise to are defeated by reasons provided by the Act. The *all-things-considered* legal 'effect' of those statutes, then, is different post-2006, but there is no gap between their communicative content and their (*pro tanto*) legal content.

It is important to (re)emphasise that the Pro Tanto view distinguishes between the legal content of a particular statute or constitutional clause – ie the legal obligations, permissions, powers, etc that they give rise to – and the legal content of the law as a whole – ie the total set of legal obligations, permissions, powers, etc in a particular jurisdiction. Because the content that a particular statute or

[31] *Metromedia, Inc v City of San Diego*, 453 US 490 (1981).

constitutional clause contributes to the (body of) law is *pro tanto*, it may look, first, as if the content of many individual enactments differs from their communicative content and, second, as if the content of the law as a whole is not just the set of legal obligations, permissions, powers, etc contributed by individual legal norms. This apparent difference, however, is explained (away) by the interaction between *pro tanto* legal content contributed by individual enactments and other legally relevant considerations – precedent, doctrine, presumption, interpretive provision, etc. In this way, the Pro Tanto view purports to explain the 'holistic' appearance of law, without giving up what is often called *atomism*: the thesis that 'individual legal norms are explanatorily prior to the content of the law as a whole'.[32]

This, then, is how the Pro Tanto view about legal content proposes to tackle the Gappiness Problem. Generally speaking, the problem comes from the fact that the intuitions of skilled legal practitioners tell us that it is not uncommon for there to be some kind of gap between the communicative content of a statute or constitutional clause and its legal content, the most manifest of which are perhaps the gaps that seem to be created by subsequent modification of legal content. On the assumption that these intuitions are reliable indicators of the relationship between the two types of content, this gives us the ingredients for the following general argument against the communicative-content theory:

> P.1 If – either necessarily or actually – the legal content of a (valid) statute or constitutional clause directly corresponds to its communicative content (via identity, constitution, grounding, or supervenience), then there cannot be a change in the legal content of a (valid) statute or constitutional clause without a change in its communicative content.
>
> P.2 There can be a change in the legal content of a (valid) statute or constitutional clause without a change in its communicative content.
>
> C. It is not the case – either necessarily or actually – that the legal content of a (valid) statute or constitutional directly corresponds to its communicative content.

The conclusion, of course, is that the communicative-content theory of law is false, in whatever version.

The Pro Tanto view allows us to resist P2 by holding that legal content provides (or consists in) *pro tanto* reasons for action, subject to possible defeat by other legal considerations, either by undercutting or outweighing. I say 'resist', because in order to demonstrate the falsity of P2, we will – depending on the modality involved – have to positively establish the impossibility of a change in the legal content of a statute or constitutional clause without a change in its communicative content, either *tout court* or within the set of possible worlds 'like ours'. Both are tall orders, each with their own challenges. However, what the Pro Tanto view does manage to show is that none of the problems described in section I suffices to

[32] For a discussion, see Greenberg (2004) 49 ff.

establish P2. In section III, I hope to put further pressure on P2, by showing how the Pro Tanto view links up fairly naturally with certain familiar claims about the foundation of authority.

Before moving on, though, I should acknowledge that the Pro Tanto view does require that we give up the claim that the actual practice of skilled practitioners is good evidence of the relation between the communicative content of an individual statute or constitutional clause and its legal content, which is arguably a significant cost. However, it does not require us to hold that the intuitions of skilled legal practitioners are wholly unreliable or irrelevant. Just as competent speakers of language have reliable intuitions about the content communicated via an utterance without having reliable intuitions about the exact semantic content of the words used and the details of how semantic content is affected by context to produce the content communicated,[33] skilled legal practitioners may well have reliable intuitions about the *all-things-considered* legal-normative 'status' of persons (ie their *all-things-considered* legal obligations, powers, permissions, etc) without having reliable intuitions about the exact normative content of the relevant legal considerations and the details of how that content interacts to produce that status. As a result, I do not think it counts against the Pro Tanto account that it does not respect the intuition of skilled legal practitioners that the legal content of the relevant provision gets modified in the cases discussed.

III. Authority, Communication and Legal Content

Having introduced the Pro Tanto view, it is time – as promised – to connect the view to a theory of authority and a principled account of how legal content is individuated. As a matter of general jurisprudence, the most fundamental claim on which the view relies is that it is among the essential functions of law to help subjects better comply with the reasons that apply to them and that the means by which law does so is by expressing views about how its subject ought to behave.[34] This mediation between subjects and reasons, of course, is the backbone of Raz's (1986) service conception of authority.[35] In what follows, I adopt a great deal of the service conception, but I do not want to commit myself to the claim that this is law's only essential function. If I'm right in what I say, the more modest claim is all I need to motivate the link between authority and the Pro Tanto view.

As a starting point, Raz invites us to consider the fact that, necessarily, the law claims legitimate authority, and that the normal way to justify authority is to claim that accepting the authority's directives as binding gives one a better shot at

[33] See eg Bach (2002) 29–32), Neale (2005) 183–84 and Soames (2008) 460–62.

[34] This claim of course itself presupposes realism about reasons, but the framework described here may well work on an anti-realist view, too.

[35] See Raz (1986) 53.

doing the right thing (relative not just to a one-off instance but to a domain of action).[36] On the assumption that it is possible to justify legal authority this way, the law must be of a certain kind, Raz says: it must be the kind of thing the directives of which, first, are (or are presented as being) 'someone's view of how its subjects ought to behave' and, second, can be identified 'without relying on reasons … on which the [directives purport] to adjudicate'.[37]

These two features each reflect the mediating role of authority, on Raz's account. Authorities issue directives that reflect a view – typically theirs – on how subjects ought to behave, a view they have come to, if they operate as they should, after considering the reasons that apply to their subjects independently of the involvement of the associated authoritative pronouncement. Raz calls such reasons *dependent reasons*. The authorities' directives, however, are not simply to be added to the balance of reasons, as suggestions or advice would be – rather, they should replace some of the reasons on which they depend. Thus, authoritative directives are reasons that preempt dependent reasons and the deliberation on the merit of performing the action prescribed (at least vis-à-vis the relevant dependent reasons).[38]

Raz's classic summary of the service conception consists in the following trio of theses:[39]

> *The dependence thesis*: All authoritative directives should be based, among other factors, on reasons which apply to the subjects of those directives …
>
> *The pre-emption thesis*: The fact that an authority requires performance of an action is a reason for its performance which is not to be added to all other relevant reasons when assessing what to do, but should replace some of them.
>
> *The normal justification thesis*: The normal and primary way to establish that a person should be acknowledged to have authority over another person involves showing that the alleged subject is likely better to comply with reasons which apply to him (other than the alleged authoritative directives) if he accepts the directives of the authority as authoritatively binding and tries to follow them, than if he tries to follow the reasons which apply to him directly.

It is important to add to this that not only are authoritative reasons preemptive, they are also *exclusionary*. Exclusionary reasons are negative second-order reasons, in the sense that they are not simply reasons to act in a certain way, but reasons not to act on reasons to act in a certain way. Thus, authoritative directives are both

[36] In formulating the service conception, Raz uses the term 'directive' in a broad sense, to include 'propositions, norms, rules, standards, principles, doctrines, and the like', rather than to refer only to the content of a directive speech-act; see Raz (1985) 303.

[37] Raz (1985), 303.

[38] Such directives, therefore, are (at least qualified) peremptory reasons. Here, I follow Shapiro (2002), *contra* Raz, in holding that deliberation is properly normative (ie it involves action-guidance) and that pre-emptive reasons and peremptory reasons are normatively equivalent, if not ontologically so.

[39] Raz (1985), 299. Note that I have changed the order of the theses so that the pre-emption thesis occurs before the normal justification thesis.

positive, preemptive first-order reasons (reasons for, say, φ-ing, which replace the positive dependent reasons) and negative second-order reasons (reasons, then, not to act on certain reasons not to φ). Raz calls such composite reasons *protected reasons*.[40]

Of special interest to us here is the service conception's corollary thesis that if it is among the essential functions of law to help subjects better comply with the reasons that apply to them, then – assuming that law is authoritative, rather than, for example, manipulative or educative – the law must be the kind of thing the directives of which are, or are presented as being, someone's view of how its subjects ought to behave. For the purposes of the Pro Tanto account, this thesis captures much of what I am after, but although I generally embrace Raz's conception of legitimate authority and its application to the legal domain, I'd like to move through some of the steps in a slightly different way, just to be able to make it transparent enough how I view the Pro Tanto account's relation to the service conception.

It is worth noting, first, that on the service conception, it is possible for A to have authority over B without A expressing a view of how B ought to behave. Such expression is needed only in order for A to *serve* B as an authority. And even so, A can express a view of how B ought to behave in many ways – some of them linguistic, some not. We probably all know the evil eye, for example – or an open palm pointed towards a dinner-ready table.[41] Heck, A could even telepathically express a view about how B ought to behave, to put an example from Alexander (2010) to my own use;[42] so long as B accepts the telepathed content as binding, A can serve her mediating role. For my purposes here, it is therefore useful to slightly rephrase the above corollary, to make it fully clear that linguistic communication is not part of the story yet (and to highlight that I don't want to insist here on analysing the relevant expression as a directive speech act, although this is indeed the analysis I favour[43]): if it is among the essential functions of law to help subjects better comply with the reasons that apply to them (via its role as an authority), then law can serve this function only if it is capable of expressing a view about how its subjects ought to behave.

A. Legally Authoritative Expression and the Semantics of Legal Statements

Now, although – on the account proposed here – law's expression is (in a sense) a given, the same of course does not apply to which forms of expression count,

[40] See Raz (1979/2002), 17–18.

[41] Note that the views in question do not have to be presented as authoritative in order to serve their role – it is enough that the 'recipient' treat the expressed view as binding.

[42] See Alexander (2010), 142 ff.

[43] Note that an authority can serve its function even if it never issues a directive – so long as its subject treat the authorities expression as a directive, the normal justification thesis is satisfied.

and whose. This is contingently determined by law itself, which is to say that the rules of recognition at the foundation of any given legal system determine, among other things, who is authorised to express views about how the law's subjects ought to behave, and what form such expression must take. In other words, the constitutive rules of the relevant system determine what counts as the *law's* expression.

Typically, of course, the law expresses views about how its subjects ought to behave in a variety of ways – most prominently via legislation and judge-made law (coupled, in some systems, with administrative agency lawmaking). And some judge-made law happens not via precedent but via custom; the law need not express itself view via a single expressive act – the view in question may emerge gradually over time, in virtue of any number of relevant acts. (Generally, I take judges to make law – as a matter of fact – even in strict civil law systems, although the process through which their decisions make law is perhaps significantly more 'recalcitrant' than in common law systems.)

I will return to the crucial issue of which forms of expression count, and whose, but for the time being what matters is that irrespective of particular modes of expression, in expressing a view about how its subjects ought to behave, the law presents a perspective from which its subjects genuinely have the specified obligations, powers, permissions, etc.

It may seem natural to take this to have specific implications for the semantic analysis of legal statements – most notably, perhaps, that it implies that when we use 'ought' in legal statements it means the same as it does when we use it in moral statements, ie that the meaning of the legal 'ought' is in some relevant sense 'moralised'. This, indeed, is Raz's view – when speakers utter legal statements in what he calls a *detached* fashion, the meaning of the statement is that, from the perspective of the law, the subject in question has a moral obligation, power, permission, etc.

Shapiro (2006) has further argued that, using Raz's analysis, we can make good sense of what we can call 'pure' legal reasons. He points out that on one reading, the modifier 'legal' functions as an adjective, on the other, as a qualifier. On the adjectival reading, a legal reason to φ is a genuine moral reason to φ, the existence of which depends on the operations of legal institutions (suitably understood). A genuine reason here is just a fact or consideration that in fact counts in favour of some action. On the qualified reading, however, one has a legal reason to φ – roughly – just in case, from the perspective of the law, one has a genuine moral reason to φ (at least partly in virtue of the law having directed one to φ).

While I think the moralised perspectival analysis does captures an important truth about (the pragmatics of) authoritative expression, I do not think it furnishes the semantics of legal statements. As Wodak (2018) points out, as a proposal about the semantics of such statements, not only does it run up against what – for good reason – has become the orthodox view in linguistics about the meaning of 'ought' and other modal expressions (due largely to Angelika Kratzer's influential David

Lewis-inspired work[44]), it also suffers from certain intractable problems related to the 'stacking' of modifiers, ie sentence constructions where modifiers embed under other modifiers.

Wodak's primary example is how the suggested account fails to provide a principled account of how, intuitively, 'legal' stacks with 'moral', as for example in the sentence 'A has a legal moral reason to φ'.[45] First, as Wodak points out, the stacking of the modifiers should clarify 'what the legal point of view is about', in a way that is analogous to effects of stacking 'Kantian' and 'moral' in, say, the sentence 'A has a Kantian obligation to φ'. But while such a clarification comes intuitively in the latter case, the same does not go for the former; the sentence seems linguistically anomalous, as it's called. Another way to highlight the issue here might be to say that whereas moving between the sentences 'From the perspective of Kantian theory, A has a moral reason to φ' and 'A has a Kantian reason to φ' is intuitive, the same does not go for 'From the perspective of the law, A has moral reason to φ' and 'A has a legal reason to φ', which spells trouble for the moralised perspectival analysis.

Proponents of the moralised analysis might respond by claiming that stacking modifiers this way for some reason forces an adjectival – rather than a perspectival – interpretation, ie an interpretation on which 'legal' marks the source of the moral reason. But, in addition to absence of a principled explanation for this, we also seem forced, then, to conclude that the following sentence is semantically (and thus necessarily) inconsistent: 'A has a legal moral reason to φ but does not have a moral reason to φ'. A proponent of the perspectival account, however, should presumably want to be able to interpret this perspectivally, and to yield a truth in some circumstances. It seems, then, that the moralised view needs to posit some very convoluted, ad hoc rules governing the use of the modifier 'legal', in particular regarding the relationship both between single and stacked occurrences of it and between 'legal' and 'moral', as types of modifiers.

The Raz/Shapiro view no doubt captures an insight about the use of legal-normative language, but it does not seem to capture its semantics, then. The orthodox view, in contrast, does – I think. As a general account of the semantics of modal expressions, Kratzer's view is motivated both by the attractiveness of a unified account of such expressions (like 'ought', 'must' and 'may') – given that their use exhibits a distinct feeling of invariance, not just in English but across languages – and by worries associated with positing indefinite polysemy (due to the vast variety of uses to which such expressions can be put). On Kratzer's view, the meaning of modal expressions is the same across different uses but specific uses of the term get their different 'flavours' due to the different contexts in which they are used. This contextual variance is complex, yet systematic – in technical parlance, 'ought' has two parameters, which get specified contextually and the

[44] See, in particular, Kratzer (1981) and (1991).
[45] See Wodak (2018) 800 ff.

interaction of which determines the relevant modal 'flavour', and with it determines the truth-conditions of the statement in question.

The truth of claims in which modals occur is doubly relative, then; first, to what is referred to as the expression's *modal base* and, second, to what is referred to as its *ordering source*. Kratzer calls these the expression's *conversational backgrounds*, which come in different kinds. Backgrounds that provide a modal base are what she calls *realistic* – they can be *epistemic* or *circumstantial*, or possibly *empty*. Semi-formally, realistic backgrounds are functions that in w assign sets of worlds that are true in w. Backgrounds that provide an ordering source are *normative*; these can be *deontic*, *stereotypical*, *teleological* or *buletic*. Normative backgrounds impose an ordering on the set assigned by the conversational background fixing the modal base, ie, they are functions that yield an *ideal* represented by the set of propositions A which induces a partial ordering on the set of worlds provided by the modal base.

On this account, necessity (for our purposes, obligation) plays out in the following way, roughly: A proposition p is a necessity iff p is true in all accessible worlds that come closest to the ideal introduced by the ordering source.[46] And possibility (for our purposes, permissibility), in turn, is defined in terms of the absence of necessity (for the negation).[47] Importantly, Kratzer's doubly relative account is also designed to capture graded modality, but we can leave that aside for our purposes here.[48]

Now, applied to legal statements, the modal base will be empty. This just means that *all* possible worlds are accessible from w. The ordering source will be deontic: namely, *what the law provides*. The ordering source, then, orders all possible worlds with respect to how close they come to what the law provides. Semantically, therefore, saying that, legally, S must φ is to say that in all possible worlds that come closest to the ideal introduced by the law, S φs. And saying that, legally, S may φ is to say that it is not the case that in all possible worlds that come closest to the ideal introduced by the law, S does not φ (ie, that in at least one such world, S φs).

On the view proposed here, the orthodox view about the semantics of modal expressions captures the meaning of legal-normative statements, while the Raz/Shapiro analysis captures a crucial part of what grounds the content of the law, ie, of the pragmatics of authoritative expression. On the assumption that grounding involves metaphysical necessitation, it may often be quite unproblematic to use these analyses interchangeably, especially if the relevant determination relation entails supervenience (either generally or coupled with domain-specific claims

[46] Kratzer (2012) 40.

[47] ibid.

[48] I should note that I make what is called the *Limit Assumption* – colloquially, that there is always a unique set of worlds closest to the relevant ideal (and thus the set of possible worlds to be considered has to be *finite*); see Lewis (1973). The Limit Assumption is controversial, but I think it is plausible in the legal domain; in any case, nothing really hangs on it, so it is safe to assume for the sake of (relative) simplicity.

about how the relevant underlying facts ground legal content).[49] As a matter of theorising, however, it pays off to take them to be compatible analyses of different, albeit intimately related, phenomena (rather than competing views about the semantics of legal statements).[50]

B. Law's Expression and the Metaphysics of Legal Content

How does the law's expression, then, create legal content? As I mentioned above, I will have to say something about particular modes of expression in order to properly ground the communicative-content thesis, but for now it will pay off to continue to approach things in a simplified way. What matters for our immediate purposes is just that the law's expression creates an *ideal* (or a constellation thereof), which now applies to its subjects. *Prima facie*, this may sound ontologically innocent, but, as I will try to make as transparent as possible below, I take such ideals to be a part of reality and, further, to be significantly distinct from the speech acts that create them, something akin to a fictional normative entity (although not fiction, per se). The individuation of legal content, therefore, is derivative of the individuation of law's expression, on this account. As a matter of labelling, the general terms 'legal content' and 'the content of the law' refer, on my account, to the set of these artifactual entities, instances of which are 'purely' legal obligations, powers, permissions, etc (or constellations thereof). Hopefully, it will become clear how this is not merely a matter of *stipulative* labelling – these entities definitely earn their label, I think.

It is important to note that the creation here is not causal, but one of metaphysical determination – (purely) legal content *exists in virtue of* the law's expression. And the account of legal content presented here is non-eliminative, since I take legal content to be something 'over and above' its underlying facts, in a sense to be made clearer below. It will be a little harder to tell with confidence whether or not the account is reductive, in part because it depends on what we take reduction to be.

One might of course have doubts either, generally, about the existence of artifacts or, specifically, about the existence of legal content. As a matter of what kind of stuff there is in the world, is there any reason to count legal content among it, rather than just the underlying speech act? The answer here, I think, comes from considering the extent to which the legal content, as an artifact, has any significant properties which the fundamental facts do not. There is a range of relevant properties that suffice to distinguish legal content as 'new stuff', distinct from the

[49] On the relation between supervenience and metaphysical dependence, generally, or grounding, specifically, see eg Jackson (1998) and Chilovi (2018) respectively.

[50] If what I have said is correct, it follows that Coleman's (2007) *moral semantics thesis* contains an important insight, even though it is not strictly correct: '[T]he content of the law can be truthfully *redescribed* as expressing a moral directive or authorization;' p 592.

underlying facts, I believe. Some of these are familiar temporal and modal differences and some are more peculiar to legal content, as such. Here are a few of the most prominent ones (for ease of exposition, I focus here only on obligations).

Unlike its underlying set of facts, a (purely) legal obligation is something which:

- endures beyond the existence of the relevant expression;
- is temporal but not spatial (albeit jurisdictional);
- can be created and repealed (ie made to exist and made not to exist);
- can be had by those subject to it (which is different from having a moral status from the perspective of the law);
- can be violated (or conformed to) by those subject to it.

In addition to giving us good reasons to think that legal content really exists, these (and numerous other) properties should also make us doubt that the relevant determination relation between the underlying speech act and the resulting legal content is that of constitution. Constitution, not being identity, of course allows for ways in which the constituted entity comes apart from its constituting facts, but it is reasonable to take the relation to still require a pretty strict sharing of properties.[51] A statue and the lump of clay constituting it have the same shape, weight, smell, and so forth, for example. I don't think we see such overlap in the case of the law's expression and legal content, in which case we need to appeal to some other, less 'tight' metaphysical relation in explaining the relation between the two sets of facts. Grounding, I think, has the best prospect of doing the relevant explanatory work. It's certainly not anything like the determinable/determinate relation, mereological parthood, functional realisation, type or token identity, etc, all of which are (for our purposes here) comparably tight to constitution – and supervenience, as I have indicated, is not a 'deep' explanatory relation, although it may of course play a role in the overall explanation of the nature of the relevant set of facts.

Now, even if legal content is real and significantly distinct from its underlying facts, nothing said so far excludes the possibility that it is *epiphenomenal* – ie, that it is metaphysically determined but does not itself metaphysically determine anything else (with some trivial exceptions[52]). To me, this is both one of the most vexing questions of general jurisprudence and one of the more significant ones, especially given recent arguments to the effect that even if there is such a thing as 'pure' legal content, there is no reason for us to appeal to it in theorising about law.[53] For any question that matters, the thought goes, we can instead appeal directly to the underlying facts, irrespective of which jurisprudential theory we hold.

[51] For a discussion, see eg Zimmerman (2002).

[52] Any instance of legal content would presumably ground the truth of a corresponding existential generalisation, for example.

[53] See, in particular, Hershovitz (2015) and Waldron (2013). Some put Greenberg (2014) in the same camp, but I think his view is significantly more radical than this.

To get some traction about how we might properly answer this question, we should consider, I think, whether – when related to legal content via grounding – the underlying set of facts (or some subset thereof) has any properties it would otherwise lack.[54] It seems to me that this is indeed the case, at least on the view proposed here. Those who propose to demote the notion of legal content often say that what we should be paying attention to is just the (genuine/real/robust) normative weight of the underlying facts, but it seems to me that, partly, the underlying facts have such weight – and/or have the particular weight that they have – in virtue of the fact that they ground legal content. If that is the case, then not only is legal content real, it is also 'metaphysically efficacious' and explanatorily indispensable.

Another way to frame this argument is to say that under certain conditions, authority becomes institutionalised and with that come criteria of legal validity. Only if expressed in the right way – as determined by the constitutive rules of the institution – does the grounding relation obtain and legal content come into being. Legal obligations, permissions, powers, etc, then, have a particular kind of institutional status, and they do so *essentially/non-derivatively*.[55] This way of putting things may allow us to state the response to the deflationist about legal content even more forcefully. If part of the explanation for why we should pay attention to the underlying facts is that the entities that these facts metaphysically determine have a certain property as a matter of essence, then, surely, those entities – and in particular that property – should have a clear place in our theorising about law. This may not be true of every theory of law, but it certainly seems to apply on the view presented here, which is enough to rebut the claim that – as a general matter – 'pure' legal content is a dispensable ontological category.

That said, what exactly *is* pure legal content, such that it is (supposed to be) real, distinct from its underlying facts, and not epiphenomenal? Fundamentally, of course, the law – when it exists – creates the equivalent of a Kratzer-style ordering source (see section III.A), simply in virtue of being a unified, normative system (partly in virtue of the fact that one of its essential functions is to help subjects better comply with the reasons that apply to them). It is in virtue of the existence of a legal system – as such – that we get an ordering on possible worlds at all. The law, we can say, is in the business of constructing ideals. Specific legal content then determines what the ordering is in fact like. Accordingly, individual contents – ie legal obligations, powers, permissions, etc – are best characterised, I submit, *by the way their creation affects the relevant ordering* (an ordering specific to a particular system/jurisdiction).

As I have indicated above, in proposing the Pro Tanto view as a response to the Gappiness Problem, I think that the interaction that determines the *all-things-considered* contours of the overall legal content of a given system is often fairly

[54] See Silver (ms) for an argument in the context of constitution.

[55] A grounded entity has a property non-derivatively just in case the property is not among the grounding facts. Plausibly, legal validity is not a property of anything in the grounding base.

complex – it is, indeed as Greenberg thinks, certainly nothing like an additive function, however complex. But it is still, *contra* Greenberg, an amalgamation of atomic entities. Focusing again just on obligations, some cases are pretty straightforward, such as when an expression with the content *that (in C) S must* φ changes the ordering of possible worlds so that, now, in all accessible worlds that come closest to the ideal introduced by the ordering source, S φs (whereas before this was not the case). In this case, the obligation to φ is wholly undefeated. In other cases, things are more intricate. Consider again, for example, the case in which common law doctrine 'adds' a *mens rea* requirement to a criminal offence. Here, an expression the content of which is a criminal statute, but the language of which does not contain a *mens rea* requirement, will create an interaction with the *mens rea* doctrine in such a way that, now, in all accessible worlds that come closest to the ideal introduced by the ordering source, no one acts in the specified way with whatever *mens rea* is taken to be relevant. In this case, the obligation contributed by the speech act is partly defeated, but – as a matter of individuation – the obligation itself is still determined by how it *would* affect the ordering, had it not been defeated.[56]

Before moving on, I want to return briefly to some of the properties I said that legal content has, or can have. It may seem entirely mysterious, for example, how people subject to the law can *have*, let alone *violate*, the sort of entity I have described. Perhaps I am making a category mistake of some sort? I don't think I am. To *have* something can mean a variety of things – I can have a headache, a reason, a sister, a cold, etc – but what is common to all these uses of the locution is some relevant sort of relation. In the case of obligations, generally, I think it is plausible to say that they relate agents and action-types in a certain way (or agents and propositions of which action-types are constituents). One *has* an obligation simply when one stands in that relation. And on the account of legal content I have just characterised, people subject to the law certainly stand in a relevant relation to action-types, I think. For one to have a (purely) legal obligation to φ, on this account, is for one to be related to φ-ing in a certain way – namely, to be an individual such that in all accessible worlds that come closest to the ideal provided by the relevant jurisdiction, one φs. Another way to describe this relation – not too convoluted, I hope – is perhaps to say that for one to have a legal obligation is for one to be related to the relevant action-type(s) in virtue of being related to the ordering source, which orders the possible worlds in such a way that in all the best worlds, one instantiates the type.

It is worth pointing out that the account presented here is not, I think, subject to what Greenberg (2004) calls the *rational-relation* constraint, ie that the

[56] We can now restate my diagnosis of the Gappiness Problem in slightly more precise terms. As I indicated above, critics of the communicative-content theory take the Gappiness Problem to be a problem in part because they take the legal content created by an authoritative expression to be determined by the effect it has on the ordering of worlds *all-things-considered*. Whereas I have argued that it is in fact determined by the way it interacts – or does not interact – with already existing legal content to affect this ordering.

underlying facts make intelligible or rationally explain that the legal facts obtain.[57] It seems to me that – *contra* Greenberg – this is a constraint which, if applicable, is applicable not to the relation between pure legal facts and their determinants but that between pure legal facts and robust normative facts. But even if it were applicable to the former, it would in fact be satisfied, I think, both in terms of how legal content is determined by the underlying speech acts and in terms of what makes this the case (the interplay between necessary facts about authority and contingent facts about rules of recognition). To use Greenberg's own example, there is – on the proposed account – indeed a (I should add 'transparent') 'reason that deleting a particular word from a statutory text [has] the impact on the law that it … in fact [has]'.[58]

So far, so good (I hope). It might still be thought, however, that I have made a category mistake. Even if legal obligations can be *modelled* by the orthodox modal semantics, isn't it taking the machinery too far to say that such semantics in some relevant sense determine what they are? Not necessarily, I think – and here the law's similarity to fiction becomes salient. In the case of genuine moral obligations, I do take the semantics to merely model reality, but in the case of the law, as I have said, we are in the business of constructing ideals (ordering sources). While not fiction, as such, the way in which the law creates these ideals is much like fiction, in the sense that 'saying so makes it so'. By expressing a view about how its subjects ought to behave, such as 'In C, S ought to φ,' the law creates an ideal – in C, S φs – which gets added to the existing body of ideals and interacts with it in more or less complicated ways. Since the ideal corresponds directly to the content of the view expressed, we have an explanation for why the legal content of an individual law corresponds directly to the content of the relevant expression, even if – taken as a whole – the content of the law has a rather 'holistic' appearance.

I should acknowledge that, as stated, the Kratzer semantics doesn't by itself capture the way in which the various (pro tanto) legal contents interact to determine the *all-things-considered* way in which they affect the overall ordering. Worse yet, it may seem like the machinery actually makes impossible the scenarios that I'm trying to capture. In the standard semantics, conflicting ideals are typically taken simply to be 'tied' and so, for example, in the *mens rea* scenario, the semantics – unamended – could be taken to yield the verdict that it is *indeterminate* whether someone who did what the criminal statute prohibited but without the *mens rea* (required by the common law doctrine) has violated their legal obligation.

The inability to capture different weights within the ordering source, and their interaction, has long seemed to be one of the stickier problems of the orthodox view.[59] As a response, a number of promising suggestions have recently been made about how best to extend the standard framework to capture this. Some, like

[57] See Greenberg (2004) 163–64.
[58] ibid, 165.
[59] See eg Lassiter (2011) and Finlay (2014).

Goble (2013), propose that we add a weight parameter to the propositions in the ordering source, while others, like Silk (2017), propose instead that we make them dependent on the absence of defeating conditions, while yet others, like Katz et al (2012), propose that we combine ('merge') any relevant ordering sources in a way that represents their priority relations. Of the three, I think the latter two are particularly attractive, especially Silk's, due to its simplicity. I suspect, however, that such extensions may not be necessary, so long as we can appropriately delegate some of the linguistic work to pragmatics. Uttering the sentence 'S must φ' on its own, the content conveyed may of course be – and perhaps even normally so – that given *everything* that the law says, S must φ. As a matter of pragmatics, it is also generally inferable in such situations that the speaker believes (and intends to communicate) – the force of the obligation to be *all-things-considered.* But modal language is flexible and sometimes – in particular when conflicting obligations are present – the content conveyed may be that given *some of* what the law says, S must φ. In such cases, the pragmatic implication is defeated and the appropriate inference regarding the force of the claimed obligation would be that it is *pro tanto.*

The following example illustrates fairly well the mechanics I have in mind. Say that S utters 'You ought to help your friend fix their fence'. Without further context, the warranted inference here is that the speaker believes and intends to communicate that given *all* the relevant considerations regarding the value of friendship, you *all-things-considered* ought to help your friend (pragmatic aspects of the content italicised). However, if S subsequently utters 'But you also ought to help your other friend move to their new flat', this cancels both pragmatic inferences; now, the appropriate inference with respect to both statements is that given *some of* the relevant considerations regarding the value of friendship, you *pro tanto* ought to help your friend fix their fence/move to their new flat. Moreover, no information is conveyed here about the relative weights of the two competing obligations. This may be added explicitly – such as by complementing the two statements by saying 'It's more important to help your friend move, so that's what you ought to do', possibly (and perhaps normally) triggering an inference that the content intended to be conveyed pertains to an *all-things-considered* obligation – or information about relative weights may be part of the conversational background.[60] Of course, in ordinary conversation, a speaker is most likely to utter two conflicting modal statements in contexts in which it is unlikely that a resolution is to be had (either epistemically or metaphysically). In theoretical analyses, however, things are quite different, so we need an account of what licenses the above inference, even if such an argument is unlikely to be made in ordinary settings. The outlined picture does a reasonably good job accommodating both types of scenarios, I submit.

[60] Note that the notion of conversational background I have in mind here is much broader than Kratzer's technical one. Indeed, I *don't* want information about relative weights to enter into the Kratzer-type backgrounds.

This has obviously been a very rough sketch of the approach I prefer. I cannot expand on it here, but should note that what – in large part – motivates this pragmatics-heavy approach is that I think that adding a mechanism for capturing the way in which *pro tanto* norms interact (intra- or intersystematically) to produce the ultimate ranking is simply asking too much of semantics – it seems both unnecessary and to give rise to worries about unrealistic demands in terms of semantic competence (a worry some have already marshalled against the unamended Kratzer semantics[61]). How normatively relevant considerations combine – whether in the case of preferences, expected utility, morality, or law, etc – is a matter of how things are in the world. Such facts of course still play a very significant role in inferring and evaluating the content conveyed by the use of modal language, but not in virtue of actually being represented in the semantic content of modal statements. In any case, for our purposes here, I will make do with the standard semantics, as they are.

As a last matter in this rather extensive sub-section, I'd like to revisit briefly the relationship not between law's expression and legal content, but between the content expressed and the content of the law. Given the extremely close relationship that I take to obtain between the two types of content, it may be natural to wonder whether in effect I'm taking the (propositional) content of law's expression to *constitute* the associated legal content. The Gappiness Problem of course puts significant pressure on constitution-based views of the communicative-content theory, but I should acknowledge that I do not think I have a conclusive argument against them.

We *can* conclusively rule out the identity view, I think, because it doesn't have the resources to explain how legal content interacts so as to explain the apparent gaps. On different grounds, we can also rule out the mere-supervenience view. Supervenience, as I have indicated, is not a deep explanatory relation;[62] the relation is also too coarse-grained for our purposes here, focusing, as it does, on types of facts (or properties), rather than on the structure of the facts themselves, as such. (I do think, though, that *pro tanto* legal content strongly supervenes on propositional content.[63]) This leaves constitution- and grounding-based views, then.

Although I do not pretend to say enough on this occasion to provide anything like a conclusive argument against constitution-based versions of the communicative-content theory, I do think that – given the extensive sharing of properties required by constitutive explanations – the properties needed in order to explain the interaction between *pro tanto* legal content (in order to respond

[61] See eg Finlay (2016).

[62] We might also add that supervenience – although transitive – doesn't allow for levels in the same way as, say, constitution and grounding do; there is no such thing, for example, as mediate versus immediate supervenience.

[63] The *all-things-considered* content of the law, however, does not, since its logic is non-monotonic. For a related discussion, see Chilovi (2018). Since I take this to hold generally for facts that combine 'non-monotonically', I take this point also to apply in the case of metaethics.

to the Gappiness Problem) are probably too distinctive to warrant a constitution claim. While legal content has weight and is able to interact with other legal content in complex ways, propositions not only lack these properties, they seem not even to have any properties that manage to robustly help explain how legal content comes to have them, which makes me sceptical that legal content is constituted by communicative content. For a (crude) illustration of the problem, consider an analogous situation involving material constitution. Say that Statue 1 and Statue 2 'combine' to form Statue 3; the shape of Statue 3 still is what it is in virtue of being constituted by Lump 3 (the product of merging Lump 1 and Lump 2). There is – I submit – no comparable story to be had in the case of a statute's propositional content and its legal content. If that's right, then the difference in properties between the two types of content simply seems too significant for the determination relation to be as 'tight' as constitution requires. Which leaves me with a view on which the legal content of a statute or constitutional clause is *grounded in* – rather than constituted by – its communicative content.

C. The 'Necessity' of the Communicative-content Thesis

For ease of exposition, I have allowed myself to simplify the discussion by abstracting away from particular modes of expression, but the version of the communicative-content theory proposed here specifically concerns statutes and constitutional clauses, so I will have to say something about the nature and role of (direct) linguistic expression and how it fits into the framework I have outlined.

As I have indicated, authority doesn't require linguistic expression, as such. Nor does authoritative expression, by itself, create legal content. However, although the conventional – and thus contingent – rules at the foundation of a legal system cannot change the fact that law is authoritative, they can operate on such expression in at least two fundamental ways. I have put this in terms of the constitutive rules of the system determining 'what counts as law's expression', but there are two distinct – albeit closely related – aspects to this notion. On the one hand, conventional rules make it the case that authoritative expression produces law; on the other hand, they determine what forms of expression count, and whose. In determining what forms of expression count, and whose, modern legal systems generally establish a specific body of officials primarily tasked with creating law and certain procedures by which these officials settle on direct linguistic means of expressing their collective lawmaking choice.

Legislation, thus, on this picture, is (*contra* Bach and Harnish (1979)) fundamentally a speech act of *two* types: it is both an effective and a directive, to borrow terminology from speech act theory.[64] Effectives are conventional and so the

[64] See also Searle (1976) 22. For further discussion, and critique of the kind of view proposed here, see Allott and Shaer (2018).

effective aspect of legislation does not – as such – depend on the communicative intentions associated with the utterance (although it does arguably depend on at least some minimal intention to make law); directives are communicative and thus the directive aspect does depend on such intentions. In relation to the legislation's effective aspect, it is important to (re)emphasise here that although convention determines that linguistic expression (following a specified procedure) counts as the right kind of expression for the purposes of law, that does not mean that the expression itself is determined by convention. That is, legal systems can shape the way in which they institutionalise authoritative expression in a myriad of ways, but they cannot change the directive nature of the relevant speech act. And directive speech acts, as such, do depend on communicative intentions, both in that the speech act succeeds (in some relevant sense) by virtue of intention recognition and – what matters more to us here – in that the content of the utterance is its communicative content. And – on the picture I favour – its communicative content, roughly, is the content that a competent, rational hearer would take the speaker to be intending to communicate in uttering the relevant words.

I'll say more about communicative intention in section III.E below, but we now have the main pillars of the argument for the communicative-content thesis, which we can summarise in the following way (for the sake of brevity, I do not present it as not a non-enthymematic deductive argument):

P1. It is among the essential functions of law to help subjects better comply with the reasons that apply to them and the law does so by expressing views about how its subjects ought to behave.

P2. When the law expresses a view about how its subjects ought to behave, the law creates an abstract normative entity (legal obligation, permission, power, etc, or some constellation thereof) that corresponds directly to the content expressed.

P3. The legal content of the law's expression about how its subjects ought to behave just is the abstract normative entity created by the law's expression.

C1. The legal content of the law's expression corresponds directly to the propositional content expressed.

P4. If C1 and the constitutive rules of a system determine that direct linguistic forms of expression, such as (the enactment of) statutes and/or constitutional clauses, count as law's expression, then the legal content of such expression corresponds directly to the propositional content expressed.

P5. The propositional content expressed by direct linguistic forms of expression is its communicative content (determined by reference to what a competent, rational hearer would take the speaker to be intending to communicate in uttering the relevant words).

C2. If the constitutive rules of a system determine that direct linguistic forms of expression, such as (the enactment of) statutes and/or constitutional clauses, count as law's expression, then the legal content of such expression corresponds directly to its communicative content (determined by reference to what a competent, rational hearer would take the speaker to be intending to communicate in uttering the relevant words).

Given the modal status of P1–P5, we can even take C2 to be a necessary truth, despite the fact that the communicative-content thesis, as stated at the outset of the chapter, is now conditioned on the existence of statutes and constitutional clauses. If what I have said is correct, it is a necessary truth, then, that if the law expresses views about how its subjects ought to behave via direct linguistic communication, then the legal obligations, powers, permissions, etc that those expressions contribute to the relevant body of law correspond directly to the communicative content of the relevant utterances. Accordingly, for those systems in which statutes and/or constitutional clauses count as law's expression, their legal content corresponds directly to their communicative content.

D. A (Worthwhile) Digression on Legal Positivism

Before I conclude with some remarks about communicative intention in the legislative context, I want to digress briefly, in order to address a significant worry related to the view I have outlined. The worry, perhaps raised most forcefully by Plunkett (2019), is that in relying on a foundational premise about the nature of authority, the view cannot really count as positivist.[65] Facts about authority – ie, facts about what it really is – are presumably appropriately classified as robustly normative facts, so if such facts are at the foundation of an account of the way in which legal content is grounded, it seems tempting to conclude that legal content is grounded in robust normative facts. While the issue is downstream from my immediate concerns in this chapter, a slight digression is still in order, I think. I do not have space to address the worry fully here, but I will sketch three promising ways to respond to it, at least as it arises in relation to the framework I have outlined above.

I should begin by noting that although it is for some purposes unproblematic to say – as I have – that law institutionalises authority, a more transparent way to express what I mean would be to say that legal systems institutionalise authoritative speech acts (well, authoritative expressions, more broadly, but for ease of exposition, I will focus here on speech acts). Setting aside wholesale scepticism about

[65] See Plunkett (2019) 118–30. Plunkett raises the worry both in the context of Raz's own theory, specifically, and in the more general context of legal positivist theories relying on claims that are arguably best characterised as robustly normative.

authority, authoritative speech acts have some interesting, non-accidental relation to authority. It is hard to determine exactly what that relation is, but as a starting point we can say that authoritative speech acts in some relevant sense 'track' facts about authority, where such facts are facts with robust normative import and tracking indicates a non-contingent explanatory relation between those facts and the relevant type of speech act. It seems plausible enough to say – again, setting aside wholesale scepticism about authority – that authoritative speech acts are what they are in some relevant sense *because* authority is what it is. Arguably, for example, it is non-accidental both that authoritative speech acts presuppose *standing* and that they involve an intention that the utterance be accepted as a binding reason by the addressee (to do as directed).[66] *That's how authority works*, we might say.

Assuming that facts about authority are robustly normative, is this enough to say that authoritative speech acts – and thereby legal content – metaphysically depend on robust normative facts? It's hard to say, but for our purposes here, an analogy will suffice to show that we seem to have good reason to think that it isn't. Consider belief-forming processes. It is common to claim that such processes are constitutively sensitive to some epistemically significant feature, such as truth, justification, or what have you, yet few would hold that particular beliefs resulting from these processes metaphysically depend on truth, justification, etc. The relationship, while non-accidental, does not seem like outright metaphysical dependence – at least not of the sort we are concerned with here. Analogously, even if authoritative speech acts constitutively track facts about authority, that does not entail that the legal content they (under certain conditions) 'produce' metaphysically depends on robust normative facts, at least not in a way that threatens positivism. The most plausible explanation, I think, is that 'tracking', here, does not amount to grounding.

In case we are not satisfied with this response, however, and think that the relationship between robustly normative facts about authority and facts about authoritative speech acts does amount to grounding, the best way to respond to the worry is to consider the rather complex grounding story involved. On the proposed view, each particular instance of legal content is immediately grounded only in the (directly corresponding) communicative content. This grounding relation, in turn, is grounded in the system's rule(s) of recognition along with the relevant speech act token. The worry, of course, is that the fact that the relevant speech act token is grounded in robust normative facts about authority means that this somehow 'transmits' to the resulting legal content, such that legal content is mediately grounded in robust normative facts. The conventionality/institutionality provided by the rule(s) of recognition, however, explains why this is not the case. In 'producing' legal content, the relevant rules of the system do not operate on the

[66] See eg Bach and Harnish (1979) 47–51.

underlying robust normative facts (assuming for the sake of argument that this is the right way to characterise things) – rather, they operate on the speech acts 'directly', and this is enough to block the potentially problematic inference.

An analogy might be useful here. Let us assume that (in some jurisdictions) *marriage* institutionalises a social-psychological phenomenon (or cluster thereof) which 'tracks' something of robust normative significance – say, committed, caring, and perhaps intimate partnerships. And that, further, this 'tracking' is robust enough for it to be plausible to say that the way we think and behave with respect to such partnerships (ie the social-psychological phenomenon) is partly grounded in their value. Declaring their commitment, for example, is something people in such relationships tend to do (at least in some cultures), and arguably for good reason. Moreover, such declarations, moreover, may be a constitutive part of the conditions for its institutional 'counterpart'), ie, a valid marriage; in England and Wales, for example, exchanging vows is a ceremonial requirement. Does it follow that each particular marriage is partly grounded in the robust normative facts about committed and caring partnerships? I don't think it does, the reason being – as indicated above – that the conventional rules that 'produce' marriages operate directly on the social-psychological phenomenon, that is on the practice of declaring commitment (where applicable), rather than on the robustly normative facts that partly ground them (if they do). A similar story goes for legal content, on the assumption – made here for the sake of argument – that robust normative facts partly ground the nature of authoritative speech acts.

We might still be worried that the above responses don't change the fact that there is clearly *some* significant reliance on robust normative facts. Perhaps such facts do not explain the obtaining of legal content, but they do seem to play some role in explaining its 'shape' – that is, that it directly corresponds to the communicative content of the relevant utterance. So perhaps facts about authority and the foundational conventions of the relevant legal system jointly ground the fact that specific kinds of utterances ground the fact that (the resulting) legal content is grounded in the communicative content of the utterance?

I think that's roughly correct, but still not enough to make trouble for positivism. The key, I think, is to recognise that not every fact that plays a grounding role in relation to some other fact is a ground of that fact. More specifically, I think that the following principle is false: if the fact that A grounds the fact that <the fact that B grounds the fact that <the fact that C grounds the fact that D>>, then the fact that A grounds the fact that D. In the context of facts about authority and the obtaining of legal content, this is indeed the case: facts about the nature of authority, along with the fact that relevant rules of recognition obtain, ground the fact that speech acts of a certain sort ground the fact that their communicative content ground the fact that a corresponding legal norm obtains. Phew! As a result, we do *not* get the implication that facts about the nature of authority ground the fact that a particular legal norm obtains, although they of course play an important role in the overall explanation of why legal norms obtain and, in particular, why they have the content that they do.

I should note that my claim that the above principle is false is not pulled out of thin air – an analogous principle for so-called *structuring causes* fails as well.[67] Consider a twist on the classic Dretske-type example of a thermostat controlling a furnace. The furnace may ignite (effect 1) because something in the thermostat triggered it, say, a switch closing the relevant circuit (triggering cause 1). But the structural conditions that enabled the triggering to happen, and the effect to come about, also had a cause – say, the engineer's hooking things up in the relevant way (structuring cause 1). Both are causes of the furnace igniting. The engineer's actions (structuring cause 1/effect 2), in turn, were triggered by certain stimuli (triggering cause 2), given her mental state. The structural conditions provided by the engineer's mental state, in turn, of course also had a cause (structuring cause 2). And so on. What matters for us here is that the cause of the engineer's mental state (structuring cause 2) is neither a structuring cause nor a triggering cause of the furnace igniting (effect 1).

We might of course posit some additional type of cause to cover such relations, but better, I think, to conclude that it is not a cause of the furnace igniting, while of course acknowledging its causal relevance. We can say that causation 'peters out', in some relevant sense, while causal relevance (arguably) does not.[68] Similarly, in the case of legal content, we can acknowledge the metaphysical relevance of robustly normative facts about authority without having to thereby accept that such facts ground facts about legal content. This response to the grounding worry of course requires the dependency explanation to be complex enough for grounding to peter out 'in time', and it may thus not work for all jurisprudential accounts that rely on claims about authority, but it is in any case a promising strategy for the view presented here, I think.

E. The Problem of Collective Communicative Intention

So far, I have taken for granted the notion of law expressing things by means of linguistic communication. In this final subsection, I want to say a bit about what I take this to involve, and stake out a middle ground between sceptics about legislative intent and those who think we can provide a robust explanation of the way in which the intentions of lawmakers ground communicative content (and thereby legal content).

Sceptics about legislative intent tend to focus either on the metaphysical or the epistemological issues relating to collective intention.[69] Some argue that the very

[67] For the classic account of triggering vs structuring causes, see Dretske (1988) and (1989).

[68] Note that this is different from the (complementary) kind of petering out proposed by Moore (2009).

[69] For a range of well-known sceptical arguments, all discussed by Ekins (2012), see eg Radbruch (1910), Radin (1930), Dworkin (1986), Shepsle (1992) and Waldron (1999). In ch 6, I discuss some related worries, as they arise in debates about textualism.

idea of collective intention is incoherent – to borrow a familiar phrase, the legislature is a 'they', not an 'it'. Others argue that even if small, close-knit groups can have collective attitudes, the same does not hold for legislatures, due in significant part to the adversarial nature of the legislative institutions in modern democratic societies. And yet others argue that even if legislatures could have such attitudes, the actual, messy context of legislation in anything resembling contemporary legal systems would make it impossible for us to reliably ascertain the content of such attitudes. (The latter two points are not always clearly distinguished.)

Much has been written in response to these worries, most of which I will not address here, but I want to highlight – and contrast my own view with – one of the most thorough replies on offer, made recently by Richard Ekins.[70] Ekins argues that despite the messiness of legislative reality, legislators still manage to act in concert so as to produce certain crucial group attitudes, which – importantly – do not reduce to any aggregation of their individual intentions; on his account, the legislature is distinctively an 'it', not a 'they', then. And these attitudes, Ekins seems to think, are generally determinate enough to robustly ground communicative content, evidenced, for example, by his argument that the law contains a myriad of cases in which the legislature manages to communicate something (and thus make law) beyond the literal content of the enacted text.

In (very) simplified terms, Ekins's main move is to argue for a general philosophical account on which individual intentions can 'interlock' in ways that ground group intentions, and to show how that account applies to the legislative context in a way that explains how the legal content produced by the enactment of text corresponds to the legislative act's objective communicative content, ie, the linguistic content that a reasonable member of the relevant audience would, knowing the context and conversational background, associate with the enactment. The key, he argues, is to recognise that individual legislators have (among other things) certain so-called *we-intentions*, individual intentions about a common goal and how to jointly achieve it.[71] In the legislative context, Ekins says, the relevant we-intentions produce (again, among other things) an irreducible, general intention to follow certain established procedures which constitutively determine what counts as more particular joint action (in the service of the common goal, which on Ekins's account is to legislate for the common good). Thus, when a proposal successfully completes the (locally determined) legislative procedure, its enactment counts as an intentional act of the legislature, irrespective of individual legislators' intentions (or lack thereof) on that particular occasion. Individual legislators may or may not contingently have such particular intentions, but vis-à-vis the legislative act itself, that's neither here nor there, Ekins thinks; it's part of the legislature's general intention that legislative procedure is adopted as a way for legislators to jointly evaluate and select a proposal, the content of which is to be understood in

[70] For a condensed statement of the view, see also Ekins and Goldsworthy (2014) 64 ff.
[71] For more detail, see Ekins (2012), in particular chs 3 and 8, and Bratman (1999) chs 5–8.

terms of its potential future promulgation. The content of legislation is thus determined by the linguistic content that a reasonable member of the community at large would, knowing the context and conversational background, associate with the enactment. This, I hope, is a faithful – if woefully brief – description of the main contours of Ekins's view.

On this occasion, I can neither do the issue nor Ekins's laudably detailed arguments justice, but I do need to say something about legislative communicative intention(s) and in the service of doing so I think it is useful to flag some main points of agreement and disagreement with him. First, although I disagree with Ekins about the nature of the function at the root of the explanation for how the enactment of a text contributes to the content of the law via legislative procedure, we seem to agree that the existence and content of law (originating in the legislature) is explained in crucial part by the combination of some necessary function of legislation and certain contingent procedures adopted and used by the legislative body to accomplish that function. On the account I favour, law's function (to help subjects better comply with the reasons that apply to them) entails that, necessarily, lawmaking is an expressive act, while which forms of expression counts, and whose, is a contingent matter, settled by the legislative procedures adopted in each system. However, unlike on Ekins's picture, on my account, the content of the legislature's utterance is not determined by any particular communicative intention, grounded in a standing intention along with specific, unanimously adopted legislative procedures. For reasons duly emphasised by the sceptics, I think that – at least in the actual world – there is insufficient agreement regarding what legislators take themselves to be doing in following legislative procedure to warrant the conclusion that the content of legislative changes in the law, and their promulgation, fully corresponds to the objective communicative content associated with the enactment of the text. That is, in the actual world, I don't think it's true that legislators conceive themselves to be jointly evaluating and voting on a proposal to be understood in terms of its potential future promulgation – at least not to the extent required by Ekins's own framework.

Moreover, even if they did, the type of group intentions at play would not suffice to ground any particular communicative intentions. A legislature's intention that the result of their adopted procedure – the content of which is determined by the content that a rational and competent reader would associate with the proposal – *count as* the content selected and promulgated does not magically create a communicative (group) intention in any particular case. At best, the legislature's general intention is an intention to be treated as having a particular communicative intention on specific occasions, which – granted – may create a *fictional* intention, but it does not suffice to ground any actual intention of that sort. However, as I read him, Ekins is after something more robust – an actual intention irreducibly grounded in the we-intentions of individual legislators (along with legislative procedure). This, I assume, is what – as a general matter – he thinks it takes in order for an utterance to have content.

On the picture I favour, however, the legislature does not need to have any actual communicative intentions. Conventional rules determine that the legislature's expression counts as law's expression and that the legislature is in control of the procedure by which it selects the linguistic items used on particular occasions of expression, but the content of the resulting law is not constitutively determined by any actual intention of the legislature, or of individual legislators; rather, it is determined by the content to which the legislature – by way of rationality – commits itself in selecting and promulgating a particular text via its adopted procedures. And the content to which it thereby commits itself is – as a general linguistic matter – the linguistic content that a reasonable member of the relevant audience would, knowing the context and conversational background, infer that the legislature intended to communicate, in selecting and promulgating that text.[72]

It is worth emphasising that while communicative content – on my account – is in some sense 'objective', I still think that communicative intentions are indispensable. I understand how it may seem that by embracing an objective account of communicative content, one significantly demotes the notion of communicative content – if the norms of rationality, along with any further particular norms present in the relevant context, do most of the work in determining the content of any given utterance, then why do we need to refer to communicative intentions at all? Why not just say that the relevant norms fix the content of the utterance?[73] The answer, I think, is that in doing so we would simply be talking about something other than meanings/communicative content. At least at the level of theory, communication necessarily involves reference to such intentions – that's just how communication works, on my view. We can of course often bypass such reference for practical purposes, but once we do so in a robust, metaphysically committed way, I think we are simply doing something other than 'gauging' meaning. We can of course still talk about interpreting acts and about assigning them significances, but I take that to be an analytically distinct activity.

Since communicative content is still determined – partly, but crucially – by reference to actual communicative intentions, the sceptics' worries will have some significant consequences for how determinate we should take legislative content to be. I will discuss pragmatic indeterminacy in some detail in chapter five, but let me say that due in part to the issues highlighted by the sceptics, and in part to worries about lack of pragmatically relevant information in the legislative context,

[72] I should note that some – arguably, eg, Harnish (2005) – take appeal to normative notions like *commitment* to mean that the relevant speech cannot be categorised as communicative. But while that may be true in the sense that the success conditions in some sense no longer depend on correct uptake, it is still the case that the content of the speech act depends on warranted inference about the speaker's communicative intentions, which – I think – makes it communicative in a sufficiently robust sense (so as to merit the label).

[73] For worries in this vein, see eg Greenberg (2010) and Levenbook (ms).

I think that indeterminacy in legislative communicative content is fairly widespread, even when the enacted text contains no extravagantly vague terms. In particular, *contra* Ekins, I do not think that (determinate) non-literal legislative speech is as widespread as he seems to think. In fact, I think it is relatively rare. That does not mean, however, that I think the law is limited to the literal content of the language used. As I will argue in chapter five, the law is often indeterminate between its literal content and some pragmatic enrichment thereof; and even in those cases in which it seems clear that the legislature intended to communicate something non-literal, it is still often indeterminate what that enriched content is. To some, this no doubt seems like a problematic picture of law, both descriptively and normatively, but I hope to show that the legislative context actually doesn't fare all that much worse than ordinary conversation in either respect. Indeterminacy, as it happens, is fairly widespread in communication generally; what matters more is that we have strategies for managing it.

2

On the Instrumental Value of Vagueness in the Law

It is natural to think that law ought not to be vague. After all, law is supposed to guide conduct, and vague law seems poorly suited to do that. Contrary to this common impression, however, a number of authors have recently argued that vagueness in the law is sometimes a good thing, because it is – in one way or another – a means to achieving certain valuable ends. Timothy Endicott argues, for example, that vagueness in the law is valuable in virtue of being a necessary means to adequately regulating certain forms of conduct, while Jeremy Waldron argues that it is valuable because it is a facilitating – or partial – means to invoking people's capacity for practical deliberation in a special way. On views like these, then, vagueness in the law is – or at least can be – instrumentally valuable.[1]

In this chapter, I want to point out what I take to be a rather common mistake underlying the attribution of instrumental value to vagueness in the law. Although I think that it does in fact have some such value,[2] it seems to me that many authors (including Endicott and Waldron) wrongly associate vagueness with instrumental roles that are really played by a closely related semantic phenomenon – what I call *incommensurate multidimensionality*. Incommensurate multidimensionality entails vagueness, so it is perhaps unsurprising that the former is sometimes mistaken for the latter. Such a mistake, however, has significant consequences when it comes to the proper attribution of instrumental value, because value only 'transmits' from ends to means but not to necessary consequences of those means.

I begin by explaining very briefly what kind of vagueness is supposed to be a valuable feature of law and how incommensurate multidimensionality entails such vagueness. Next, I examine the arguments made by Endicott and Waldron, arguing that their key premises are based on a mistake – incommensurate multidimensionality, rather than vagueness, facilitates the relevant legal ends. I devote most of my discussion to Endicott's argument and then go on to show how my critique carries over to Waldron's. After that, I consider what seems like the most natural general response to my critique: to argue that because using vague terms is a necessary consequence of using multidimensional terms, using the former is actually

[1] Throughout this chapter, 'instrumental value' refers to the value that something has in virtue of its being a means to something good – in this sense, then, not all means have instrumental value.

[2] See chapters 3 and 4, this volume.

a necessary means to using the latter. Given the transitivity of the *is-a-means-to* relation, it would follow that value does in fact transmit from the relevant legislative ends to vagueness. I argue that there is a general reason why this strategy fails: it is not generally true that if something is a necessary consequence of a means to some end, then it is also a means to that end. Finally, I note that – independently of any considerations of means and ends – Standard Deontic Logic (SDL) validates a principle that, given my concession that incommensurate multidimensionality is sometimes a good thing, seems to force on me the conclusion that vagueness is sometimes a good thing, too. I mention in brief a number of ways to avoid this conclusion, in order to acknowledge that – and illustrate how – in making claims about how to reason with value statements, one incurs significant commitments in the logic of value.

I. Incommensurate Multidimensionality, Extravagant Vagueness and Endicott's Argument from Instrumental Necessity

Many natural language expressions are associated with multiple dimensions; consider, for example, the term 'crowd', the proper application of which (in a context) depends on the number of people and the density of the relevant gathering. It is also quite common that two or more of the dimensions of such expressions are *incommensurate* – that is, to use Timothy Endicott's phrase, they correspond to 'attributes that cannot be measured in common units'.[3] There is no non-arbitrary way, for example, to measure how the decrease in the number of people in a gathering can be offset by an increase in its density so that it still counts as a crowd.

According to Endicott, incommensurate multidimensionality entails vagueness. The reason, he says, is that incommensurability across associated dimensions entails partially defined comparatives ('is more/less *F* than'), which in turn entail the absence of a sharp boundary between the relevant predicate's determinate extension and determinate anti-extension (ie, there is no sharp boundary between the *F*s and the non-*F*s).[4] And if there is no such boundary, then the relevant predicate is vague. Further, as the number of incommensurate dimensions increases, the indeterminate cases will start to crowd out the determinate ones, and, eventually,

[3] Endicott (2000) 42. Two attributes can fail to be measurable in a common unit in at least two ways: (i) the attributes may each have a natural numerical ordering, but there is no common unit to which the relevant scales can non-arbitrarily be reduced, and (ii) the attributes may not have any natural numerical ordering.

[4] See ibid, 36 (esp n 6). The basic idea is that if the attributes associated with a term cannot be measured in common units, then for every (actual or possible) *x*, there will be some (actual or possible) *y*, such that it is indeterminate whether *x* is more/less *F* than *y*. If so, then there will be no *x* such that (i) for every *y* that is *F*, *x* is less *F* than, or just as *F* as, *y*, and (ii) for every *z* that is not *F*, *x* is more *F* than *z*.

we get what Endicott calls *extravagant vagueness*, which he primarily associates with normative terms. Paradigmatic examples of extravagantly vague terms in the law include, for example, 'neglect' and 'reasonable', both of which are associated with multiple incommensurate dimensions, and both of which are common in tort, contract, and administrative law (and the latter even in commercial law).[5]

Endicott argues that extravagant vagueness of this kind is instrumentally valuable to law. The primary motivation for this conclusion is the following claim: extravagant vagueness is a necessary means for achieving general regulation of a widely varying range of conduct.[6] In many legislative contexts, he says, precise schemes of regulation are impossible, and so the only means for regulating the relevant forms of human conduct is to issue vague norms. Thus, according to Endicott, lawmakers sometimes have to use extravagantly vague terms, if they wish to regulate. In order, for example, to adequately prevent, and punish, conduct that is especially damaging to children, he says, the law must use terms like 'neglect' and 'abandoned' (or approximate – and usually non-exhaustive – definitions thereof which are themselves extravagantly vague). Assuming – as we certainly can in this case – that it is valuable to prevent such conduct, it follows that extravagant vagueness is an instrumentally valuable feature of law, despite the fact that such vagueness is likely both to produce borderline cases that are practically consequential and to generate serious and deep disputes over the relevant norm's principles of application. Or so Endicott argues.

Let us say that the law adequately regulates undesirable conduct if it prevents an adequate number of instances of it and adequately punishes the instances that do occur. We can then analyse Endicott's argument in the following way:[7]

P1. Adequately regulating conduct that is especially damaging to children is good.

P2. Vagueness in the law is a necessary means to adequately regulating conduct that is especially damaging to children.

P3. Value transmits from ends to means.

C. Vagueness in the law is (sometimes) instrumentally good.

I am prepared to accept the argument as valid, and I certainly do not wish to dispute P1. The principle P3 – which I take to be an axiom in the logic of value – is also pretty solid, so long as we take it to transmit *pro tanto* value: if *x* is all-things-considered good and y is a necessary means to *x*, then *x* is *pro tanto* instrumentally good.[8] What I have to do, then, is to cast doubt on P2: that is, to show that – despite

[5] In addition to it being unsettled how the relevant dimensions of such terms 'interact', with respect to their proper application, it is often significantly unsettled exactly what the relevant dimensions are. Thanks to an editor at *Ethics* for pressing me to address this point.

[6] See Endicott (2011) 28.

[7] Thanks to Olav Gjelsvik for helpful discussion about Endicott's argument.

[8] Thanks to Henry S Richardson and an editor at *Ethics* for helpful comments regarding P3. Note that one could choose to limit the conclusion to vagueness in the law being *pro tanto* good, subject

appearances to the contrary – vagueness is not a necessary means to adequately regulating conduct that is especially damaging to children. My focus will be on the term 'neglect', as it is used in child care law, since this is one of Endicott's favourite examples of vague terms that lawmakers have to use, if they are to properly regulate human affairs.[9]

II. Incommensurate Multidimensionality is Doing the Real Work

According to Endicott, the issue that is immediately relevant to determining the instrumental value of vagueness in the law is that terms like 'neglect' cannot possibly be replaced by precise phrases that are sufficiently similar to these terms in their extension, or by any disjunctions thereof. In general, only terms that have one or more totally ordered dimensions, or that are otherwise significantly correlated with such an attribute, can be so replaced. 'Citizens are required to drive safely', for example, can be replaced with 'Citizens are required to drive at no more than *n* mph' in tandem with a host of other more or less precise rules, because speed is such a weighty factor in safe driving, and the resulting scheme of laws can still be said to have the purpose of preventing automobile-related accidents/injuries/damage. This is similarly true with 'Only mature citizens may vote' and 'Only citizens older than *n* years of age may vote' (even though age is only a significantly correlated attribute, since age is not something in virtue of which one counts as mature).

Vague terms or phrases that are not associated with any attribute that can be quantitatively measured, on the other hand, do not generally admit of replacement by relatively precise alternatives, nor do terms that are associated with a relatively insignificant proportion of such dimensions, since – in most cases – the resulting regulation could not properly be said to be a regulation of the conduct in question (more on this below, in section IV). Arguably, 'neglect' falls in the latter category, since, although time (spent with or away from one's children) and age (of, say, babysitters) are certainly relevant attributes, these dimensions – along with other totally ordered dimensions – do not suffice to make for an adequate replacement. In these cases, vagueness is indeed necessary for the relevant regulatory ends. But that, I hope to show, does not suffice for vagueness to have value, even if the ends in question are valuable.

to possible outweighing, or one could go further and agree with Endicott that its *pro tanto* goodness outweighs whatever *pro tanto* badness it may have, concluding – as Endicott does – that vagueness in the law is (sometimes) good, all things considered. Note also that I leave it open how much value P3 transmits from ends to means. For a valuable discussion of transmission principles for 'ought'/reasons and related problems, see Kolodny (2018).

[9] I should also note that my discussion owes a great deal both to Kolodny (2018) and to Soames (2011) 31–57.

Let me begin by saying that what lawmakers have to do in order to regulate a wide variety of conduct with a general standard is not – in the first instance – to use terms that are vague. Rather, it is to use broad general terms associated with multiple incommensurate dimensions, or perhaps to use approximate (and usually non-exhaustive) definitions thereof which are themselves highly general and multidimensional. (It is important to note that non-exhaustive definitions do not replace their definienda; rather, they are meant to be guidelines for application.) Endicott even indicates as much in at least two places. He claims, for example, that the relevant issue regarding negligence law is the 'sheer, mind-boggling variety of ways in which people can create more or less unreasonable risks to other people' and that the relevant issue regarding child care law is the 'daunting variety of things that a child needs from its parents [which] corresponds to a wide variety of ways in which a parent may more or less neglect a child'.[10]

Now, I think that Endicott is right that extravagantly vague laws generally do not have any relatively precise replacements, since terms tend to be extravagantly vague due to the fact that they have multiple dimensions that cannot be measured in a common metric (and some are bound to be impossible to measure in any reasonable way, at least cardinally). But I think he is wrong in maintaining that this is the issue that is relevant to determining whether vagueness has value in virtue of being a necessary means. The reason, I will argue, is that vagueness is not the semantic feature that helps bring about this 'general regulation of a widely varying range of conduct'.[11] Rather, incommensurate multidimensionality is doing the real work.

To see this, consider the following general features of the relevant lawmaking scenarios, where, again, the law adequately regulates undesirable conduct if it prevents an adequate number of instances of it and adequately punishes the instances that do occur. First, lawmakers need/want to adequately regulate a (possibly open-ended) set of multiple related types of behaviour. Second, there exists a term denoting the relevant set, a highly general term with multiple incommensurate dimensions.[12] Third, it is not possible for lawmakers to compile a list – precise or not – of less general terms, such that (disjunctively) they adequately cover the relevant set, vis-à-vis the relevant legislative purposes.

In Endicott's favoured example, for instance, lawmakers want to prohibit certain forms of conduct in order to prevent certain types of harm to children (and to punish instances that do occur), namely (something like) those types that

[10] Endicott (2011) 24, 25.

[11] ibid, 28.

[12] Note that worries about family resemblances are premature, since it suffices for this characterisation that, for example, 'game' denotes a property that is informative and necessary of all instances of every subtype of game – such as chess, solitaire and golf. It is only in relation to the exact nature of this property that issues about family resemblances come up, since no one would deny that, necessarily, chess, solitaire and golf are all games.

constitute unreasonable failure on behalf of parents to pay attention to the needs that their children have in virtue of their parent–child relationship. And indeed there exists a term that covers the relevant forms of behaviour – namely, 'neglect'. Owing to the nature of such conduct, however, it is not possible for lawmakers to devise a list of less general terms – precise or not – that disjunctively covers an adequate amount of the relevant behaviour (ie, an adequately coextensive list of action-type terms). As Scott Soames notes:

> [O]ne who undertook the task of more precisely delineating either [the class of clear neglect or the class of clear nonneglect] using only more highly-focused language designating specific behavior – about the regularity and content of meals, frequency of trips to doctors, time with parents, age of baby-sitters, and the like – would ... find it stupefying at best, and practically impossible, at worst.[13]

If lawmakers were to try to use any such attempted list, they would likely get things gravely wrong; they would probably end up failing to prevent (and punish) a significant amount of harmful conduct as well as prevent (and punish) a significant amount of non-harmful conduct. That is, any attempt to come up with a list would result in excessively over- and under-inclusive regulation.[14] Lawmakers, then, should not attempt to specify the set of action types intended to be prohibited. Given that they want to adequately prevent (and punish) harm that is especially damaging to children, they should rather use the term 'neglect' or some approximate – and presumably non-exhaustive – high-level definition thereof.[15]

III. The Impossibility of Specification

There are, of course, a variety of ways in which something can be impossible, and so far I haven't said anything about in what sense it is impossible for lawmakers to devise an adequate, more specific, list of terms. Is it metaphysically impossible or epistemically impossible or perhaps simply practically impossible?

It may be tempting to think that the impossibility of compiling an informative list of sub-types of neglect has to do with the context-sensitive nature of evaluation. And presumably it does have something to do with it. However, the immediate issue of unspecifiability has nothing to do with evaluation, as such. To see this, let us say that someone who utters 'The Smiths have been neglectful toward their child' succeeds in communicating the proposition *that the Smiths*

[13] Soames (2011) 40.

[14] The law does have some tools for handling errors like these – such as the necessity defence; more on this in section IV below.

[15] That, for example, is what UK lawmakers did when they drafted the Children and Young Persons Act 1933; Endicott (2011) 24.

have unreasonably failed to pay attention to the needs of their child.[16] We can – at least for practical purposes – separate the evaluative aspect of this (rough, but sufficient) analysis from the descriptive aspect and focus just on the latter (ie, on the proposition *that the Smiths failed to pay attention to the needs of their child*). With respect to unspecifiability, 'neglect' is in an important sense no different from many purely descriptive terms: just as there is a vast variety of ways, for example, in which people can walk to work or use a firearm, so there is a vast variety of ways in which people can, as parents, fail to pay attention to the needs of their children (in part due to the diversity of a child's needs). In general, there is nothing distinctively evaluative about the inability to list exhaustively the ways in which one can realise a given action type, even if the relevant term is properly characterised as evaluative; we could repeat this line of reasoning, for example, with 'cruel', 'lewd', 'unjust' and so forth.

Now, this inability could merely be practical. Perhaps there is a finite number of ways in which parents can fail to pay attention to the needs of their children, but for practical reasons we just can't list them. Or there is a countably infinite number of ways, and so it is impossible to know what a complete list looks like. If so, then it will of course also be impossible to construct one. Or perhaps the number is uncountably infinite, in which case any sort of complete list is impossible (try, for example, to imagine counting possible worlds), let alone knowable or humanly constructible.

To be sure, when it comes to normative terms, there is a further – potentially significant – complication: we are only interested in those instantiations of the relevant types that have the further property of being unjustified (whatever property that turns out to be). If parents, for example, for justifying reasons do not feed their children regular nutritious meals – say, during a widespread famine – then presumably we wouldn't complain that they are being neglectful.[17] So, what we are ultimately after is a list of action types in (types of) circumstances: A1 in C1, A2 in C2, and so on. Each item on this more complicated list, then, is what is correctly said to be less general than 'neglect', even if the relation isn't straightforwardly taxonomic (like it is with 'tiger' and 'mammal').

Thus, even if we had a reasonable list of action types that corresponds to the ways in which parents can fail to pay attention to their children's needs, we would need to revise that list so as to include only unreasonable instantiations of those types. And here, we are faced with a problem similar to the immediate one described above, in that we need a list of exceptions, determined by a theory of right and wrong action. Depending on one's metaethical view, however, such a list

[16] I say 'communicates' because I wish to remain neutral about the 'linguistic location' of the evaluative aspect of such an utterance. That is, nothing turns on if the evaluative aspect is part of the semantics of the term or if it gets attached pragmatically (by way of pragmatic enrichment, implicature, or presupposition).

[17] Or consider the morality-based motivation for allowing battered mothers to seek a defence of duress or of diminished capacity against prosecution for failure to protect.

may be finite, countably infinite, or uncountably infinite. Only if the list of exceptions is finite and practically manageable can we expect an adequate specification of 'neglect'. This is a tall order, and probably not to be expected. As Pekka Väyrynen has pointed out, outside ethics it has not proved promising to provide finite lists of exceptions to *ceteris paribus* generalisations, and there is no a priori reason to think that ethics is special in that respect.[18]

If what I have said in this section and in the section before it is true, then we have good reason to believe that using terms that are associated with multiple incommensurate dimensions is a necessary means for adequately regulating, for example, conduct that is especially damaging to children. This, of course, does not suffice to show decisively that Endicott's P2 is false, since A's being a necessary means to C does not preclude B from also being a necessary means to C, but it does very strongly suggest that vagueness is not what is really doing the work, vis-à-vis the regulation of the relevant forms of conduct. If that is correct, then – at the very least – the support for P2 goes away.

In the next section, I want to tackle an issue that I have left unaddressed so far. I have been taking it pretty much for granted that using a certain set of terms is indeed a necessary means for regulating conduct that is especially damaging to children and that the primary issue is what semantic aspect of those terms is doing the work. But, as I hope to show below, it is not obvious that this is true. In many cases, it is better to regulate conduct with terms or phrases that are associated with relatively few dimensions – and which are therefore relatively precise – than with vague multidimensional terms. The question is why this is not also the case when it comes to regulating conduct that is especially damaging to children. Why exactly are there supposed to be no good proxies for terms like 'neglect', as it is used in child care law?

IV. Are Incommensurate Multidimensionality and – Hence – Vagueness Really Necessary?

Let us suppose, on the basis of what I said in the previous section, that it is in fact – at a minimum – practically impossible to compile a list of action types (in circumstances) that is necessarily coextensive with 'neglect'. It is natural to wonder whether this is any different from other forms of conduct that lawmakers have an interest in regulating. Surely, in many cases, lawmakers do the right thing by trying to replace general terms with something more specific – and thus often better action guiding – even if it results in a specification that is likely to be both over- and under-inclusive. Sometimes, it is simply better to settle for some sort of rough approximation. When it comes to drinking and voting age, for example,

[18] Väyrynen (2009) 91–132, citing, eg, Fodor (1991) 19–34; and Pietroski and Rey (1995) 46, 81–110.

it would make bad sense to formulate the law in terms of maturity. Given the extent to which people would be at the mercy of officials and the cost of evaluating each case, it is better to avoid that mess and make age the legally relevant factor, as was done in the National Minimum Drinking Age Act (23 USC §158 [1984]) and in the Twenty-Sixth Amendment of the US Constitution.

Why shouldn't we do something similar with 'neglect'? Couldn't we, for example, either construct an admittedly under-inclusive but manageable list of relevant action types or find some quantifiable aspect – such as the minimum age of babysitters, minimum number of visits to the doctor per month, minimum number and nutritional value of meals per day, and so on – and rely on available legal tools, such as legal defences, to mitigate any over- and under-inclusiveness? The significance here of settling this issue is that if neither incommensurate multidimensionality nor vagueness is strictly necessary for the relevant lawmaking, then Endicott's P2 is straightforwardly false, and it would be superfluous for me to argue that despite its necessity vagueness does not inherit any value from the relevant ends. In addition, one of the main sources of appeal of Endicott's argument is that it is an argument from instrumental necessity and, accordingly, promises to be significantly stronger than arguments from facilitation.

In the case of neglect, I do not think it is possible to do away with incommensurate multidimensionality/vagueness in the way suggested, and I think we can see why if we attend to the fact that the relational notion of being an adequate proxy has – for our purposes – two relevant dimensions. Let us say that a term t_1 is an adequate proxy for a term t_2 if and only if it is not the case that the product of the number of errors and their disvalue resulting from the use of t_1 > the product of the number of errors and their disvalue resulting from the use of t_2.[19] What makes the suggestions in the previous paragraph inadequate proxies has, I think, primarily to do with the gravity of the resulting errors – that is, with the gravity of the over- and under-inclusiveness (and the limits of legal tools to mitigate these; more on this below). It seems to me that, on any reasonable theory of value, what is at stake in adequately preventing child neglect is considerably weightier than what is at stake in preventing, say, immature people from voting or drinking.

By saying this, I just mean that the interest that children have in not being subject to neglect (underinclusion) and the interest that parents have in not being held legally responsible for morally permissible or excused conduct (overinclusion) is weightier or stronger than any comparable interests that may be present in the context of voting and drinking. If so, then it is reasonable to think that instances of over- and underinclusiveness in the attempt to regulate child neglect will be quite serious. And given that any attempt to provide a fairly specific, but manageable, list of relevant conduct is likely to be widely off the mark, if not entirely so, we can reasonably say that the resulting over- and underinclusiveness would be excessive. Given the number of errors and their disvalue, it is too off

[19] Note here that '*ti*' can denote either what we would normally call a single term or a set thereof.

the mark to count as a means to the lawmakers' end of adequately preventing and punishing child neglect. This provides, I believe, a reasonable explanation why nothing will make for a relatively precise proxy for 'neglect', as opposed, for example, to 'mature'.

It is worth emphasising here that whether a term is an adequate proxy for some other term of course depends on a multitude of factors. My argument above, for example, presupposes that subjects, courts and agencies are more or less competent to respond reasonably to regulation using a term like 'neglect'. But if such regulation were shown to systematically prompt parents, judges, or agency officials to make biased or prejudicial decisions regarding the welfare of children, then it would perhaps no longer be so clear that 'neglect' lacked an adequate proxy. Under such circumstances, we might conceivably do equally well or better to try to come up with a relatively specific list of behaviours to prohibit, even if this would in fact result in a significant number of grave errors. Now, as a matter of fact, I do not think that this is the case – there really is no adequate proxy for 'neglect' in child care law, I believe. It is important, however, to stress that *adequate proxyhood*, as I have defined it, is a comparative relation and that a great variety of things (including, for example, the competence of officials) may affect whether one term is an adequate proxy for another, because they affect the number and gravity of errors resulting from the use of the relevant terms.[20]

This brings me to another possible objection to my claim that 'neglect' has no adequate proxy vis-à-vis child care law. I have said that any attempt to provide a fairly specific, but manageable, list of relevant conduct is likely to result in excessive over- and underinclusiveness, given the number of errors and – most significantly – their great disvalue. I have also said, however, that the law does have some tools for handling errors like these – most notably legal defences that aim at exculpating those who break the law excusably or justifiably (such as Insanity and Necessity, respectively). The potential problem for me here is that if such tools reliably reduce the number of errors, then it makes sense – especially in this particular case, given the emphasis on gravity – to ask whether I may be overestimating the negative outcome of enumerating a set of relatively specific requirements as a proxy for prohibiting 'neglect'. Does perhaps such an enumeration qualify as an adequate proxy once we take into account established legal tools designed specifically to remedy over- and underinclusiveness?

Although the law is indeed capable of remedying some of the relevant errors, the answer – I think – is still no. The reason is that the relevant legal tools are subject to several significant limitations. The necessity – or 'lesser evils' – defence, for example, which allows for acquittal in case the defendant's best course of action really was to break the law, is in general not known to people, and authorities arguably have an interest in keeping it that way.[21] This means that circumstances

[20] Thanks to a reviewer at *Ethics* for pressing me to highlight this aspect of being an adequate proxy.
[21] For a discussion, see Dan-Cohen (1984).

in which subjects will do what is best – by breaking the law – are likely to be relatively rare. And even if people did know about the defence, they would presumably be very hesitant to take the risk and hope for a successful outcome. In fact, it seems that they should be hesitant, since – as Gideon Yaffe has pointed out – the calculation of lesser/greater evils is far from consistent between courts, because it is not settled (in any jurisdiction) what standards are to be employed in evaluating the alternatives or what it is exactly that needs to be better than what.[22]

In addition to all this, legal defences can only mitigate the effects of overinclusion. But in the case of neglect, in contrast to most other legislative scenarios,[23] underinclusion is arguably the more serious side of the coin (or at least equally serious), and the only possible way of mitigating underinclusion seems to be the employment of expansive purposive legal interpretation. But this presupposes that cases of underinclusion reliably reach the courts, and much has to happen for a case that is not covered by the law (but which should be) to get that far in the system. It is probably not an exaggeration to say that most cases of underinclusion will stay out of the courts' reach, and, as a result, judicial interpretation is a rather inefficient tool for dealing with underinclusion.

From all this, it seems to me appropriate to conclude that in the case of neglect, using a list of fairly specific action types is not an option that is available to lawmakers, given their end to adequately regulate the relevant form of conduct. I won't venture to define the threshold that – no doubt, vaguely – divides courses of action into means and non-means, relative to ends, but I do think we can say that, whatever that threshold is, using a set of fairly precise requirements just cannot be considered a means to adequately regulating conduct that is especially damaging to children. It is just too far off the mark.

As I have hinted at, I do not think that lawmakers are required to use the term 'neglect' undefined, as UK lawmakers, for example, did in the Children and Young Persons Act.[24] It may well be that although no manageable list will count as an adequate proxy, some sort of approximating high-level definition will. In the United States, for example, the federal government provides a non-exhaustive definition of 'neglect' that constrains any state legislation:

> the term … means, *at a minimum*, any recent … failure to act on the part of a parent or caretaker, which results in death, serious physical or emotional harm, sexual abuse or exploitation, or … failure to act which presents an imminent risk of serious harm (my emphasis).[25]

[22] See esp Yaffe (2009) 43(3), 369–90, 372–78. I should note that Yaffe doubts that the necessity defence is best characterised as a justificatory defence. Rather, he thinks, it is a procedural estoppel defence, much like the defence of double jeopardy. If the government were to find the defendant guilty, its conduct would be 'inconsistent in some way with some prior government conduct with respect to the defendant' (371) vis-à-vis its authority over her.

[23] As Husak (2008) notes, there is in law a presumption against overinclusion/overcriminalisation (see 154); such a presumption, however, can be justified only if overinclusion is generally worse than underinclusion.

[24] See n 15.

[25] See the Child Abuse Prevention and Treatment Act, 42 USC §§ 5101, 5116 et seq.

To be sure, when non-exhaustive definitions are provided, they do not replace their definienda, and many states (such as California, Connecticut and Kentucky) have followed the federal government in defining 'neglect' in this incomplete way (with some variation of course).[26] However, several states (including New Jersey, Texas and Utah) do provide what appear to be complete high-level definitions of 'neglect', that is, definitions that do replace the 'ordinary meaning' of the term even if they are intended to capture or approximate it.[27] Given these (seemingly adequate) proxies, what should we make of the claim that incommensurate multidimensionality – and, hence, vagueness – is necessary in order to adequately regulate conduct that is especially damaging to children?

The answer, I think, is this: for every way in which you can reasonably formulate a legal text that aims to adequately regulate conduct that is especially damaging to children, it is the case that, necessarily, if lawmakers enact a norm using a text formulated in that way, then the resulting law contains terms that are associated with multiple incommensurate dimensions and, hence, vague. Or, to put it another way, there are more or less general ways, as well as more or less informative ways, in which lawmakers might try to achieve the relevant purpose, but the law will be multidimensional – and therefore vague – no matter which one of them is chosen. In fact, I believe that in the case of neglect, the law will be extravagantly vague, just as Endicott claims, since any proposal that can be considered a means to the relevant end has to be multidimensional in much the same way as 'neglect'. The US definitions of 'neglect' mentioned in the previous paragraph are good examples of this.[28] And multidimensionality of that sort entails extravagant vagueness, if Endicott is right.

I hope to have made a reasonable case for the claim that expressions that cover classes of widely varying conduct do so not in virtue of the fact that they are vague but rather in virtue of the fact that they are associated with multiple – and often incommensurate – dimensions. To be sure, the vagueness of the relevant terms is, by necessity, tied to their multidimensionality, but not in a way that makes vagueness central in our explanation of how the law can, or should, achieve regulation of very broad classes of conduct. Rather, vagueness is a necessary consequence of the feature that actually does facilitate reference to these classes. To use vague terms, then, is something lawmakers have to do in order to achieve certain valuable ends – it is indeed a practical necessity in some sense – but that does not make their vagueness a means to those ends.

Next, I want to turn to what I take to be a broader payoff of the foregoing critique. It is a payoff, I think, that applies not just to Endicott's argument but also to a number of related arguments regarding the instrumental value of

[26] California Welf & Inst Code § 300; Connecticut Gen Stat § 46b-120; Kentucky Rev Stat § 600.020.

[27] New Jersey Ann Stat § 9:6-8.21; Texas Fam Code § 261.001; Utah Ann Code § 78A-6-105.

[28] Note that what makes these definitions multidimensional is not that they are disjunctive but rather that each disjunct contains a term associated with multiple (incommensurable) dimensions.

vagueness in the law. If I am correct, these arguments also wrongly attribute value to vagueness on the grounds that it is a means to some end that is valuable for law.

V. Waldron's Argument from Facilitation

It is sometimes said that vagueness in the law can be a good thing because it enables lawmakers to enact norms that are 'flexible', 'openended', 'elastic' or 'adaptable'. In a recent paper, for example, Jeremy Waldron says that open-ended standards invoke people's capacity for practical deliberation in both structured and unstructured ways – that is, it incentivises them to act according to their own practical thinking in certain circumstances.[29] A vague traffic provision, for example, may require one to make some appropriate – but unspecified – modification to one's driving behaviour whenever a particular circumstance occurs. Such a provision thus relies on, and – if internalised – invokes, the capacity of human agents to determine what behaviour is appropriate given the provision and the relevant circumstances.[30] In doing so, Waldron says, the law directs subjects to consider a multitude of factors that may combine in various ways to determine what they ought – by law – to do. As he explains, a great variety of things – such as the narrowness of the roadway, the amount of traffic, and the presence of children playing on the road – may play a part in determining what modification a driver ought to make to her driving behaviour, given a traffic provision requiring people to drive at a 'reasonable or proper' speed.[31]

Our general capacity to deliberate about action in this way is, according to Waldron, a valuable one – in fact, it is what the dignity of a human agent consists in. The law, in issuing vague norms, he says, respects this dignity by '[crediting] the subject with the sophisticated ability to adapt [her] agency to [her] own practical thinking when this is required of [her]'.[32] In doing so, the law recognises the moral standing that a person has in a society.[33]

On the basis of this, Waldron concludes about the value of vagueness in the law that

> [it] is good to focus on the need for legislative flexibility [in certain areas] … The adaptability of law, secured precisely by what others would call its indeterminacy, is … a

[29] Waldron (2011) 58–82.
[30] ibid, 64.
[31] ibid.
[32] ibid, 65.
[33] Waldron (2012) 201–02. I should note that in Waldron's view, dignity is not a value concept but rather a status concept, designating what he calls *high-ranking social status*. For the purposes of my discussion in this chapter, however, this difference is immaterial, since Waldron clearly believes that it is a good thing to assign such high rank to everyone and that it is – consequently – one of law's virtues that it facilitates and protects such an assignment.

> valuable legislative resource and a respectful one too, for it works in tandem with the most sophisticated understanding of people's powers of practical reasoning.[34]

Thus, Waldron takes vagueness to be valuable for law on the grounds that enacting extravagantly vague norms makes the law flexible and open-ended, which in turn invokes a capacity the exercise of which realises the dignity of human agents. According to Waldron, then, vagueness in the law is a good thing because it is a facilitating – or partial – means to invoking people's capacity for practical deliberation in a special way.[35]

In the interest of clarity, let us analyse Waldron's argument in the following way:

> P1. Invoking people's capacity for practical deliberation in a way that realises the dignity of human agents is good.
>
> P2. Vagueness in the law is a facilitating – or partial – means to invoking people's capacity for practical deliberation in a way that realises the dignity of human agents.
>
> P3. Value transmits from ends to means.[36]
>
> C. Vagueness in the law is (sometimes) instrumentally good.[37]

Structurally, the argument is nearly identical to Endicott's, except that the second premise is a claim about facilitating means, rather than necessary means. I will argue that Waldron's conclusion about the value of vagueness in the law rests on a conflation of two distinct notions of flexibility and open-endedness, one properly associated with vagueness and the other with multidimensionality. If what I say is correct, the support for Waldron's instrumental premise (P2) goes away – we will have reason to be sceptical that vagueness is a means to invoking people's capacity for practical deliberation in the relevant way. Instead, as before, multidimensionality seems to be doing the work.

To be sure, as several authors have noted, vagueness in an important sense does allow for flexibility and open-endedness in the law.[38] Sometimes, lawmakers – for various reasons – do not want to settle beforehand how to classify borderline cases. It is better to deal with them in the courts, if and when they come up, since that allows decision makers to evaluate, for each case, whether it (and sufficiently similar ones) should be within or outside the reach of the law (and for

[34] Waldron (2011) 82.

[35] Thanks to a reviewer at *Ethics* for helpful comments on this section.

[36] As in the case of Endicott's argument, I take P3 to transmit *pro tanto* value; see discussion in section I.

[37] Also as in the case of Endicott's argument, I take it that Waldron is assuming that the *pro tanto* goodness that vagueness in the law has is not outweighed by any *pro tanto* badness it may have. Alternatively, we can limit the conclusion to *pro tanto* goodness.

[38] See eg Soames (2012) 95–108; and ch 3, this volume.

what reasons). This is indeed appropriately characterised as flexibility or open-endedness, and vagueness does help bring this about.

However, this is not the only way in which it is valuable that the law is flexible or open-ended. Often, the relevant – and usually more pressing – matter is that lawmakers do not want to draw sharp lines that make determinate cases fall on the wrong side of law's boundary, vis-à-vis the relevant law's rationale. If there is an indefinite variety of ways, for example, in which one can neglect a child, the worry is not that using more specific language will arbitrarily settle borderline cases of neglect but rather – as we have seen – that some determinate cases of neglect will not be covered by law and that some determinate cases of non-neglect will be. And this matter has to do with multidimensionality, rather than vagueness.

If we attend to why it is that terms like 'reasonable' invoke the deliberative capacity that Waldron appreciates, we see that his argument really concerns this latter notion of flexibility and open-endedness:

> The legislature does not want [certain] norms pinned down to a precise and exact meaning that will govern all future cases; that would detract from the very *elasticity* that it is aiming at and it would detract from the sort of active consideration by citizens that it is seeking authoritatively to elicit … If someone asks about the meaning of 'reasonable' or 'appropriate', all we can do is indicate that these are *flexible* all-purpose predicates of evaluation that invite us to consider a *number of possible factors in an open-ended way*.[39]

It may of course vary between legal contexts whether it is – ultimately – a good idea to rely on subjects themselves to make potentially complex judgments about what kind of behaviour is required of them in particular circumstances. Perhaps it turns out that traffic provisions using terms like 'reasonable' and 'proper' are generally a bad idea, whereas it might – as we have seen – be a good idea to protect the interests of children using terms like 'neglect'. In Waldron's view, however, there appears to be something distinctly valuable in invoking the capacity of human agents to determine how they ought to behave, a value that is to some extent independent of considerations regarding the adequate regulation of conduct that eludes specification. A multidimensional traffic provision, for example, might turn out to be a bad idea all things considered, but it would still require people to act according to their own practical thinking and thereby help realise the dignity of human agents, on Waldron's account. Thus, if Waldron is right, there is something valuable about laws containing multidimensional terms even in cases in which such law is ultimately undesirable, a value deriving from the fact that it directs people to consider a multitude of possible factors in an open-ended way, in an effort to determine what they ought – by law – to do in the relevant circumstances.

Now, one might of course disagree with Waldron that invoking people's capacity for practical deliberation in this way genuinely realises the dignity of human

[39] Waldron (2011) 74; my emphasis.

agents. That is, one might want to reject Waldron's P1. For the sake of argument, however, I am at least prepared to accept that it may be true. It may also be true that the value of employing terms like 'reasonable', 'proper' and 'neglect' in legal provisions has been underestimated, due to a failure to see how such provisions respect the dignity of human agency. However, even if both these claims were true, Waldron's conclusion about the value of vagueness in the law would not follow. The reason, I hope to have shown, is that the argument trades on a conflation of the two notions of flexibility and open-endedness mentioned above. Thus, Waldron – and whoever argues in a similar vein – wrongly associates vagueness with an instrumental role that is really played by multidimensionality and, as a result, wrongly attributes instrumental value to vagueness, at least in significant part.

I should note that at a certain point in his paper, Waldron indicates that there is – so far as his argument is concerned – no need to distinguish between 'unclarity, vagueness, and imprecision' or between 'ambiguity, vagueness, and contestability'.[40] One might think, therefore, that I am being somewhat uncharitable to Waldron – perhaps he is using the term 'vagueness' as we often do in ordinary conversation, to cover all sorts of cases in which an utterance might provide insufficiently specific information relative to the purpose of the relevant conversation (broadly construed).

However, although it may be the case that Waldron is primarily using the term 'vague' in a broad sense, rather than the technical sense it has in logic and philosophy of language, I still think his argument is a fair target for my critique. The reason is that even if this is the case, his claim that there is – for the purposes of his argument – no need to distinguish between, for example, ambiguity, vagueness and contestability clearly indicates that he thinks that vagueness in the technical sense is one of the sources of vagueness in the broader sense. But if that is the case, then introducing the former into the law is a facilitating means to doing so with the latter. Given the transitivity of the *is-a-means-to* relation, it follows that vagueness in the technical sense is a facilitating means to invoking people's capacity for practical deliberation in a way that realises the dignity of human agents, which is exactly P2 above. Further, since value transmits from ends to means, establishing that vagueness in the broad sense can be a good thing suffices to establish that vagueness in the technical sense can, too. Thus, I take it that Waldron really is concerned with the value of vagueness in the technical sense, despite the fact that he may also have something broader in mind.

As in Endicott's case, what I have said here does not decisively show that Waldron's P2 is false, but it gives us good reason to be sceptical. In any case, I hope to have showed that the premise is unsupported by the considerations discussed by Waldron.

[40] ibid, 62, esp n 16.

VI. Possible Reply: Vagueness Really is a Means to the Relevant Ends

The most natural response to my critique of Endicott and Waldron would, I think, be to argue that, since incommensurate multidimensionality entails vagueness, using vague terms is really a necessary means to using multidimensional terms and that – given the transitivity of the *is-a-means-to* relation – value therefore does in fact transmit from the relevant legislative ends to vagueness. If that is correct, then vagueness in the law is still instrumentally valuable, although its value is perhaps not as 'immediate' as we might have thought.

This strategy certainly has some appeal, in particular in Endicott's case – evidenced, for example, by the intuitive force of the following claim: in order to adequately regulate conduct that is especially damaging to children, lawmakers have to use vague terms. If this statement of practical necessity strikes us as true – and I have argued that it should – then that seems to lend some support to the claim that vagueness is after all a necessary means to the relevant legislative end. Perhaps, necessary consequences of means to ends are also means to those ends – which, if true, vindicates the instrumental premises of the two arguments. Or so this line of response goes.

Despite its prima facie plausibility, I think we have good reason to think that this strategy won't work. As I hope to show, practical necessity sentences are not confined to expressing means–ends relations, even if they are perhaps most commonly used in that way, and so true statements of practical necessity don't suffice to guarantee transmission of value. The best explanation for this, I believe, is that it is not generally true that if something is a necessary consequence of a means to some end, then it is also a means to that end – not even if it is something that one has to do in order to achieve that end.

Let me borrow and adapt an example from Jaegwon Kim to substantiate these claims.[41] Say that Meletus sees to it that Socrates dies. By doing so, he also sees to it that Xanthippe becomes a widow. But there is no causal relationship between Socrates' dying and Xanthippe's becoming a widow – the dependence is of another sort.[42] Imagine also, for the sake of argument, that in order to protect the youth of Athens, Meletus has to see to it that Socrates dies. Given the relation between seeing to it that Socrates dies and seeing to it that Xanthippe becomes a

[41] Kim (1974) 41–52.

[42] This sort of dependency is often called *Cambridge dependency*; see eg ibid. For those who don't like Kim-style events and prefer Davidson-style events instead, I can make the same point by arguing that value talk and reasons talk is intensional rather than extensional. This isn't very hard, since SDL assumes that only logically equivalent descriptions can be substituted for one another. So even if we have theoretical reasons for saying that the lawmakers' using an incommensurately multidimensional term is in fact identical with the lawmakers' using a vague term and the former is instrumentally valuable, it does not follow that the latter is also (since these events are identical without being logically equivalent).

widow, Meletus also has to see to it that Xanthippe becomes a widow in order to achieve his end – it is in some sense a practical necessity.

Suppose, then, that it is in fact valuable that Meletus sees to it that the youth of Athens are protected and that – consequently – it is valuable that he sees to it that Socrates dies. It would seem odd to say that, by the same token, it is valuable that Meletus sees to it that Xanthippe becomes a widow. Although her fate is something that has to be brought about in order to achieve a valuable end, it is not a means to that end – there is no interesting relation between her being or not being a widow and the youth of Athens. Rather, Xanthippe's becoming a widow is just a necessary by-product of something that does help bring the relevant end about: Socrates' dying. Hence, her fate seems to be a practical necessity to which no value transmits. And the best explanation for this, it seems to me, is that making Xanthippe a widow is not a means to killing Socrates.

Vagueness, I want to claim, is to lawmakers much like Xanthippe's becoming a widow is to Meletus. What is going on in law, on my account, is that by using terms with multiple incommensurate dimensions, lawmakers also use terms that are (extravagantly) vague. Thus, if the former is something that lawmakers have to do in order, say, to adequately regulate conduct that is especially damaging to children, then so is the latter. However, in order for value to transmit in the required way, practical necessity is not enough – vagueness must also in some relevant sense help bring about the relevant legislative ends. And vagueness, if I am right, is not doing any of the work relevant to Endicott's argument – that is, there is no relevant connection between the vagueness of the relevant terms and the ability of lawmakers to use them to adequately regulate the relevant forms of conduct.

Granted, the relationship between incommensurate multidimensionality and vagueness is tighter than the relationship between Socrates' dying and Xanthippe's becoming a widow – after all, had Socrates not been married, Xanthippe's fate would have been quite different. However, there are two general reasons why I don't think this affects my point. First, among the main general lessons to draw from the Xanthippe example is that it is not generally true that if something is a necessary consequence of a means to some end, then it is also a means to that end, because not all such consequences help bring about the relevant ends. This, I have tried to show, is the case with vagueness in the law – at least the kind discussed by Endicott. Neither does it directly help bring about the relevant legislative ends, nor does it do so indirectly – it is not the case that by using vague terms one helps bring about that one uses terms with multiple incommensurate dimensions. Second, if the relevant consequence in question isn't doing any instrumental work, then there is simply nothing in virtue of which it has instrumental value, relative to the end in question. And this explains, I submit, why value fails to transmit from the relevant regulatory ends to vagueness, just as it explains how value fails to transmit to Xanthippe's becoming a widow.

These considerations carry over straightforwardly to Waldron's case: if value doesn't generally transmit from ends to necessary consequences of necessary means, then we have no reason to expect that value transmits from ends to necessary consequences of merely facilitating – or partial – means. The reason, as before, is that it is not generally true that if something is a necessary consequence of a means to some end, then it is also a means to that end. This applies equally to necessary means and merely facilitating means and, thus, equally to the envisioned amendments of the two arguments.

VII. Another Possible Reply: The Logic of Value Validates Closure under Necessary Consequence

In the previous section, I was concerned with showing that it is not generally true that if something is a necessary consequence of a means to some end, then it is also a means to that end. On the assumption that value only transmits from ends to means, but not to necessary consequences of those means, this allowed me to resist the conclusion that vagueness in the law is a good thing. In this final section, I want to consider what implications it has for my arguments in this chapter that Standard Deontic Logic (SDL) validates closure under necessary consequence.[43] Assuming we have at least a prima facie reason to expect the logic of 'good' to mirror the logic of 'ought' in significant (if not all) respects, the problem I face is that it makes sense to ask – given that I have conceded that incommensurate multidimensionality is sometimes a good thing – whether the logic of value forces on me the conclusion that vagueness is sometimes a good thing, too.

I don't think it does; there are a number of ways to block the inference, some of which require rejecting SDL and some of which do not. The purpose of this final section, however, is not to catalogue the different possible responses but rather to acknowledge that – and illustrate how – in making claims about how to reason with value statements, one incurs significant commitments in the logic of value.

First, we could reject closure under necessary consequence for both the logic of 'ought' and the logic of 'good', which would amount to rejecting SDL altogether. This would not be a novel move – many authors have provided reasons for thinking that distribution over conjunction (from which closure under necessary consequence is crucially derived) is problematic in the case of 'ought'. In particular, many of the so-called paradoxes of deontic logic arise because of distribution over conjunction.[44] These paradoxes can more or less be reproduced using value statements instead of ought statements, and so distribution over conjunction seems equally problematic in the logic of value. However, SDL happens to be a comparatively well-studied logic, being – as it is – a normal modal logic, and so this strategy entails a very significant commitment: to provide a workable logic for both 'ought' and 'good', alternative to SDL.

Second, we could claim that the logic of 'ought' is closed under necessary consequence but that the logic of 'good' is not. However, although it allows us to retain

[43] For a discussion of SDL, see eg Hilpinen and Føllesdal (1971) 1–35.
[44] For an overview of the paradoxes, see eg McNamara (2014).

SDL, this second strategy generates even further commitments than the first, since we would incur a commitment both to provide a workable logic for 'good' that does not validate closure under necessary consequence and to explain why the logics of 'ought' and 'good' diverge so radically. To be sure, there are significant natural differences; for example, the phrase 'it is good that' is presumably factive, whereas 'it ought to be the case that' is not. However, although such a difference will of course make for a difference in the logics of the two notions, it is not so radical as to make one a normal modal logic and the other not.

Third, we could hold that the logic of intrinsic value is closed under necessary consequence but that the logic of instrumental value is not. And since we are here concerned with the instrumental value of vagueness, the problematic conclusion doesn't follow. Perhaps, necessary consequences of intrinsically good states of affairs are also themselves good, but the same is not true of states of affairs that are merely instrumentally good. This is an attractive strategy but would generate a commitment – in particular – to provide a workable logic of instrumental value, alternative to SDL.

Fourth, we could distinguish between types of value claims of the form 'it is good that *p*' and '*x* is good' and argue that only the former distributes over conjunction. Given my concession that it is good that lawmakers use terms that have multiple incommensurate dimensions, it would then follow that it is good that lawmakers use terms that are vague. This conclusion, however, tells us nothing about the value of vagueness, as such; it just tells us – to a rough approximation – that the possible worlds in which lawmakers use vague terms are better than some contextually determined standard or better than sufficiently many other possible worlds in some relevant comparison class. That is, while the conclusion does tell us something about the 'normative status' of the relevant possible worlds, it doesn't tell us anything about in virtue of what they have that status. Thus, nothing follows about the value of vagueness, as such: on this account, that it is good that lawmakers use vague terms does not entail that vagueness is good.[45]

As I said, the purpose of this final section is neither to catalogue nor to thoroughly discuss the possible responses to the apparent problem posed by the attractiveness of closure under necessary consequence in the logic of evaluative notions. It is important to emphasise, however, that in making claims about how to reason with value statements, one incurs deep commitments in logic. What I mean by this is not that deontic logic – or the logic of evaluation, more broadly – is somehow theoretically prior to value theory or theories of practical reasoning. Rather, I mean that logic serves as a significant constraint on such theories, in the sense that it counts significantly against a theory if the resulting logic proves unworkable. It should be clear, therefore, that limiting the principle of value transmission to the means–ends relationship – as I have done here – is not without significant further commitment.

[45] And – on this account – *that incommensurate multidimensionality is good* and *that incommensurate multidimensionality entails vagueness* do not together entail *that vagueness is good.*

3

Vagueness and Power Delegation in Law*

In 'Vagueness has no function in law',[1] Roy Sorensen argues that it is a mistake to think that vagueness has a constructive function in law, such as delegating limited lawmaking power to officials[2] or eliciting certain kinds of desired behaviour on the part of subjects.[3] It merely *appears* to be functional, Sorensen says, due to 'a cluster of logical and linguistic errors' about its nature. In addition, he thinks that vagueness in the law often generates serious problems, and so cannot have a function in the law, on the understanding that something has a function in a system if, and only if, its presence is explained by how it serves a goal of the system. Thus, for Sorensen, the issue is whether vagueness is valuable vis-à-vis law's aims, ie whether the presence of vagueness in the law does or can promote the common good.[4] The main problems he identifies are that (i) vague legislation is often used in a way contrary to the promotion of the common good,[5] and (ii) vague legal language, in genuine hard cases, forces serious judicial insincerity.[6] Sorensen believes, then, that he can explain away the evidence for the claim that vagueness has a function in law, and, further, produce evidence for the contrary claim that it has no such function.

One of the main aims in this chapter is to examine one of Sorensen's primary claims: that vagueness in the law – properly understood – cannot be justified by appeal to the value of power delegation. Sorensen appears to think that the delegation of power to officials is justified *only if* these officials are in a better position to discover the right answer in the relevant cases. Since vagueness proper entails that there is no answer to be discovered, power delegation will not be justified, he says. If he is right, then he will have taken away what is traditionally thought to be the main reason for thinking that vagueness can have a constructive function in law.

In section I, I will present Sorensen's epistemic account of vagueness, his distinction between absolute and relative borderline cases, and his argument that

* Chapter 3 has been reproduced with permission of OUP through PLSclear: 'Vagueness and Power-Delegation in Law: A Reply to Sorensen' in M Freeman & F Smith (eds), *Current Legal Issues, Vol 15: Law and Language* (Oxford University Press, 2013).

[1] Sorensen (2001a) 385.

[2] Raz (2001) 419.

[3] See Endicott and Spence (2005) 664 and Hadfield (1994a) 545.

[4] Sorensen (2001a) 398.

[5] ibid, 399.

[6] ibid, 388–92.

absolute borderline cases do not have a constructive power-delegating function in law. I should note that the examples I present are mine, except for *Brown v Board of Education*. So in case any of them are unpersuasive, Sorensen is not at fault.

In section II, I will examine his argument, arguing that it is unsound. More specifically, I will argue that the following claim is false: delegation of decision-making authority, vis-à-vis borderline cases regarding something's being *F*, is valuable *only if* the relevant delegates are in a better position to answer the question whether *x* is *F* than those delegating the power. Delegation of decision-making authority *can* be valuable, I hope to show, *even if* the relevant delegates are *not* in a better position to answer the question whether *x* is *F*. The key to seeing why is to acknowledge that when faced with absolute borderline cases, the courts must engage with a related *normative* question – whether *x ought*, relative to the purposes of the law, to *count* as an *F*.

I will try to show that, under certain circumstances, it is indeed better to let the relevant delegates answer the normative question – ie whether *x* ought, relative to the purposes of the relevant law, to count as an *F*. If I am successful, then there are situations in which delegation of decision-making authority is valuable *even if* the relevant delegates are not in a better position to answer the question *whether x is F* than those delegating the power. That is, if I am correct, then Sorensen's argument is unsound.

I. Sorensen's View

It is standard to define vagueness with reference to *borderline cases*, in the sense that most writers on vagueness hold either that *a term is vague only if it has possible borderline cases* or that *a term is vague if, and only if, it has possible borderline cases.*[7] Since Sorensen is committed to the latter claim, and nothing in this particular chapter hangs on which one of these claims is true, I will assume it here for the sake of accurately representing his argument.

The nature of borderline cases is controversial, but most theorists would accept the characterisation that these are cases in which there is inherent uncertainty regarding whether or not the relevant term applies. They will vary, however, in how they think this uncertainty ought to be understood. Some will say that the appropriate explanation is fundamentally epistemic (ie concerns what we can know), others that it is linguistic (ie concerns the rules of language), and yet others that it is at bottom ontological (ie concerns the way the world is).

[7] Sorensen himself accepts the stronger claim that a term is vague *if, and only if,* it has possible borderline cases, but several authors on vagueness take the existence of borderline cases alone to be insufficient for vagueness (see eg Soames (1999)). It is also important to distinguish between *intensional* vagueness – the possibility of having borderline cases – and *extensional* vagueness – actual borderline cases. Vagueness is properly characterised in terms of the *possibility* of borderline cases. This distinction will also play a role in determining the value of vagueness for law.

Sorensen thinks that the proper explanation of vagueness is primarily epistemic. A borderline case, unlike a clear case, is a case in which the question regarding whether a predicate '*F*' applies to an object *o* has no knowable answer. The reason that the question has no answer is that there is nothing that makes either a positive or negative answer correct. For example, in case $\langle F, o \rangle = p$ and p is a borderline proposition, p will lack a truth-maker (and, thus, so will $\sim p$). Here, a truth-maker is something 'in the world' which makes the relevant truth true; Joe's being bald, for example, makes the proposition *that Joe is bald* a true proposition (which in turn makes the sentence 'Joe is bald' a true sentence). In general, truth-makers are also the entities via which we come to know the truth-values of propositions. On Sorensen's view, the borderline proposition p will still have a truth-value – it's either true or false – but since we cannot, via any truth-maker (*o*'s being *F*), access this truth-value we are irremediably in the dark as to what that truth-value is.[8] This is what makes Sorensen's approach epistemic. Since one cannot, even in principle, justifiably believe that a borderline sentence is true (or false), it follows that one cannot, even in principle, come to know the relevant proposition. In borderline cases, then, one's lack of knowledge is irremediable.

A. Absolute Borderline Cases, Relative Borderline Cases and Answering Resources

But, says Sorensen, there are borderline cases and there are borderline cases. He distinguishes between *absolute* borderline cases – in which the ignorance really is irremediable – and *relative* borderline cases – in which the ignorance is remediable – and he thinks that confusing the two may mislead one to believe that genuine vagueness is functional in law.[9]

A term is genuinely vague if, and only if, it has absolute borderline cases, and a term has absolute borderline cases if, and only if, it has cases that are borderline given any means of answering 'Is *x F*?' That is, in principle, there exist no resources for us to answer this question with respect to genuine borderline cases. Relative borderline cases, on the other hand, are not evidence of vagueness proper, since the ignorance in such a case is remediable by some means or other (which may or may not be available at a given time).

Sorensen thinks that most borderline cases are relative ones.[10] Relative cases include, for example, ignorance as the result of a 'measure-by-eye' test for whether an *x* falls in this or that size category, which may be resolved by a 'measure-by-ruler' test. An *x* may be categorised as borderline relative to the former test (ie the test doesn't, for the relevant *x*, return an answer to the question 'Is *x F*?'), while

[8] Borderline cases, in Sorensen's view, therefore do not involve truth-*value* gaps, but truth-*maker* gaps.

[9] Sorensen (2001a) 392–400.

[10] Sorensen (2001b).

relative to the latter it may be categorised as a member or non-member of the relevant set (ie that test may return an answer to the question 'Is *x F*?'). Imagine, for example, a couple of fishermen determining by eye whether a given fish is big or not. From what they can determine by eye, the fish may be borderline big. Yet, if later measured by a ruler, it may turn out that it does fall within the category *big fish*. If so, then the case was a relative borderline case.

To take a legal example, consider the Pollution Prevention Act 1990, under which 'pollution that cannot be prevented should be recycled in an environmentally safe manner whenever feasible'.[11] Owing to the complexity of environmental matters, it is clear that there are a great many possible cases that lawmakers could not categorise as safe or unsafe, but that experts nevertheless could. That is, relative to the body of information available to the average member of Congress, there may be many cases that are borderline without being borderline relative to the evolving body of information available to an agency like the Environmental Protection Agency.

Things are different when it comes to absolute borderline cases. Such cases include, for example, borderline patches of colour in between, say, yellow and green (chartreuse). Here, arguably, the ignorance – as to whether or not a chartreuse patch is green – resulting from a 'measure-by-eye' test cannot be remedied by appeal to another test. It is not to be expected, for example, that a measurement of the spectrum of reflected light waves – or any other imaginable test – will provide us with an answer to whether or not a patch of chartreuse really is green. Likewise, there will presumably be some absolute borderline cases of 'environmentally safe recycling'. In such cases, no body of information – no matter how sophisticated – can settle whether or not it is safe. Absolute cases are resistant to *any* further inquiry.

Measuring devices, bodies of information, sets of inference rules, etc are *answering resources* – considerations capable of furnishing an answer to a question of the form 'Is *x F*?'[12] Such a resource may, eg, provide a test for being F (eg *if condition C is satisfied, then x is F*). A test, of course, may be more or less fine-grained. Less fine-grained ones are likely to yield more borderline cases. And a case that is borderline relative to a certain answering resource may not be borderline relative to some other – perhaps more fine-grained – resource, as we have seen.[13] If there is *some* answering resource relative to which a case is not borderline, then the case is only relatively borderline. Cases in which no answering resource is capable of returning an answer, on the other hand, are absolute borderline cases.

[11] 42 USC §13101–13109.

[12] Sorensen (2001a) 392.

[13] Sorensen says that formal systems in which a statement which is undecidable in one but provable in another show clearly this structural relationship. Thus borderline cases are spawned by *incompleteness* of the relevant answering system: Sorensen (2001b), 23.

B. Borderline Cases and the Delegation of Power

Sorensen thinks that legal theorists are really interested in the functionality of relative borderline cases, since the relevant ignorance *can* be remedied by appeal to an appropriate answering resource. Delegation of power to administrative agencies, eg by means of introducing relative borderline cases into the law, is valuable, Sorensen claims, only because the relevant agencies have answering resources equipped to answer the question whether *x* is *F*. In these cases, he says, legislatures typically make it the case that certain cases are borderline relative to the answering resources provided by law, ie the law will provide no test that will, for every *x*, provide an answer as to whether *x* is *F*. But this doesn't mean that alternative non-legal answering resources aren't available. 'What is undecidable relative to current law,' he says, 'may be decidable with the help of supplementary premises and procedures.'[14] If I understand Sorensen correctly, I take it that, for example, the legislature may in certain cases not have the resources to answer whether or not a recycling process is 'environmentally safe' – ie the law does not tell us under which conditions such a process is safe – while scientific studies may indicate at least some such conditions. That is, it may be the case that there exists no specific regulation defining what is or is not environmentally safe, in which case an appropriate answer cannot be given by the law, yet it may be had by appealing to 'extra-legal' answering resources. The important thing is this: if such resources are in principle available, then the relevant case isn't an absolute borderline case – it is merely borderline relative to existing law.

Sorensen's own main legal example is *Brown v Board of Education*,[15] a case in which the Supreme Court ordered that school desegregation proceed 'with all deliberate speed'. The court did not provide any explanation of what this phrase meant and there was no precedent to furnish legally clear cases of things happening with the required speed. In some cases, of course, a superficial test may suffice, for example if it is clear that almost everybody would think that desegregation clearly had, or had not, happened with all deliberate speed. Such a case does not call for a finer, more discriminating test. But it may also happen that it is neither immediately clear that it hadn't happened with all deliberate speed nor that it hadn't. In this case, the courts may, for example, appeal to explanations of what it 'really is' for something to happen with such speed. But in some cases, ie genuine borderline cases, no acceptable theory or resource of any other type will furnish an answer to the relevant question.[16] It is these sorts of case that typically bother philosophers of logic and language. So it seems that the phrase 'with all deliberate speed' is genuinely vague.

[14] Sorensen (2001a), 399. I am not sure why these additional answering resources cannot count as legal, assuming that officials are authorised to consult them, but for the sake of argument I'll go along and agree that these are somehow 'beyond the law'.

[15] 347 US 483 (1954).

[16] Although, as Sorensen notes, Dworkin would deny this, since, on his view, *all* alleged hard cases concern relative borderline cases.

However, the flexibility that this phrase was supposed to facilitate does not, Sorensen says, have to do with genuine vagueness, ie it does not have to do with absolute borderline cases, which exist due to the inability to answer the question whether *x* is *F*. Rather, the utility of the vague phrase has to do with relative borderline cases and the ability to furnish answers to the relevant questions. In *Brown*, the flexibility that the phrase allows is relevant to cases in which the people closest to it are in a position to say whether a particular case of desegregation has, or has not, happened with the required speed. That is, the decision of the Supreme Court allows the law to rely on the people who deal with the actual case to furnish the relevant answer, which is arguably better than if the Court had come up with some definition of the phrase, or used instead a more precise one. The complexity and unforeseeability of such matters as school desegregation make it the case that it is reasonable to delegate the task of finding out whether '*x* is *F*' to those with special experience and/or who are in close proximity with the actual situation. Such individuals arguably have better discriminatory abilities – that is, they are better equipped to classify the relevant cases – and so delegating certain legal powers to them is in an important respect analogous to utilising a more fine-grained test for *F*-ness. Cases that may seem borderline relative to a rather limited body of information possessed by the legislature (or the Supreme Court) may turn out not to be borderline relative to a richer body of information available to the relevant officials. So relative borderline cases may well have a valuable power-delegating function in law.

Absolute borderline cases, on the other hand, do not have any such power-delegating value, Sorensen says, since no answering resource is capable of providing an answer to whether the relevant *x*s are *F*. Hence, no one could ever be in a position to answer the relevant question and the delegation of power to agencies or the courts would be useless (for the purposes of settling the matter). The phrase 'endangerment to the health of persons',[17] for example, presumably has absolute borderline cases, but there is no benefit, Sorensen would say, in delegating power vis-à-vis absolute borderline cases of such endangerment, since no one can be in a better position than any other with respect to determining whether or not such a case constitutes endangerment in the relevant sense. Not even the best experts. The same goes for absolute borderline cases of 'with all deliberate speed'.

Let me conclude section I by summarising Sorensen's argument:

P1. Delegation of decision-making authority, vis-à-vis borderline cases, is valuable only if the relevant delegates are in a better position to answer the question whether *x* is *F* than those delegating the power.

P2. When *x* is an absolute borderline case of 'F', it is not the case that the relevant delegates are in a better position to answer the question whether *x* is *F* than those delegating the power.

[17] See the Federal Water Pollution Control Act 1948, 33 USC §1364(a).

C. Therefore, when *x* is an absolute borderline case of 'F', it is not the case that delegation of decision-making authority, vis-à-vis *x*, is valuable.

Sorensen's conclusion from all this, then, is that the notion of power delegation cannot be used to show that vagueness – proper – can be a valuable feature of law.

Sorensen's distinction between absolute and relative borderline cases is quite interesting and the argument indeed threatens to take away what is traditionally taken to be the main reason for thinking that vagueness can have a constructive function in law. If the benefits of being able to delegate limited law-making power are had by introducing relative borderline cases into the law, rather than absolute ones, then power delegation won't be a benefit due to vagueness proper. Moreover, the distinction does not depend on Sorensen's particular theory of vagueness – rather, it is one that any broad theory of vagueness should take seriously. More particular to our purposes here, it seems to me that P1 and P2 are jointly consistent with any viable theory of vagueness. Thus, we cannot avoid the problem posed by Sorensen's argument simply by arguing against his account of vagueness. It must be tackled some other way.

Sorensen's P2 seems safe enough. In fact, it is arguably entailed by any respectable theory of vagueness, whether epistemic, supervaluational, psychological, or indexical/contextual. As far as absolute borderline cases go, all theories will claim that for every cogniser *x*, every cogniser *y*, and every borderline proposition *p*, it is *never* the case that *x* is epistemically better situated than *y* vis-à-vis the truth value of *p*. P2 is simply a limited case of this general claim.

Now, I agree with Sorensen that the distinction between absolute and relative borderline cases is often overlooked and that, as a result, value that is appropriately associated with relative borderline cases is wrongly associated with absolute ones. Still, I think that there *are* cases in which the delegation of power – and the resulting discretion – is justified *even if* the relevant delegates are *not* in a better position to find out whether *x* is *F*. In certain cases, it may well be better to leave the *stipulation* as to whether *x* is *F* – ie the decision whether *x* ought, for the purposes of the law, to count as an *F* – up to competent delegates. In section II, I try to explain some conditions under which this is the case. If I succeed, then P1 of Sorensen's argument will be false.

II. The Value of Vagueness

Sorensen recognises that absolute borderline cases prompt judicial discretion, and characterises this discretion as discretion to substitute the question whether *x* is *F* with the question whether *x should count as an F*. If a court is faced with a borderline case of, say, 'business establishment' – as it was in the case of *Curran v Mount Diablo Boy Scouts*[18] – the courts may relativise the concept in question

[18] 17 Cal 4th 670 (1998).

to suit the purposes of the law, Sorensen says.[19] In *Curran*, for example, such relativisation led to the Boy Scouts being counted as a business establishment. If I understand Sorensen correctly, he has in mind the practice of the courts to use phrases of the following sort: 'for the purposes of [such-and-such a statute], *x* is *F*'. The Boy Scouts, then, presumably counted as a business establishment *for the purposes of California's Unruh Civil Rights Act* (1959).[20] For an example in the constitutional realm, many have argued (and the Supreme Court has agreed) that *for the purposes of the First Amendment*, flag burning counts as speech (and so is protected).[21] These, of course, are not answers to whether *x* is *F*, but to whether *x* should legally count as an *F* relative to some particular aims of the law. Thus, in absolute borderline cases, the question is – implicitly or explicitly – changed. Moreover, it is changed to one that in many cases has better prospects of being answered (ie a non-zero probability, unlike 'Is *x F*?').

The reason I bring this up is that I have a hard time seeing why this question-changing discretion may not be valuable. In fact, I believe that legislators often rely on this pervasive judicial response. When legislatures deliberately use vague language, they are not asking the courts to find out whether absolute borderline *F*s really are *F*s; rather, they are asking the courts to do exactly what Sorensen describes, to engage with the *normative question* whether *x* ought – relative to the purposes of the law – to count as an *F*. And I fail to see any argument in Sorensen's paper to the effect that the judicial response to this legislative 'request' cannot, under certain circumstances, be valuable. And if it can be shown that discretion to change the question can be valuable, then – since such discretion is due to absolute borderline cases – vagueness *proper* will have a constructive function in law.

One issue which may be in the back of Sorensen's mind is, I think, the following. It seems that if it is valuable to let the courts figure out whether *x* should count as an *F*, then that is because there is an answer to whether *x* should count as an *F*. And if there is an answer to whether *x* should count as an *F*, then it seems that there is a fact of the matter whether *x* is a case that ought to be regulated, on the narrow understanding that a case *c* is regulated by a rule *R* if, and only if, *c* is included in *R*'s domain of application. But, and here is the catch, if the immediate aim of the lawmakers is to regulate everything *F* and *x* is absolutely borderline *F*, then there is arguably no fact of the matter whether *x* ought or ought not to be so included. Thus, combine the relevant immediate regulatory aim with the absolute borderline status of *x* and you may have a hard time explaining how it could be valuable to let the courts decide whether or not it should be regulated. If there is a truly arbitrary distinction to be made, it seems better simply to make it at the legislative level.[22]

[19] Sorensen (2001a), 414.

[20] Cal Civ Code §51.

[21] See *Texas v Johnson*, 491 US 397 (1989), and *US v Eichman*, 496 US 310 (1990).

[22] There is a potentially important general issue here regarding the question whether *x* ought to be regulated. When we ask this question, we can be asking (at least) two things: (i) ought it to be the case

I suspect that the answer here lies in the question-changing element of the judicial response to absolute borderline cases. In some cases, it may be that *x* ought to be included in the relevant rule's domain of application not simply in virtue of its being *F* – since it is borderline – but in virtue of a combination of factors (of which borderline *F*-ness may be one). Even if the legislature chose vague language in order to be able to regulate everything *F* (their immediate aim), background regulatory aims or justifications may dictate that particular borderline *F*s be regulated. The background justification of the well-worn fictional 'No vehicles in the park' statute, for example, may suffice to answer the question whether a skateboard ought to count as a vehicle. In case the background justification includes, say, to minimise noise pollution in the park, then that may point in favour of skateboards counting as vehicles 'for the purposes of the statute'. If, on the other hand, the aim was to reduce exhaust pollution and/or risk of fatal accidents, then that seems to clearly count in favour of not counting them as vehicles.

Now, it may of course happen that the relevant background aims do not determine a verdict either way – that is, they may fail to resolve the matter. Consider the normative question once again: Ought *x* to count as an *F*? Let's semi-formalise the question in the following way ('O' here reads 'It ought to be the case that'): *O*(*x* counts as an *F*)? We can then construct a complex predicate [λx *O*(*x* counts as an *F*], which may have borderline instances, both relative and absolute – just as *F*, by hypothesis, does. This, however, is not a theoretical problem, and should in fact be expected. I would be highly sceptical of an account that predicted otherwise. My claim is not that looking to legislative purpose can in all borderline cases guide judicial decision – that is, I am not suggesting a uniform practical decision procedure for all borderline cases. Nor need I suggest one in order to reply to Sorensen. I am merely pointing out that while it may be arbitrary with respect to *F*-ness whether *x* ought to count as an *F*, it may happen – and probably often happens – that it is not arbitrary with respect to the purposes of the law.

I should note that the law seems to embrace this question-changing resolution strategy in other varieties of hard cases too, even ones in which the particular behaviour is within the determinate anti-extension of the relevant predicate. It seems appropriate to understand both the doctrines of transferred intent and wilful blindness as prescriptions to treat particular cases in certain ways, *for the purposes of the law*. Take for example the case of a person A who intends to harm another person B, but who – by accident – ends up harming yet another person C. In such a case, the law often treats A as having intended to harm C. This is known as transferred intent (or transferred malice, in English law). Consider the case

that there is some rule *R* such that *x* is regulated by *R*? or (ii) for some particular rule *R* and case *x*, ought it to be the case that *x* is regulated by *R*? The former question concerns whether *x* ought to be regulated by law (at all), while the latter concerns whether *x* ought to be regulated by some particular law. It is possible that, in some cases, this distinction matters – since lawmakers have an unconstrained choice of rules, while the discretion of the courts is limited to precisifications of particular (already enacted) rules – but I will not pursue these matters here.

of *Bradshaw v Richey*,[23] in which Richey was found guilty of aggravated felony murder on the basis of this doctrine. Richey had intended to kill his ex-girlfriend and her boyfriend but ended up killing a little girl, Cynthia Collins, instead. That is, Richey's intended violation of the law failed and instead he killed a person he had no intention of killing. Still, he was found guilty of murdering the girl, a felony that requires *intent*.

The doctrine of transferred intent arguably operates on the premise that the behaviour to which it applies is *just as bad as* the intended behaviour. Thus, the question facing the courts is a version of the normative question: ought *x* – for the purposes of the law – to count as an *F*? The purpose, in this case, is to prevent or punish behaviour that is equally as bad as intended violations of the law (assuming attempt). In *Richey*, for example, the question was whether Richey's unintentional killing of young Cynthia Collins was – given the fact that it was the result of an attempt to murder another person – equally as bad as the intended murder.

The doctrine of wilful blindness operates on a similar premise: the doctrine is supposed to apply if a defendant's deliberately ignorant violation of the law is just as bad as a knowing violation. In *US v Jewell*,[24] for example, Jewell was convicted for knowingly transporting marijuana across the US–Mexico border in his car, despite the fact that he deliberately avoided positive knowledge of what was in the car's compartment. In this case, too, the court opted to 'change the question', from a factual one to a normative one: ought Jewell's violation – relative to the law's purpose of preventing or punishing behaviour that is equally as bad as knowing violations of the law – to count as a knowing violation?

The reason I am mentioning the doctrines of transferred intent and wilful blindness is that they arguably show that the question-changing strategy shows up in different sorts of hard cases. That is, it is not a strategy particular to borderline cases, although the particular context of the normative question is different because – in the typical cases where transferred intent or wilful blindness are taken to apply – the relevant behaviour is within the determinate anti-extension of the relevant predicates and the background purpose is a quite particular one. In vagueness-related cases, the courts can of course also ask if the relevant behaviour is just as bad as behaviour that is within the determinate extension of the predicate in question, but I see no reason to suppose that the resolution of borderline cases is restricted to that particular purpose. There may be all sorts of reasons why *x* ought – for the purposes of the law – to count as an *F*.

Now that we have relieved the arbitrariness worry, by proposing a strategy grounded both in normative theory and in practice, we can ask whether the normative question is ever better left to the courts or administrative agencies. If it is, then Sorensen's argument will be unsound.

[23] 546 US 74 (2005).
[24] 532 F2d 697 (1976).

A. Evaluating the Value of Vagueness in Terms of 'Better Than'

I want to start this section by focusing on what kind of questions it is appropriate to ask when we are considering the value of vagueness in the law. The reason is that Sorensen's framework for talking about law and vagueness can sometimes make for misleading questions. In particular, Sorensen's strict notion of function is poorly suited for asking the appropriate questions regarding the value of vagueness in the law. His criterion of function was this: something has a function in a system if, and only if, its presence is explained by how it serves a goal of the system. This prompts an unhelpful way to think about the value of vagueness, since we are in effect forced to ask whether the presence of absolute borderline cases is valuable relative to the aims of the law. It is unhelpful since it seems odd from the get-go to even entertain the thought that somehow the *presence* of a particular absolute borderline case in the law is a good thing. What value does a particular hard case promote? This way of conducting the inquiry makes claims about the value of vagueness seem dubious from the start and so should be rejected and substituted by a more sensible way of asking the relevant questions. If we don't, we run the risk of not getting to the real issues.

I propose that we evaluate the value of vagueness in law using the comparative phrase 'better than', which underlines the fact that the value of using terms that have absolute borderline cases depends on the alternative options available to the lawmakers. The appropriate question is, I think, whether it is better to leave a law vague and let the courts deal with borderline cases than to have the legislature work out a more precise alternative. Or, to put it another way: is it ever better to leave it to the courts (or administrative agencies) to answer the question whether *x* ought to count as an *F* (assuming *x* is a genuine borderline case)? As for Sorensen, he must think that an answer can be affirmative only if the relevant delegates are in a *better position* to answer it than the legislators. This, however, would also be a misleading way of framing the issue. *That A is in a better position than B* to answer a question does not – as the phrase seems to superficially suggest – entail that A has better *knowledge* than B. A can also be in a better position if A has better tools than B for finding an answer, or if A's cost of finding the answer is lower than B's. This latter notion of *answering cost* may be particularly helpful, I think, in understanding the benefit of letting delegates answer the question whether a borderline *x* ought to count as an *F*. And since the answering cost we are concerned with here has to do with a practical question – whether to count *x* as an *F* – we can presumably substitute it with the more familiar notion of *cost of deliberation*.[25]

[25] For the time being, I am including under the heading of 'cost of deliberation' the *appropriateness* of the deliberator. That is, the extent to which the deliberator is inappropriate for the task of deliberating will figure in the cost of deliberation. Ultimately, this cost should perhaps be considered separately, but I'll leave that discussion for a later occasion.

Now, in some cases it is clearly *not* better to let delegates decide whether or not particular borderline cases ought to be regulated. When it comes to drinking age, for example, it would make bad sense to formulate the law vaguely ('Only adults are permitted to purchase and publicly possess alcoholic beverages') and have the courts or law enforcement agencies deal with borderline adults, by asking whether or not this or that person should count as one. The overall cost of deliberation would be enormous. Better to avoid that mess and make a somewhat (but not totally) arbitrary cut-off point by mentioning a particular age – say, 21. That may of course be done in at least two ways, either by leaving out any mention of adults in favour of explicit age, as was done in the National Minimum Drinking Age Act 1984,[26] or by defining 'adult'.

In other cases, however, it may be better to stick with a vague formulation and let the courts change the question to whether *x* ought to count as an *F* relative to the purposes of the relevant law. Let me try out a fictional example.

The federal code concerning drive-by shooting related to major drug offences specifies, among other things, that if one fires a weapon into a crowd '[causing] grave risk to any human life', then one shall receive such-and-such punishment.[27] The phrase 'grave risk' here is vague, mainly in virtue of the term 'grave'. As a borderline case, we can imagine that someone, in relation to a major drug offence, fires rubber bullets into a crowd and that, given the nature of the projectiles and the circumstances of the shooting, it is indeterminate whether the shooter caused grave risk to human life. In other words, the shooting constitutes an absolute borderline case of the behaviour prohibited by the statute.

Now, it seems to me that it would be a bad move for the legislature – whose aims presumably include the reduction of danger to innocent bystanders and of the public fear that drive-by shootings induce – to try to work out a precise alternative statute. In addition to the fact that it would be very cumbersome, it is very likely, due to the multiplicity of factors that make for the absence or presence of risk, that any attempt to come up with a formula that isn't excessively over- or underinclusive is bound to fail.[28] Also, substituting the vague law with a more precise one would mean to exclude in advance some unpredictable borderline cases and include some, thereby eliminating the possibility of determining – when they come up – whether the law has an interest, vis-à-vis the purpose of the code, in regulating them.

To put this point more generally, it seems to me a bad bargain, all in all, to have legislators try to deal with *intensional* vagueness instead of letting the courts deal only with *extensional* vagueness. No matter how many concrete cases end up in the courts, they will always be far fewer than even the most modest sets of possible absolute borderline cases. That is, *the cost of deliberation associated with determining in advance what to do regarding possible borderline cases will in most*

[26] 23 USC §158.
[27] 18 USC §36(b1).
[28] I say 'excessively' since most laws are arguably both over- and underinclusive to some extent.

cases greatly exceed the cost of deliberation associated with determining what to do regarding actual borderline cases when they come up. Although, as we saw above, sometimes the foreseeable actual borderline cases are so many that it is better to draw a simple bright line, as long as this 'cheaper' rule is sufficiently acceptable (with respect to the relevant legislative aims). But sometimes, such a strategy is not feasible and the better option is to leave the language vague and let the courts deal with extensional vagueness on a case-by-case basis.

If this is correct, then Sorensen's argument against the claim that vagueness proper can have power-delegating value is unsound. In particular, it is not the case that the delegation of limited lawmaking power is justified only if the individuals or entities to which the power is delegated are in a better position to find out whether x is F. Also, it seems that – at least in some cases – we can, using Sorensen's own strong notion of function, say that the occurrence of absolute borderline cases in the law is indeed explained by how they contribute to the promotion of the aims of the law. They do so *not* by delegating to the courts the task to find out whether x is F. Rather, they do so by delegating to them the task to find out whether x ought, relative to the purposes of the relevant law, to count as an F.

The above example regarding drive-by shooting is of course very limited. But there are other, more wide-ranging, cases in which similar reasoning applies. Take for example the general requirements of culpability, as defined by the Model Penal Code s.2.02. In s.2(a),[29] the vague ordinary term 'purposely' is defined partially in terms of *awareness*, *belief*, and *hope*. Now, there will be both relative and absolute borderline cases of persons purposely violating the law in the ordinary sense of 'purposely'. The definition used in the Model Penal Code is arguably a precisification vis-à-vis relative borderline cases, ie the definition supplies a somewhat helpful answering resource. But I fail to see that the definition helps eliminate absolute borderline cases in any meaningful sense. At best, it trades one set of cases for another, since 'awareness', 'belief' and 'hope' are at least as vague as 'purposely' (I'm not assuming that we have a clear theoretical way of comparing vagueness – I only mean that the following holds: If 'purposely' is vague, then so are the other terms).

The question I want to ask here is this: Which of the following options seems better?

(1) The legislature tries to pre-empt the occurrence of absolute borderline cases by adding further, non-circular, definitions of 'awareness', 'hope' and 'belief', stipulating meanings in order to eliminate absolute borderline cases of purposely violating the law.
(2) The legislature – at some fairly coarse-grained level – leaves the provision vague and gives judges the discretion to ask whether actual absolute borderline cases that reach the courts ought – relative to the purpose of the code – to be regulated and thus to be counted as being purposeful.

[29] MPC §2.02(a).

It seems to me that (2) is the better option. Option (1) is feasible only if the lawmakers are able to evaluate a significant number of possible borderline cases or if it makes sense to halt deliberation and opt for a cheap and simple bright-line rule. The former isn't feasible given the high cost of deliberation and limited cognitive resources of normal human beings. And the latter isn't feasible given the high likelihood of error – ie of drawing an unacceptable boundary, relative to the relevant regulatory aim. Better to opt for (2) and let the courts deal with borderline cases incrementally, by dealing with actual borderline cases of purposeful violations as they reach the courts.

If what I have said is correct, then Sorensen's argument against the power-delegating function of vagueness is unsound. Vagueness may indeed have such a function, and, moreover, this function seems to be significant rather than marginal. I do agree, however, that many power-delegating instances are valuable because there is hope that the delegates will in fact discover whether *x* is or is not *F*, and that we should be careful to distinguish the value of relative borderline cases from that of absolute ones.

III. Summary

In section I, I introduced Sorensen's epistemic account of vagueness and his distinction between absolute and relative borderline cases, and explained his argument for the claim that absolute borderline cases do not have a constructive power-delegating function in law. The argument was summarised in the following way:

> P1. Delegation of decision-making authority, vis-à-vis borderline cases, is valuable only if the relevant delegates are in a better position to answer the question whether *x* is *F* than those delegating the power.
>
> P2. When *x* is an absolute borderline case of 'F', it is not the case that the relevant delegates are in a better position to answer the question whether *x* is *F* than those delegating the power.
>
> C. Therefore, when *x* is an absolute borderline case of 'F', it is not the case that delegation of decision-making authority, vis-à-vis *x*, is valuable.

My reply, presented in section II, was to argue that P1 is false. Delegation of decision-making authority can be valuable even if the relevant delegates are not in a better position to answer the question whether *x* is *F* than those delegating the power. The key to seeing why, I claimed, is to acknowledge that when faced with absolute borderline cases, the courts must engage with a related *normative* question – whether *x ought*, relative to the purposes of the law, to *count* as an *F*.

I tried to show that, under certain circumstances, it is indeed better to let the relevant delegates answer the normative question – ie whether *x* ought, relative to the purpose of the relevant law, to count as an *F*. It is better when both of the following options are worse: (i) lawmakers consider in advance possible borderline cases and work out a sophisticated, more precise, alternative; (ii) lawmakers halt deliberation early on and opt for a cheap and simple bright-line rule. These options are typically worse if option (i) incurs extravagant costs of deliberation and option (ii) is likely to result in a rule that is unacceptable relative to the relevant regulatory aim. If I am correct that there are situations in which neither of these options is feasible, then there are situations in which delegation of decision-making authority is valuable even if the relevant delegates are not in a better position to answer the question whether *x* really is *F*.

4

Vagueness, Uncertainty and Behaviour

In this chapter, I continue to examine the power-delegating value of vagueness in the law, but my primary concern will be the relationship between vagueness, uncertainty and (desirable) behaviour, focusing on arguments by Endicott (2011), Hadfield (1994a) and Sorensen (2001a). I argue, first, that Endicott's argument for the power-delegating value of vagueness is problematic to the extent that it relies on assumptions about special judicial competence. I also argue that, although I think he – and other writers influenced by law and economics, such as Hadfield – is in important respects right about the way vague law affects people's behaviour in potentially desirable ways, due attention to issues like the highly contingent nature of behavioural incentive shows that but we should be careful not to over-estimate this value. I then address some significant general concerns – raised by Sorensen – about the efficacy of vagueness-related uncertainty in the law. All in all, the chapter offers a qualified endorsement of the arguments provided by Endicott and Hadfield.

I. Endicott's Argument from Comparative Value

In chapter two, I argued that Endicott's argument for the instrumental necessity value of vagueness did not succeed. This is not necessarily fatal to his overall view, however, since he may still be right – in important respects – about its comparative value. As we saw in chapter two, some forms of human conduct arguably cannot be regulated by precise norms, but in other situations, when both precise and vague schemes of regulation are available to lawmakers, they must determine whether, in a given scheme of regulation, the consequences of precision are worse than the consequences of vagueness.

In his argument for the comparative value of vagueness in law, Endicott identifies three ways in which precision and vagueness may be (comparatively) valuable.[1] I will start by listing and briefly explaining them in the abstract and then move on to a more detailed discussion.

(1) From the perspective of the *law's subjects*, the value of precision is that it lets them know their legal rights and obligations and the value of vagueness is

[1] Endicott (2011) 28.

that it can encourage desirable forms of behaviour. Vague law can, Endicott says, give people incentive to be innovative in avoiding liability or to cost-efficiently contract out of liability. He calls these values *guidance value* and *private ordering value*, respectively.

(2) With respect to *officials*, the value of precision is that it lets them know how to apply the relevant norm and the value of vagueness is that it can appropriately delegate to them limited lawmaking power. According to Endicott, vagueness for example allows the courts to work out the details of the law, which may be preferable in domains where the courts satisfy certain competence conditions. He calls these values *process value* and *power allocation value*, respectively.

(3) With respect to the *purpose* of the relevant norm, the value of precision is that it constrains the discretion of officials and the value of vagueness is that it allows officials to act in a way that is faithful to that purpose. In certain borderline cases, the background purpose, or purposes, of the law may dictate an outcome; unlike precision, vagueness affords a case-by-case determination of borderline cases, and so may sometimes be better suited to bring the law closer in line with its underlying purposes. Endicott calls these values *constraint value* and *fidelity value*, respectively.[2]

It is by reference to these three types of values that lawmakers must determine whether the consequences of precision are better or worse than the consequences of vagueness. That is, these values form the 'basis of calculation' vis-à-vis the comparative value of vagueness in the law. To be sure, vagueness is often worse than precision. When it comes to drinking and voting age, for example, it would make bad sense to formulate the law vaguely and have the courts or law enforcement agencies deal with borderline adults, by asking whether or not this or that person should count as one. Given the extent to which people would be at the mercy of officials and the cost of evaluating each borderline case, it is better to make a somewhat (but not totally) arbitrary cut-off point by mentioning a particular age – say, 21, as was done in the *National Minimum Drinking Age Act 1984*, or 18, as was done in the *26th Amendment* of the US Constitution.[3] However, the value of precision can sometimes be negligible compared to the value of vagueness, or so Endicott argues.

A. Arbitrariness: The Cost of Precision May Be Greater than the Cost of Vagueness

Endicott's primary examples of vagueness comparing favourably to precision come from contract law, negligence law and child care law. The Unfair Contract

[2] Endicott (2011).
[3] 23 USC §158 and US Const, Am 26, respectively.

Terms Act 1977 in English contract law, for example, uses vague terms like 'reasonable' and so on.[4] The purpose, according to Endicott, was to 'delegate to courts the power to determine the reasons for which limitation of liability clauses were to be permitted or not'.[5] This delegation is justified, he says, given that judges have special expertise in developing norms of contract law, that the doctrine of precedent is well suited to facilitate such development, and that the courts are in a position to hear the arguments of disputing sides. In other words, the courts are in a better position than lawmakers to develop the details of contract law norms. The Act's low process value is negligible, then, compared to its high power allocation value. Moreover, if the Act were replaced with a more precise alternative, the increased process value would be negligible compared to the low fidelity value – making the law easier to apply would make it significantly less faithful to its underlying purpose.

The Act also provides service providers with an incentive to be innovative in avoiding liability. They may decide that it is in their best interest to accept liability or to take out insurance, or they may devise various contract clauses that (at least attempt to) make reasonable exclusions of liability. This sort of desirable creativity in the private domain would not have been encouraged by a precise scheme of regulation. The Act's low guidance value is negligible, therefore, compared to its high private ordering value, Endicott says.

In negligence law, vague schemes of regulation are necessary, according to Endicott, but there is still a choice about whether to try to incorporate some precise norms. It is here that comparative judgments must be made. Endicott argues that the uncertainty arising from relatively vague schemes may encourage private parties to avoid creating risks to others or to cost-effectively contract out of liability, thus assigning responsibility for action where it best belongs. Precise standards, on the other hand, do not encourage this sort of behaviour, but instead encourage people to do no more than just what is required. In cases where private persons are in a better position than lawmakers to devise ways of avoiding harm to others, it is therefore better to refrain from including a precise standard. In these cases, the low guidance value is negligible compared to the high private ordering value.

Endicott is not explicit about how vagueness compares with precision with respect to officials, but it is plausible to take him to believe that the delegation of power in negligence law is justified for the same reasons as in the case of contract law – the courts are in a better position than lawmakers to develop the details of negligence law norms, due to the fact that judges have special expertise in developing such norms. If that is correct, the low process value is negligible compared to the high power allocation value.

[4] It is reasonable to assume that what applies in the case of the Unfair Contract Terms Act in English law carries over to the unconscionability clause of the Uniform Commercial Code in US law.

[5] Endicott (2011) 26.

In child care law, vague schemes are – as in negligence law – unavoidable, on Endicott's view. But, as before, it remains to be determined whether to incorporate certain precise norms – like, for example, a norm prescribing the minimum age of babysitters. Endicott argues that refraining from including such a norm may allocate responsibility to the persons who ought to have it, ie to the appropriate persons. Refraining from specifying a minimum age for babysitters, for example, appropriately assigns certain responsibilities to parents, which makes it the better option. In this case, and in similar ones, the low guidance value is negligible compared to the high private ordering value.

As for the power allocating value of vagueness, it is low with respect to the courts, since they do not have any special expertise in this domain. However, it is presumably high with respect to social services officials (if they function well), although Endicott does not say anything about the latter. I would not go so far as to say that the low process value is negligible compared to the high power allocation value, but aggregating all of the relevant values will presumably still yield that vagueness is preferable to precision.

These examples constitute Endicott's main case for the comparative value of vagueness. I think he is right about a number of things, but would like to voice a couple of worries. One concerns the highly contingent nature of economic incentives; the worry is that vagueness may give subjects incentive both to undercomply and to overcomply, both of which gives us reason not to overestimate the *private ordering value* of vagueness. The other concerns judicial competence; the worry here is that there is reason to doubt that courts have any special expertise with respect to either contract law or negligence law, which gives us a reason not to overestimate the *power allocation value* of vagueness.

Before I go on to discuss these worries, however, I would like to make a remark about Endicott's threefold distinction of value. Value, as we saw, was distinguished by its relation to (i) law's subjects, (ii) officials, and (iii) legislative purposes. The reason I want to start here is that I think the third category is undermotivated, and to some extent obscures rather than clarifies the relevant lawmaking scenarios. Endicott himself says very little about this category, and the two associated values – *constraint value* and *fidelity value* – seem primarily to have to do with the presence or absence of private or official discretion/responsibility. I think it would be better to recognise just two domains of value – value with respect to private persons and value with respect to officials – and to construe Endicott's third category as identifying the *source* of those values. This would also eliminate the problem of associating a source of value with that third category.

It seems to me best to say that *guidance value*, *private ordering value*, *process value*, and *power allocation value* are all determined by the (sometimes conflicting) purposes of the law, both law's general (contingent and/or necessary) purposes – such as guiding action and assigning responsibility for action where it best belongs, etc – and specific legislative purposes – such as ensuring that only mature individuals vote, and so on. Vagueness and precision have value, then, insofar as they promote law's ends. And this seems right.

B. Vagueness and Undercompliance

Recall Endicott's argument that vagueness in negligence law, under certain circumstances, gives private persons incentive to avoid creating risk to others or to contract out of liabilities in cost-effective ways. On Endicott's view, then, one of the consequences of enacting vague law is that it gives efficient incentive, in the sense that it motivates agents to take courses of action that are considered desirable from the point of view of the law. In many circumstances, this may be right. Recent work, however, on the ways in which people *actually* behave in the face of vague law seems to suggest that the relevant uncertainty contributes less to such motivation than Endicott (and others) have predicted. Feldman and Teichman (2008), for example, report a study that they designed in order to test the hypothesis that the type of uncertainty with which a legal subject is faced does not matter vis-à-vis the calculation of probability of liability (conditional on taking a particular action), which is – within the framework of Rational Choice Theory – the probability used to determine incentives given by law.[6]

Rational Choice Theory has traditionally treated uncertainty about the law's content as being on a par with – or fungible with respect to – uncertainty about enforcement. As Feldman and Teichman note, traditional theories assume that '[t]he expected sanction if illegality is certain and the probability of detection is fifty percent is identical to the expected sanction if detection is certain and the *probability of illegality is fifty percent*'.[7] Endicott is not explicit about whether he adopts this view, but it appears to me to be implicit in his arguments. Although the study and the reported findings should be taken with a grain of salt, it did show a significant positive difference between the percentage of people willing to follow through with a borderline illegal course of action (given certain enforcement) and the percentage of people willing to do so when the probability of enforcement is .5 (given certain liability).[8] Insofar as it is not desirable (from the point of view of the law) that people engage in borderline legal behaviour, it is appropriate to call this statistically significant pattern of behaviour a tendency to 'undercomply' in borderline cases.

Feldman and Teichman seem to have shown that we cannot expect uncertainty about the legal status of a given course of action to contribute to the expected sanction to the same extent that uncertainty about enforcement does. It is not clear how the uncertainty should be modelled, but we can nevertheless infer that if vague law is – in borderline cases – able to give the same incentives as other (better understood) types of legal uncertainty, it seems that the sanctions for violating such laws would have to be raised.[9] This, however, is not feasible since most of the

[6] For a description of the study, see Feldman and Teichman (2008) 985–86.
[7] ibid, 985.
[8] See, in particular, ibid, 1001–02.
[9] Unless people tend to behave irrationally in borderline cases, in which case it is not clear that any remedy is possible.

cases that reach the courts will presumably be clear ones, and imposing higher sanctions *only* for borderline behaviour is remarkably problematic. Because it is not feasible to raise sanctions, it seems that, in borderline cases, the uncertainty associated with the legal consequences of the relevant course of action will often not give the incentive that Endicott identifies in his arguments.

I take the findings reported by Feldman and Teichman to indicate that Endicott may not have taken account of circumstances under which people have the incentives that frustrate law's purposes. I do not want to suggest that Endicott did not consider undercompliance at all, but it is reasonable to conclude, given the fact that he does not discuss it, that he thinks the relative frequency of undercompliance – prior to the consideration of the circumstances discussed by Feldman and Teichman – is negligible. But if Feldman and Teichman are right, then the relative frequency of such cases is presumably non-negligible.

It is an open question to what extent this affects Endicott's conclusion, but if he is correct in his claim that the value of enacting a precise scheme of negligence regulation is negligible compared to the value of enacting a vague one, then it is reasonable to expect that, although taking account of the possibility and disutility of undercompliance will reduce the expected value of the vague alternative, vagueness will still be preferable to precision. Nevertheless, if the reduction can plausibly be shown to be sufficient – or further negative consequences need to be taken account of – it will prove hard to argue that vagueness has significant advantage over precision. This, however, is not currently the case, and so I will take the consideration regarding undercompliance not to be fatal to Endicott's argument, but to give us a definite reason not to overestimate the comparative value of vagueness.

C. Vagueness and Overcompliance

As noted by Calfee and Crasswell (1984), uncertainty about the content of the law may, under certain circumstances, give people incentive to overcomply, relative to standards supplied by economic theory. In the domain of negligence law, people may for example take excessive care (relative to these standards) – a strategy known as 'safe harbour' – in order to avoid negligence liability. That is, it can pay for agents to make sure that their behaviour falls within the determinate anti-extension of the predicates used in the relevant legal texts, and they may do so in ways that have nothing to do with innovation or efficient contracting-out – they just spend an inefficient amount of resources on taking precaution.

I take this to indicate that Endicott may have overestimated the proportion of cases in which people are given sufficient incentive to behave in ways considered to be desirable from the point of view of the law (like innovation and contracting out). Now, I do not want to suggest that Endicott overlooked safe harbour strategies. Instead, I take Endicott's silence regarding this type of incentive to indicate that he thinks that the relative frequency of such behaviour is negligible. Crasswell and Calfee's work suggests that it may not be.

As in the case of undercompliance, it is an open question to what extent the possibility of overcompliance affects Endicott's conclusion. My view is that it varies by domain. But, again, if Endicott is correct in his claim that the value of enacting a precise scheme of negligence regulation is negligible compared to the value of enacting a vague one, then – as before – it is reasonable to expect that, although taking account of the possibility and disutility of overcompliance will reduce the expected value of the vague alternative, vagueness will continue to be preferable to precision. In any case, since I expect everyone to agree that undercompliance with law is generally worse than overcompliance (because overcompliance is generally more likely than undercompliance to promote law's ends), the comparative value of vagueness is less affected by the current argument than by the undercompliance argument. Consequently, I will take the consideration regarding overcompliance not to be fatal to Endicott's argument, but to give us *some* reason not to overestimate the comparative value of vagueness.

D. Do Courts have Special Expertise?

There is also a worry regarding the extent to which courts in fact have the sort of special expertise that is necessary for vagueness to have significant power allocation value. Since Endicott's claim about judicial competence in negligence and contract law provides much – though not all – of the basis for his claim that vagueness is valuable compared to relative precision in these domains, due to the high power allocation value, worries about judicial competence – relative to law's purposes – are potentially serious.

I will assume that we have an adequate idea about how courts are likely to behave in the face of vague legislation in contract and negligence law. The relevant question, thus, is not what courts are likely to do, but whether what we can reasonably take them to do is faithful to law's *purposes*. The practical authority of expertise is, after all, based on the premise that the recommendations of the expert allow people to better act in accordance with the reasons that apply to them. So, in order for the power allocation value of vagueness to be as high in negligence and contract law as Endicott claims, it must be the case that the courts have special expertise with respect to the underlying purposes of those areas of law.

I think there are at least two reasons to doubt that courts in general have such expertise. One is that it is not settled what the purposes of these areas of law really are. Is the goal of negligence law to provide a mechanism for corrective justice or for distributive justice, or perhaps to minimise the sum of the cost of accidents and the cost of avoiding them? And what about contract law? Legal practice does not seem to give settled answers to these questions. Thus, claims about *special* expertise on behalf of judges seem overly optimistic.

Another reason, downstream from the first one, is that claims about special judicial expertise are hard to justify given *any* of these possible fundamental goals. For example, courts are – on average – definitely not experts on principles of economic efficiency. As Craswell (1993) notes, since public utility commissions – whose dedicated job it is to ensure reasonable rates for utility services – have not managed to inspire confidence among economists, we have no reason to think that common law courts would do any better at determining *general* economic reasonableness.[10] Nor are courts experts on distributive or corrective justice. These are moral-political goals, and if there are indeed any experts at all on these matters, I see no reason to think that the courts have *more* expertise than the legislature does.

Now, even if I am correct, this does not mean that all power allocation value is lost with respect to these areas of law. As we saw in chapter three, it is sometimes better to deal with borderline cases when they come up than to try either to consider in advance possible borderline cases and work out sophisticated, more precise alternatives, or to halt deliberation early on and opt for cheap and simple bright-line rules. And, as Endicott rightly points out, the courts are well suited to do just that. But this is true even if judges do not have any special expertise in the relevant area of law.

II. Hadfield on the Value of Vagueness-related Uncertainty

Endicott's argument – or at least certain aspects of it – can be construed more generally as an argument that vagueness can be valuable to law since it entails (or consists in) uncertainty. The unifying element of this general type of argument is that vagueness-related uncertainty generates unpredictability that somehow promotes certain important legal ends. Hadfield (1994a) provides another argument of this sort, arguing that – under certain circumstances – adopting vague rules over precise rules will, over the long run, produce legal standards that are comparatively close to optimal ones, partly in virtue of the varying behavioural incentives that vague rules give to those subject to the relevant laws.

When the law is precise, Hadfield says, subjects can, relative to all possible behaviour, assign the probability 0 or 1 to the proposition that they will incur liability. This, of course, is not the same as *being held* liable, the probability of which may be somewhere between 1 and 0 due to factors like imperfect enforcement etc. – that is, to factors that are the product of official discretion. In the case of

[10] See Craswell (1993) 20, fn 36. For a discussion about the limited competence of courts to identify economically efficient outcomes in cases concerning incomplete contracts, see Hadfield (1994b). It should be noted, however, that in some legal systems there are courts specialised, for example, in commercial law, it which case the courts may have significantly greater expertise in the relevant matters than the average lawmaker (since the relevant judges will in most cases be well trained in matters economic). These courts, of course, have more expertise than the *legislature* – as an *institution* – only if lawmakers do not have reliable access to advice from comparable economic experts (assuming that economic efficiency is the underlying goal of commercial law). Thanks to Burkhard Schafer for bringing this point to my attention.

vague legal rules, Hadfield says, this uncertainty is amplified, partly because it is not possible – *even in principle* – for people to assign, relative to all possible behaviour, the probability 0 or 1 to the proposition that they will incur liability and partly because official discretion is inevitable in borderline cases.

As we saw above, the mainstream view among law and economics scholars working on unclear law and deterrence used to be that the effect of the type of uncertainty described in the previous paragraph is that it leads to undercompliance, but recent work in that field seems to show that – if the uncertainty resulting from the enactment of vague rules is not too great – it may instead, at least under certain conditions (especially if agents are risk averse), lead to overcompliance.[11] In Hadfield's words, '[t]he decrease in probability of being held liable gained by overcompliance may be substantial enough to offset the personal cost of overcompliance; it can therefore make sense for an individual to overcomply in order to reduce expected damages'.[12] This behavioural strategy, as already noted, is known as 'safe harbour'.

However, Hadfield says, vague rules don't lead exclusively to undercompliance or overcompliance – the behavioural incentive that they give is more nuanced than that. What vague rules do, and which may be desirable on Hadfield's view, is to correlate small changes in behaviour with small changes in the probability of liability. The cost of compliance along with the probability of liability will, for each subject, determine whether complying is the optimal thing to do. As Sorensen (2001a) puts it, 't]he uncertainty of the vague rule [is supposed to create] a *spectrum* of expected utilities that varies gently with the cost of compliance'.[13] Precise rules, on the other hand, steer people either into the same safe harbour or, if that is too costly, causes people to ignore the rule altogether. The result of such legislation will be 'excessive compliance or nil'.[14]

In certain domains of law – in particular in domains in which it is likely that, if lawmakers would choose precise rules, they would choose sub-optimal ones – it is better, Hadfield argues, to enact vague law. For example, in cases in which there is 'uncertainty among lawmakers and regulators about what constitutes optimal behaviour', enacting a vague law encourages a 'small degree of experimentation by individuals acting on the margin', which 'introduces variability into the types of cases heard by courts or regulatory agencies' and thereby 'gives these institutions more information about the nature of the activity regulated, thus improving their ability to develop law'.[15]

When it comes to choosing, for example, between strict liability – which is a bright-line rule – and a rule of negligence – which is a vague rule – for product liability, there are good reasons to choose the latter, Hadfield (1994b) argues. A strict

[11] See Calfee and Craswell (1986).
[12] Hadfield (1994a) 544.
[13] Sorensen (2001a) 410 (my emphasis).
[14] Hadfield (1994a) 545.
[15] Hadfield (1994a) 549.

liability rule to a large extent ignores the various factors that determine the most efficient outcome in particular cases – such as relative costs and benefits of precautionary measures and the potential for the manufacturer to innovate new safety mechanisms – by introducing a 'blanket standard', while a rule of negligence allows sensitivity to those factors by '[directing] the court to explicitly weigh the expected costs and benefits of preventing an accident'.[16]

However, it isn't necessarily that the vague standard – as is – is the optimal standard. Rather, what it allows for – and the precise one doesn't – is that, in practice, it is eventually 'reduced to collections of refined rules when applied to any particular subset of facts'.[17] That is, over time, the vague standard is precisified in a principled manner – a manner which, at least in some domains, eventually makes for a standard (or a collection thereof) that is closer to an optimal standard than any precise standard chosen at the outset would have been.

III. Sorensen on Vagueness-related Uncertainty and Legal Unpredictability

As we saw previously in this chapter, I have some worries about this line of reasoning. But since I have already discussed these worries in relation to Endicott's argument, I will let it suffice here to briefly explain what Sorensen (2001a) thinks is – *in general* – wrong with arguments of the sort offered by Hadfield and Endicott and then go on to provide what I take to be a rebuttal of his argument.

Sorensen's main objection to views that take vagueness-related uncertainty to have value in the legal context is that, due to the tendency of the courts to treat like cases alike, whatever unpredictability is generated by vague legislation will (unlike proper randomisation) not be sufficient to promote the relevant aim. Judges, he says, are poor randomisers, even by informal standards, both because normal human beings are bad at producing sufficiently random-like results and – more importantly – because judges will attempt to decide problem cases in a *principled* fashion.

Sorensen's argument is brief and he does not provide any detailed explanation of why vague law fails to generate sufficient unpredictability. However, the argument raises important questions about one of the primary reasons that vagueness has – especially by scholars influenced by law and economics – been taken to be valuable to law, and so I think that it merits careful dissection. If we take care to reconstruct Sorensen's argument, we will be able both to identify certain problematic assumptions that he makes and to see why – despite the attempt of judges to decide problem cases in a principled fashion – vague law can still often generate uncertainty sufficient for it to be valuable.

[16] Hadfield (1994b) 610.
[17] Hadfield (1994b) 610.

We can reconstruct Sorensen's main argument in the following way:

P1. Vagueness-related uncertainty is valuable in law only if the resulting unpredictability regarding probability of (criminal or civil) liability gives subjects incentive to engage in desirable behaviour.

P2. It is not the case that the unpredictability regarding probability of (criminal or civil) liability resulting from vagueness-related uncertainty gives people incentive to engage in desirable behaviour.

C1. It is not the case that vagueness-related uncertainty is valuable in law.

P1 seems fairly safe, and I will treat it as such here. I will therefore – like Sorensen – focus on P2 and argue that it is false.

Sorensen's argument for P2 is as follows:

P3. The unpredictability regarding probability of (criminal or civil) liability resulting from vagueness-related uncertainty gives people incentive to engage in desirable behaviour only if judges/courts behave sufficiently like unbiased random-decision generators.

P4. Judges/courts do not behave sufficiently like unbiased random-decision generators.

C/P2. It is not the case that the unpredictability regarding probability of (criminal or civil) liability resulting from vagueness-related uncertainty gives people incentive to engage in desirable behaviour.

On the face of it, it may seem that P3 is dubious and that P4 is plausible. In fact, however, I think it is the other way around. We see why if we examine the arguments for P3 and P4. Let's start with P3:

P5. The unpredictability regarding probability of (criminal or civil) liability resulting from vagueness-related uncertainty gives people incentive to engage in desirable behaviour only if it is sufficiently hard to detect patterns in decision-making in borderline cases.

P6. It is sufficiently hard to detect patterns in decision making in borderline cases only if judges/courts behave sufficiently like unbiased random-decision generators.

C/P3. The unpredictability regarding probability of (criminal or civil) liability resulting from vagueness-related uncertainty gives people incentive to engage in desirable behaviour only if judges/courts behave sufficiently like unbiased random-decision generators.

P5 is the safe premise here. P6 may seem less safe, but once we acknowledge the *sufficiently* qualification, it turns out to be very plausible. Judges/courts don't have to really be unbiased random-decision generators, they simply have to appear to be.

That is, as long as decision-making patterns are *sufficiently hard to discern for the relevant group of people*, the relevant requirement is satisfied. Thus, it suffices that judges/courts be so-called *pseudo*-random-decision generators relative to the relevant perceiver. In casinos, for example, pseudo-random-number generators are used because – for the purposes of running a gambling facility – they behave sufficiently like genuine unbiased random-number generators: they make it hard enough for the majority of people to detect patterns in the relevant set of outcomes. P3, therefore, is fairly plausible.

Turning to P4, I think we start to see where the problem lies with Sorensen's argument. It is also here that we get to the issues that are most interesting from a legal-theoretic perspective. Here is a reconstruction of the support that Sorensen provides for P4, ie for the claim that judges/courts do not behave sufficiently like unbiased random-decision generators:

P7. When judges/courts make an effort to treat like cases alike, they are trying to act in a conscientious, principled fashion.

P8. When judges/courts try to act in a conscientious, principled fashion, they do not behave sufficiently like unbiased random-decision generators.

C5. When judges/courts make an effort to treat like cases alike, they do not behave sufficiently like unbiased random-decision generators.

P9. Judges/courts make an effort to treat like cases alike.

C/P4. Judges/courts do not behave sufficiently like unbiased random-decision generators.

I think that P8 is where Sorensen's argument goes wrong (I will treat P7 and P9 as unproblematic). I don't think that the way in which judges/courts attempt to act in a conscientious, principled fashion entails that they don't behave like pseudo-random-decision generators relative to subjects – even relative to subjects well-informed about precedent. My *main* reason for thinking so is twofold. One reason is that even if the courts make an effort to treat like cases alike, the doctrine is – as such – substantially empty.[18] That is, the doctrine cannot be used to predict the decision of a court unless the predictor has good evidence of the criteria of similarity that the court will use in determining whether or not two cases are alike. However, since the criteria of relevance are contestable and often controversial, the doctrine of treating like cases alike alone won't ensure that courts fail to behave with sufficient unpredictability in borderline cases. Further, although in rare cases, subjects with good knowledge of precedent and of the inclinations of particular courts can perhaps predict what the court will decide, this will not *generally* be the

[18] See Duxbury (2008) 143. See also Schauer (1987) 596–97.

case – especially since judges are likely to disagree about the relevant substantive criteria for determining the likeness of cases.[19]

An additional reason to doubt P8 is that even if we concede that courts in general attempt to treat like cases alike and that there is rough agreement about the relevant criteria, this is by no means the only consideration that courts take into account when deciding cases. In particular, predictability is often significantly undermined by the practice of *distinguishing* – ie the practice of not following precedent even though the *ratio* of the earlier case applies to the facts of the present case. When cases are distinguished, it is claimed that the present case has a property that relevantly distinguishes it from prior precedent-setting cases, warranting a contrary decision. To be sure, the probability that a court will distinguish is often lower than the probability that it will follow precedent, but if we add this measure of uncertainty on top of the frequent uncertainty regarding the criteria of similarity, then this common judicial practice helps make it the case that – at least in many cases – there will be significant unpredictability regarding court outcomes. Or, in Sorensen's jargon, the fact that courts try to act in principled ways does not guarantee that they do not behave sufficiently like random-decision generators. For the reasons mentioned above, it may be sufficiently hard for many subjects to detect any reliable patterns in the decisions of courts in borderline cases. Thus, P8 is false, which leaves C4/P4 and C2/P2 unsupported, which in turn leaves Sorensen's main conclusion – that vagueness-related uncertainty is not valuable in law – unsupported.

A third reason to treat P8 with scepticism – although not as weighty as the combination of the two preceding ones – is that although it may be true that in general people don't reliably produce sets of outcomes that closely resemble genuinely random ones, they don't reliably detect patterns either. As psychological research has shown,[20] people tend to see patterns where there aren't any and fail to see those that are there. That is, in general, the pattern-recognition capabilities of normal human beings generate a great deal of both false positives and false negatives. It is of course controversial whether and to what extent these experimental results generalise to different spheres of human life,[21] but they – at the very least – suggest that even if judges don't come very close to resembling genuine random-decision generators, the cognitive capacities of normal legal subjects will often

[19] It may of course happen that, in particular areas of law, there is significant general predictability about outcomes in borderline cases. In American criminal law, for example, the Rule of Lenity presumably makes it fairly likely that a borderline case will be decided in favour of the defendant. However, such fairly settled rules are rare outside the domain of criminal law.

[20] See eg Gilovich et al (1985), Kahneman and Tversky (1972), Bar-Hillel and Wagenaar (1991) and Hahn and Warren (2009).

[21] For a general discussion of the application of general experimental results to judicial cognitive behaviour, see Schauer (2010).

guarantee that they aren't able to reliably predict future outcomes based on their perception of previous judicial behaviour.[22]

I should emphasise that I am not arguing that vagueness – and hence uncertainty – in the law isn't diminished by judicial decisions. Of course it is. But all Hadfield's argument requires, for example, is that, initially, vague law creates incentive for people to experiment 'at the margins', thus providing legal institutions with better information about how to develop the law in the courts. And as the law is precisified through judicial decision-making, thereby decreasing uncertainty and – if Hadfield is correct – sometimes getting the law closer to optimality, it seems to me that we are simply trading one reasonably good thing for another. In addition, I take the considerations I have mentioned to show that although court outcomes in borderline cases do precisify the law, the increase in predictability gained from each individual outcome is fairly modest.

If what I have said above is correct, we have good reason to believe that Sorensen's argument for the claim that vagueness-related uncertainty is not valuable in law is unsound. What is more, what I have said in fact seems to support the opposite conclusion. In particular, it seems to support the falsity of P2, ie of the claim that the unpredictability regarding probability of (criminal or civil) liability resulting from vagueness-related uncertainty does not give people incentive to engage in desirable behaviour. On this occasion, however, I will not attempt to provide my own counterargument to Sorensen's claim. I will instead take it that both Endicott and Hadfield provide us with good reasons to believe that vagueness-related uncertainty can be a valuable feature of the law, although – as I argued – we should be careful in not overestimating that value. Thus, I counter Sorensen's claim only implicitly, in my qualified endorsements of both Endicott's and Hadfield's arguments.

[22] It is interesting to note that one fairly recent study comparing the reliability of model vs expert panel prediction about US Supreme Court cases showed that the expert panel had only a 59% accuracy rate, which isn't all too impressive. It should be noted, however, that *within* the expert panel there were certain identifiable sub-groups that had significant accuracy rates – most notably a group of appellate attorneys. See Ruger et al (2004) 1152, 1163–71.

5

On the Possibility of Non-literal Legislative Speech

Like the preceding three chapters, the existing literature on indeterminacy in the law focuses mostly on the use of vague terms.[1] There is another form of indeterminacy, however, that appears to have been somewhat neglected.[2] As I aim to show, not only is the content of a legislative utterance often indeterminate, it is often indeterminate what the content of such an utterance is. The reason, I'll argue, is that because legislative contexts generally contain little unequivocal information about legislative intent, it is often indeterminate whether the content of a law is its literal content or some pragmatic enrichment thereof.

In sections I and II of the chapter, using a recent argument by Andrei Marmor as my starting point, I discuss in some detail the conditions for successful non-literal speech and address the question whether these conditions are satisfied in the legal context.[3] I argue that – generally, albeit with certain qualifications – due to the fact that legislative contexts generally contain little unequivocal information about legislative intent, interpreters are typically not warranted in taking the legislature to have intended to communicate something non-literal.

In section III, I consider what I take to be the strongest case against my argument. Ekins (2012) offers a wealth of actual cases in which the courts have taken the content of the law to be something other than its literal content, seemingly based on relatively straightforward inferences about the legislature's communicative intentions. As I hope to show, however, only one of Ekins's examples is as straightforward as he suggests. If that is correct, his accumulative empirical argument from examples does not go through.

In the final section, section IV, I argue that the revised argument has important consequences for the extent to which we should take the content of the law to be determinate. The basic idea is that sometimes the audience of a speaker's remark ought to withhold belief regarding her communicative intentions, in which case the primary content of the relevant utterance is indeterminate between the literal

[1] See eg Hart (1958), Bix (1993), Waldron (1994), Endicott (2000), Endicott (2011), Waldron (2011) and Soames (2011).

[2] With some recent exceptions, see eg Poscher (2012), Marmor (2014) ch 4, and Marmor (2016). Endicott (2000) also dedicates a few pages to this type of indeterminacy; see pp 50–55.

[3] Marmor (2008).

content of the sentence uttered and some pragmatic enrichment thereof.[4] This has significant implications for the analysis of a number of important but controversial legal cases, which I discuss in some detail.

I. The Conditions for Non-literal Speech and the Legislative Context

In ordinary conversation, it frequently happens that speakers assert something other than what they literally say. When I utter the words 'I haven't had breakfast' to the waiter at the airport café, for example, it is obvious that I don't intend to assert that I haven't had breakfast *ever*. Rather, I am asserting that I haven't had breakfast *today*, perhaps in the hope that he tells me they are still serving. Given the ubiquity of this phenomenon, it makes sense to ask whether it also frequently happens that *legislatures* assert something other than what they literally say.

Consider for example the *Federal Tort Claims Act*, which guarantees the government immunity from '[a]ny claim arising in respect of … the detention of any goods, merchandise, or other property by any officer of customs or excise or any other law enforcement officer'.[5] On a literal reading of the Act, it guarantees immunity from claims arising in respect of certain actions on behalf of law enforcement officers of *any kind*. But it is reasonable – given the context of the Act – to wonder whether the legislature intended to communicate something slightly different, namely that immunity is guaranteed in respect of certain actions on behalf of law enforcement officers *working in customs or related domains*. The difference in content is significant. Abdus-Shahid MS Ali, for example, wanted to sue the government because prison officers lost property belonging to him, but this would require a non-literal reading of the Act. The Supreme Court held that a literal reading was appropriate and Ali was not allowed to sue.[6]

Or consider the US Criminal Code, 18 USC § 922(g)(1), which makes it 'unlawful for any person … who has been convicted in any court, of a crime punishable by imprisonment for a term exceeding 1 year … to … possess … any firearm'.[7] Read literally, there is no restriction on the location of the conviction – a conviction in *any* court will do. But, again, it makes sense to ask whether the legislature intended to communicate something slightly different from the literal content of the statute, namely that possession of a firearm is unlawful if one has been convicted in a *US* court. As before, the difference in content is significant. Gary Small, for example, had

[4] The primary content of an utterance is the content that a speaker counts as having primarily communicated, as opposed to secondarily (such as by implicature). This may be the literal content of the speaker's remark, but may also be – or may even have to be – some non-literal enrichment of that content. For a discussion, see Recanati (2012).

[5] 28 USC 2680(c).

[6] *Ali v Federal Bureau of Prisons*; 552 US 214 (2008). I discuss this case in more detail below.

[7] 18 USC § 922(g)(1).

been convicted of violating 18 USC § 922(g)(1), but the Supreme Court reversed the decision on appeal, on the basis of a non-literal reading of the Code.[8]

These cases are by no means unique – there is a wealth of cases the outcome of which turns on whether the legislature can reasonably be said to have asserted something other than what it literally said. Thus, questions about the existence and extent of non-literal assertion in the law have considerable practical, in addition to theoretical, significance.

A. Marmor's Scepticism about Non-literal Legislative Speech

Marmor (2008) argues that it *rarely* happens that the law asserts something other than what it literally says.[9] (As I understand him, what he means by 'rare' is not so much that it almost never occurs – although a few passages in the text suggest this – but rather that non-literal legislative speech is infrequent in comparison to non-literality in ordinary conversation.[10]) He substantiates his scepticism by first contrasting successful cases of pragmatic enrichment with unsuccessful ones, in an effort to identify the feature that the former cases have and the latter cases lack, and by then showing that – typically – this feature is absent in the context of legislative utterances. The distinguishing feature, Marmor thinks, is *obviousness*: typically, in cases in which a speaker successfully asserts something other than what she literally says, it is – due to a sufficiently rich conversational background – just obvious that she couldn't be intending to assert the literal content of her remark. It is *this* feature that Marmor thinks is – for the most part – absent in the context of legislation.

Marmor begins by noting that in ordinary conversation, we often come across examples like the following, in which the assertive content clearly goes beyond what is literally said:[11]

(1) A doctor examining a gunshot wound tells the patient: 'Don't worry, you are not going to die.' Clearly, the doctor did not assert that the patient is never going to die, but only that he is not going to die from this particular wound.

(2) When I get home in the evening and my wife asks me 'Have you eaten?' it is quite clear that she is asking me if I have already eaten dinner tonight, not whether I have ever engaged in the activity of eating.[12]

[8] *Small v United States*; 544 US 385 (2005). I also discuss this case in more detail below.

[9] Marmor (2008) 424–29. For an interesting – and relatively early – discussion of non-literal legislative speech and epistemic constraints, see Goldsworthy (1994) esp 168–70.

[10] Thanks to Jeffrey Goldsworthy and Lawrence Solum for pressing me to clarify this.

[11] Note that the following examples and their analyses assume that the literal content of the relevant utterances are complete propositions. This assumption is controversial, and some would be inclined to argue that the literal content is incomplete (ie not truth-evaluable). For a discussion, see eg Soames (2010) 155–56. Here, however, I will – for the sake of argument – assume that the literal content of the utterances in examples (1) and (2) *are* complete propositions.

[12] Marmor (2008) 426. As Marmor notes, these examples are slight variations of examples discussed by Bach (1994) and Soames (2008).

What makes these cases obvious is in large part that certain information is taken for granted by the participants in the conversation, including information about the purpose of the exchange, and partly that other interpretations would make the respective utterances less than fully co-operative (given the purpose of the relevant conversation). (Generally, I will refer to this information either as *background assumptions*, *conversational background*, *common ground*, or just *context*.) For our purposes, the general lesson to take away from these examples is the following, according to Marmor: 'A speaker would *normally* succeed in conveying assertive content that differs from what he says, *when it would be obvious to the hearer, in the particular context of the conversation, that it just cannot be the case that the speaker asserts exactly what he says*.'[13]

Obviousness of this sort, then, is – according to Marmor – a *sufficient* condition for non-literal speech (on the assumption that certain other background conditions are satisfied). It is clear, however, that Marmor thinks that, in normal circumstances, the obviousness criterion is also a *necessary* condition for such speech. To borrow his example, it is quite possible that in uttering 'Have you had blackberries?' a speaker can be meaning to ask whether or not the hearer has *ever* had blackberries or can be meaning to ask whether or not the hearer has had blackberries *that day*. If the contextual background is not sufficiently rich to make it obvious which question is intended, Marmor says, and it would consequently make sense for the hearer to ask for clarification, then 'this would be a clear indication that [the speaker has] not succeeded in asserting some content that differs from what [she] said'.[14] Obviousness, then, is supposed to be central in explaining our intuitions regarding successful cases of asserting something other than what is literally said – like (1) and (2) above – as well as our intuitions about unsuccessful cases – like the 'blackberry scenario'. The focus here, however, will be on obviousness as a necessary condition for successfully asserting something other than what one literally said.

In order to illustrate his general claim that legislatures rarely succeed in asserting something other than what they literally say, due to the fact that very little can jointly be taken for granted by the legislature and its audience(s), Marmor discusses the famous case of *Church of the Holy Trinity v US*.[15] In *Holy Trinity*, the relevant question was whether the *Alien Contract Labor Act* of 1885,[16] which prohibited the importation of 'labor or service of any kind' except 'professional actors, artists, lecturers or singers' and 'persons employed strictly as personal or domestic servants', prohibited the importation of people intended to serve as rectors or clergymen. The circuit court for the southern

[13] Marmor (2008) 428; my emphasis.
[14] Marmor (2008) 428.
[15] 143 US 457 (1892).
[16] 23 Stat 332 (codified as amended at 29 USC §2164 (1901)), *superseded by* Act of March 3 1903, Pub L No 162, 32 Stat 1213.

district of New York held that it did, while the Supreme Court held that it did not. As Justice Brewer put it, in delivering the opinion of the court: 'It is a familiar rule that a thing may be within the letter of the statute and yet not within the statute, because not within its spirit nor within the intention of its makers.'

Marmor asks whether it is plausible to argue – in the spirit of Justice Brewer's remark – that in enacting the *Alien Contract Labor Act*, the legislature asserted something different from what it said. That is, can we argue that although the importation of rectors and clergymen was prohibited according to what the law literally said, the *assertive* content of the legislative utterance was different, in that it did not apply to such conduct? Marmor thinks that for a couple of reasons it would be a stretch to argue this, and I think he is quite right. Given Marmor's obviousness requirement, we can say that the primary reason for this is that the context in which the *Alien Contract Labor Act* was enacted has a number of features in virtue of which it makes sense to ask whether Congress could have had in mind to prohibit the importation of foreign clergymen.[17] And if that is so, then it cannot be *obvious* that it did not mean to assert what it literally said. So in case Congress really did intend to assert something different from what it literally said, it did not succeed. Or so Marmor argues.

Now, as Marmor recognises, it is perhaps not entirely fair to pick *Holy Trinity* as the only case study. And I think that is correct. He believes, however, that we get the same results with simpler examples (assuming they are sufficiently realistic, of course[18]). For our purposes, it is not important how these examples go. Marmor's explanation for why the law – in these cases – does not succeed in asserting something different from what it literally says is the same: 'the context is not rich enough to make it obvious and transparent that the legislature could not have meant/asserted what it said.'[19]

B. Assertion, Warrant for Belief, and the Obviousness Requirement

On the picture under scrutiny, then, reinterpreting a speaker to be asserting something other than what she literally said is warranted only if it is obvious to a rational and informed hearer that the speaker could not be intending to

[17] For more detailed discussion of *Holy Trinity*, see section IV.A below.

[18] It is quite possible, I think, to invent cases in which lawmakers and their audience(s) share a wealth of beliefs/knowledge and that – consequently – the law has no problem asserting something other than what it says. But this does not affect Marmor's argument, since he is only committed to the claim that, *given the way the law tends to work*, such cases will be relatively rare.

[19] Marmor (2008) 429.

assert what she literally said, conditional on the assumption that she is being co-operative:[20]

OBVIOUSNESS Normally, a speaker asserts something other than what she literally says only if it is obvious to her that the speaker cannot be intending to assert what she literally says.

To be sure, this requirement seems to be satisfied in many cases in ordinary conversation. The question, however, is whether it is true of *all* normal cases in which a speaker asserts something other than what she literally says that it is *impossible* – relative to the body of information available to the hearer – that she could be intending to assert what she says. It seems to me that it isn't. As I will explain below, I think that there is a distinctive set of cases of successful non-literal assertion in which it is clearly not obvious – albeit *significantly more likely than not* – that the speaker is not intending to assert what she literally says. These cases, I will argue, give us good reason to reject OBVIOUSNESS in favour of a weaker, more flexible requirement.

In order to get at what I take to be the heart of the matter, we need to dissect OBVIOUSNESS a little further. First, Marmor and I both accept an account of assertion on which the following principle is true:

ASSERTION A speaker asserts *p* only if a rational hearer, knowing the relevant conversational background and context, is warranted in taking her to be intending to assert *p*.[21]

On this account, the epistemic position of the hearer plays a central role in determining the content of the speaker's assertion.[22] That is, it is partly *in virtue of* facts about epistemic justification that a speaker counts as having asserted a particular proposition.[23]

[20] I should note that Marmor is not alone in positing comparably strict pragmatic requirements – we have something rather similar, for example, in Paul Grice's pragmatic framework. Assuming that Grice would have classified the examples we are concerned with as examples of conversational implicature (rather than assertion), it follows from Grice's (1989) definition thereof that the relevant speech acts are successful only if the hearer *must* reinterpret the speaker's remark in order to make it consistent with the Cooperative Principle (see Grice (1989) 30–31)). See also Bach and Harnish (1979) 12, 61.

[21] See eg Marmor (2013) 55.

[22] Several authors – many of whom accept the basic tenets of Grice's framework – embrace this partly objective account of assertive/communicative content; see eg Goldsworthy (2005), Soames (2011) and Marmor (2013). Many devout Griceans, however, favour a subjective account, on which a speaker means, says, asserts, etc what he intends to mean, say, assert, etc; see eg Schiffer (1972), Neale (2005) and Bach (2006).

[23] Note that, although this is one sense in which the relevant account of assertion is properly said to be normative, this is different from the normativity associated with the so-called *norms of assertion*. While the norms of assertions are partly constitutive of an utterance's being an assertion, the normative considerations I am discussing in this section concern what it takes for an utterance not just to be an assertion but to be an assertion of *p*. That is, it concerns the content of a given utterance.

In the case of non-literal assertion, the above requirement takes the following form:

ASSERTION* Normally, a speaker asserts something other than what she literally says only if a rational hearer, knowing the relevant conversational background and context, is warranted in taking her not to be intending to assert what she literally says.

Marmor's obviousness requirement is produced when we combine ASSERTION* with the following principle:

STRICT WARRANT Normally, a rational hearer, knowing the relevant conversational background and context, is warranted in taking a speaker not to be intending to assert what she literally says only if it is obvious to her that the speaker cannot be intending to assert what she literally says.

It is *this* principle which brings out what I believe is really at issue here. *Contra* Marmor, I think that there *are* in fact perfectly normal instances of successful non-literal assertion in which it is less than obvious to a rational and informed hearer that the speaker could not be intending to assert the literal content of her remark. If I am able to find counter-examples to STRICT WARRANT, I will by the same token have found counter-examples to OBVIOUSNESS. I turn to this task next.

C. Low-stakes Loose Talk Scenarios as Systematic Counter-examples to STRICT WARRANT?

I should begin by explaining what sorts of case I believe make for the most plausible counter-examples to the principle STRICT WARRANT, and consequently to Marmor's obviousness requirement. In the first instance, these have to be cases in which it is not obvious that the speaker just cannot be intending to assert the literal content of the sentence she utters, yet in which nothing appears to be amiss, pragmatically speaking. That is, they must be cases in which the communicative act can reasonably be said to have gone well.

A case like this goes reasonably well – I submit – if (but not necessarily only if) (i) the speaker intends to assert something other than what she literally says, (ii) it is, relative to the epistemic position of a rational hearer, knowing the relevant conversational background and context, significantly more likely than not that the speaker is so intending, and (iii) the hearer in fact takes the speaker to be so intending. In many cases of this sort – as I will illustrate below – the hearer may not have any significant reason to ask for clarification, although it may perhaps not be outright silly to ask for it either. In such cases, it would seem that things have gone well and so I see no reason to say that the speaker did not succeed in asserting something other than what she literally said. It seems to me that the speaker succeeded in doing what she intended to do.[24]

Let us fix the relevant ideas by trying out an example in which the speaker is speaking 'loosely'. Imagine that my friend Kory tells me that he can only stay for 20 minutes or so for the premiere of my wife's new orchestra piece and that he asks me how long the piece is. Imagine also that in response I utter the following: 'It's 12 minutes long.' In this context, it is surely *possible* that I am intending to speak literally, i.e. it is not obvious that I just cannot be intending to communicate that the piece is *exactly* 12 minutes long. Yet, it is – given what is 'required by the accepted purpose of the conversation' – significantly more likely than not that I am intending to communicate that the work is *approximately* 12 minutes long. Thus, it is true both that (1) in uttering the relevant sentence in the relevant context, I have given Kory significantly more reason than not to believe that I intended to communicate that the piece is approximately 12 minutes long and that (2) it doesn't matter much, for the purposes of the conversation, if I in fact intended to communicate that the piece is exactly 12 minutes long; since Kory is able to stay for the entire piece, nothing hangs on it.

It seems to me that there is no reason here to claim that Kory is not warranted in taking the speaker (ie me) to be intending to assert something other than the literal content of the sentence uttered. In case Kory infers that I intended to communicate that the piece is approximately 12 minutes long, nothing appears to be amiss – and nothing appears to be amiss because nothing *is* amiss. Further, if Kory has any reason to ask me to clarify what I meant to communicate, this reason will be grounded exclusively in his desire to know for certain what I meant. If all this is correct, then STRICT WARRANT is false – the bar for successful assertion is sometimes lower than postulated by OBVIOUSNESS.

The scenario I have just described is not out of the ordinary – it is a perfectly normal case of successful non-literal assertion. The same reasoning, I maintain, can be applied to many, if not all, low-stakes loose-talk scenarios – and such situations appear to occur quite frequently, at least frequently enough to make them non-exceptional.[25] It seems, therefore, that we have a robust and systematic set

[24] I should note that if I am right about these cases, then Marmor's 'clarification test' for successful non-literal assertion is too strict: a speaker successfully asserts something other than what she literally said only if it would be silly of the hearer to ask for clarification about what the speaker meant. Sometimes, as I hope to show, non-literal assertion is successful despite the fact that it would not be outright silly to ask for clarification. These are cases in which the hearer has a reason to ask the speaker for clarification *only if* that reason comes from the hearer's own desire to know for certain what the speaker intended to communicate.

[25] For a second example, imagine that someone asks an artist how her show went and that in response she utters the following: 'Nobody came to my show!' In most situations, a rational hearer would infer that the artist intended to communicate that *almost* nobody came to her show. But it's not outright *impossible* that the artist is intending to assert that zero people showed up. However, given that it is rare that absolutely nobody shows up for a show, the artist has given her interlocutor good reason to believe that she is intending to communicate that *almost* nobody came to the show – it is significantly more likely than not that she is so intending. Moreover, it does not matter – vis-à-vis this particular context – which

of counter-examples to Obviousness, in which case Marmor's argument for the conclusion that non-literal legislative speech is rare is unsound.

As a matter of general theorising about language, the most natural way to proceed, I think, is to opt for a weaker, more flexible requirement, one that can accommodate both the examples that prima facie motivate Obviousness and the examples that I take to constitute counter-examples to it:

Flex A speaker asserts something other than what she literally says only if it is *significantly more likely than not* that she is intending to do so.

It is a virtue of the resulting account that it is able to explain our intuitions both about the cases in which the hearer is, despite uncertainty, warranted in drawing conclusions about the speaker's intention to assert something other than what she literally says and about the cases in which the hearer is warranted in doing so only if it is obvious that the speaker is so intending. Rather than to postulate a strict invariant requirement for all types of case, this account allows some flexibility in what it takes to be warranted in drawing conclusions about a speaker's communicative intentions, a flexibility determined by what is at stake in each case.

Before I go on to discuss whether lowering the epistemic bar in this way is fatal to Marmor's line of thought or the revised requirement can be used to reconstruct something akin to his argument, I want to consider a possible reply to my argument against Obviousness – one that seeks to show that, in my loose-talk scenarios, the hearer is warranted only in believing to a certain degree that the speaker intends to assert something other than what she literally says, but not in believing it outright. If that's true, then these scenarios are not counterexamples to Strict Warrant, on the assumption that this allows the objector to deny that they constitute examples of successful assertion.

D. Degree of Belief vs Outright Belief: Pragmatic Encroachment on Utterance Content

In my loose-talk example, I reasoned in the following way about the hearer's warranted belief about speaker intention. Given that the relevant sentence was uttered in the relevant context, it is significantly more likely than not – relative to Kory's epistemic position – that I am intending to assert that my wife's new piece is approximately 12 minutes long (rather than intending to assert that it is exactly 12 minutes long). That is, I provided Kory with good evidence of my

proposition the artist in fact intended to communicate; either way, the artist has conveyed that the show didn't go well, which suffices for the purposes of the conversation. As before, it may not be outright silly to ask the artist whether she meant that *absolutely* nobody or *almost* nobody showed up, but in the stipulated scenario there is – given what is 'required by the accepted purpose of the conversation' – no reason to ask for clarification that is independent of the interlocutor's desire to know for certain. This further indicates that *Strict Warrant* is false, and that successful non-literal assertion does not require obviousness – at least not across the board.

non-literal communicative intention – good enough so that he was warranted in taking me not to be intending to assert what I literally said on the basis of that evidence.

This line of reasoning, however, invites the following question. If the evidence supports the conclusion that it is significantly more likely than not that I am intending to assert something other than what I literally say, why do I say that Kory is warranted in outright believing that I so intend? That is, why is Kory's epistemic warrant in this case not confined just to the appropriate degree of belief? The problem for me is that if it is, then my loose-talk example isn't a genuine counter-example to STRICT WARRANT, because it would no longer be safe to assume – as the principle does – that something has been successfully asserted.

One attractive way to respond to this objection originates in theories that attempt to explain what has come to be known in epistemology as *pragmatic encroachment*. For my purposes here, *any* theory that manages to explain how pragmatic factors – what is at stake in a context – can affect an agent's warrant for outright belief without affecting her warrant for degrees of belief will do, but on this occasion I will make use of an account of belief proposed by Ross and Schroeder (2012): the *Reasoning Disposition Account*. This account attempts to explain pragmatic encroachment by arguing that, because of the function that outright belief serves for human beings, such belief is warranted as long as the relevant proposition is significantly more probable than its negation and the cost of being wrong is not too great.[26]

The *Reasoning Disposition Account* is motivated by the intuitive normative difference between low-stakes cases and high-stakes cases of the following sort:[27]

> Low: Five minutes ago, Hannah made three sandwiches and placed them in the refrigerator. She told Sarah that she placed the peanut butter sandwich on the left, the tuna sandwich in the middle, and the almond butter sandwich on the right. Hannah then departed just as Sarah's friend Almira arrived for lunch. Sarah knows that Almira has no allergies. Almira says: 'I'd love an almond butter sandwich.' And so Sarah opens the refrigerator door, points to the sandwich on the right, and says: 'The sandwich on the right is an almond butter sandwich. You can have it.'

> High: This case is just like Low, except here it is Sarah's nephew Algernon who is visiting for lunch, and he has a severe peanut allergy. He asks Sarah for a sandwich. Sarah knows that the peanut butter sandwich would be fatal to Algernon, but that the almond butter sandwich would be harmless. She also knows that he would slightly prefer the almond butter sandwich to the tuna sandwich. When Sarah goes to the fridge, she can tell, by visual inspection, which is the tuna sandwich, but she cannot tell, by visual inspection, which is the peanut butter sandwich and which is the almond butter sandwich. So she gives him the tuna sandwich.

[26] See Ross and Schroeder (2012).
[27] These cases are described in Ross and Schroeder (2012) 261.

As Ross and Schroeder note, one of the most natural explanations for the difference between the two cases seems to be that in Low, Sarah knows that the sandwich on the right is the almond butter sandwich, while in High, she doesn't. The explanation for this difference in knowledge is taken to be that in Low, Sarah is warranted in believing that the sandwich on the right is the almond butter sandwich, while in High, she is not. Without going into detail, the *Reasoning Disposition Account* grounds this explanation by claiming that in both scenarios the evidence warrants a dispositional belief, but that only in Low does it also warrant an occurrent belief – in High, the warrant for outright belief is overridden because the cost of being wrong is particularly salient.[28]

On the *Reasoning Disposition Account*, outright beliefs have a distinct functional role, due to the competing ends that they serve for human beings. Belief, on this account, serves two competing ends: to allow the believer to arrive at good deliberative conclusions and to prevent the cognitive overload that would result from reasoning in an ideal Bayesian manner on the basis of degrees of belief alone. The optimal balance seems to be struck by something like the following principle: an agent is permitted to treat a proposition *p* as true in her reasoning if the evidence significantly favours *p* over its negation and the cost of being wrong isn't too great. Treating these uncertain propositions as true in our reasoning (ie believing them), then, is a sort of optimal heuristic, justified by its benefit over the long run.[29]

The *Reasoning Disposition Account* allows me to argue that – in my loose-talk scenarios – the hearer has, given the evidence available in the context and the low stakes, a warranted non-overridden disposition to believe the speaker intended to assert something other than what she literally said, from which it follows that she (the hearer) is warranted in occurrently believing it.[30] We can call this *pragmatic encroachment on utterance interpretation*, which – if we assume that the epistemic position of the hearer plays a central role in determining the *content* of the speaker's assertion (as per Assertion) – entails *pragmatic encroachment on utterance content*. This will prove particularly significant in the fifth and last section of the chapter, where I discuss the implication of what I say for how determinate we should expect the content of legislative utterances to be.

II. Revising the Argument: Restrict, Reconstruct, or Both?

There are, I believe, two rather straightforward ways in which to respond to my objection to Marmor's argument for the claim that the law rarely asserts something

[28] See Ross and Schroeder (2012) 271–73.

[29] ibid, 273–75.

[30] I should emphasise that nothing hangs on the adequacy of the *Reasoning Disposition Account*; for my purposes, any account that allows for pragmatic encroachment will do.

other than what it literally says. One is to *restrict* the argument to the legal context and claim that, *in law*, the stakes are high enough so that obviousness is indeed required for successful non-literal assertion, and the other is to *reconstruct* the argument using another, related requirement instead of OBVIOUSNESS.

Both options provide significant departures from Marmor's line of argument and are worth examining in some detail. Doing so will allow us see more clearly exactly what features of the legislative context make it difficult for lawmakers to issue determinate non-literal legal directives. I will argue that neither strategy is sufficient on its own, but that conjoining them will provide a plausible argument for the claim that successful non-literal legislative speech is rare. It is quite plausible that, *in law*, a speaker succeeds in asserting something other than what she literally says only if she shares a great deal of *relevant* common ground with her intended audience – more specifically, sufficiently unequivocal information regarding the 'all-things-considered' purpose of the legislative utterance. And that – I agree – is rarely the case in law.

A. Restricting the Argument: Is Obviousness Required in Law?

In the previous section, I spent a great deal of effort casting doubt on OBVIOUSNESS and – at least as a matter of general theorising about language – proposed to replace it with FLEX, a somewhat weaker, more flexible requirement. The basic idea was that a speaker succeeds in asserting something other than what she literally says only if it is *significantly more likely than not* that she is intending to do so. What counts as significantly more likely than not, I argued, depends on the practical context – on what is at stake. If nothing much is at stake, the epistemic constraint is relatively low, but if *enough* is at stake, then obviousness may indeed be required for successful non-literal assertion. It makes sense, then, to ask whether, *in law*, the practical context is such that obviousness is required. If it is, then it is possible to simply restrict FLEX to the legal context, and the argument will be sound.

On the face of it, this amendment is quite plausible. In fact, it seems to be in the nature of law that it deals only with practically significant matters. It is very natural to assume, for example, that legislative utterances are made for good normative reasons and that something significant is at stake in all cases in which legal interpretation is called for. Despite the strong *prima facie* plausibility of this suggestion, however, I think we have reason to believe that the obviousness requirement fails here, too. Typically, a legal system will contain a considerable amount of relatively insignificant run-of-the-mill legislation, such as littering laws and pet identification regulations, to name some examples. While there is of course generally good reason to have laws of this sort, the stakes associated with their interpretation are in most cases not very high – certainly not high enough to provide sufficient support for the claim that, in law generally, successful non-literal assertion requires obviousness.[31] (It is important to keep in mind that the need for legal interpretation is not confined to court cases; officials often have to interpret the law in situations with little or no danger of evolving into full-fledged legal disputes. In many cases, the absence of such danger is exactly due to the relatively low stakes, or so I submit.)

Granted, this kind of regulation is most common in civil law and it therefore makes sense to ask whether we could just put a further restriction on the requirement and limit the argument to criminal law. However, legal systems typically also have a number of relatively insignificant criminal laws; laws with low fine-only options provide a good case in point. We have good reason, then, to conclude that simply restricting the linguistic premise of Marmor's argument – whether to law in general or specifically to criminal law – does not make for a sufficient revision.

Of course, if it were somehow settled by legal practice that non-literal legislative speech requires obviousness, then that would be sufficient to ground a restricted obviousness requirement, given that law – as Kelsen put it – regulates its own creation and content. However, I do not know of any jurisdiction in which legal practitioners robustly treat legislative speech in such a way as to genuinely establish such a requirement. As a matter of fact, the issue of epistemic constraints on legislative speech is distinctly under-addressed, both in judicial opinions and in scholarly literature. And the few authors that have discussed the issue all have more or less different opinions about what it is, or should be.[32]

B. Reconstructing the Argument: The Richness Requirement

On Marmor's view, OBVIOUSNESS produces a further requirement on the success of non-literal assertion when combined with the principle that it is obvious to a competent hearer that a speaker is intending to assert something other than what she literally says only if the speaker and hearer share a great deal of (relatively) specific background assumptions:

RICHNESS Normally, a speaker asserts something other than what she literally says only if the speaker and hearer share a great deal of (relatively) specific background assumptions.

[31] Thanks to Dale Smith for emphasising this point in conversation.

[32] Barak (2005), for example, thinks that the standard of proof for propositions of law is the preponderance of evidence, while Greenawalt (2010) believes that the standard is higher in cases of purported non-literality. And while Lawson (1992) argues that it ought – for political reasons – to be as high as obviousness, Alexander (1992) argues that there is no good reason that the standard of proof of law should mirror the standard of proof of fact, and that even in criminal law obviousness may be too strict a requirement.

Now, if Obviousness does not obtain, then richness is not derivable in the way proposed by Marmor. One way, however, to reply to my critique is to say that although this requirement cannot be *derived* from Obviousness in the intended way, it is still *independently* plausible. It might even be argued that *whatever the epistemic constraint on non-literal assertion turns out to be*, that constraint is satisfied only if the conversational background is relatively rich. If that is correct, then Richness – in place of Obviousness – can be used to construct something akin to Marmor's original argument. The revised argument then states that legislatures rarely assert something other than what they literally say because they rarely share a great deal of (relatively) specific background assumptions with their audience.

For the sake of argument, I will provisionally accept it as true that legislatures rarely share a great deal of (relatively) specific background assumptions with their audience, although it may vary across the different legal contexts – and, indeed, systems – how much information is shared between speaker and audience. Presumably, the legislature shares more common ground, for example, with administrative agencies and courts than it does with ordinary citizens. And, quite plausibly, the British Parliament shares more common ground with administrative agencies and courts than the United States Congress does.

That, then, leaves the question whether successful non-literal assertion always requires speaker and audience to share a great deal of information. I will argue that it does not. I will make my case in two steps, which is intended to highlight the two analytically distinct roles that shared information plays in non-literal assertion: the role it plays in determining *that* the speaker intends to assert something other than what she says and the role it plays in determining *what* the speaker intends to assert (instead).

Let us start with the first role. In order for it to be significantly more likely than not that a speaker isn't intending to assert what she literally says, all the speaker has to do – assuming certain background conditions obtain – is to utter a sentence the semantic content of which is incompatible in *some* way with *some* part of the conversational background (things presupposed, purpose of the conversation etc.). *Strictly speaking*, then, all that is required – vis-à-vis the common ground – is that the speaker and hearer knowingly share *one* bit of information. They may, of course, normally share all sorts of information – both knowingly and unknowingly – but what is *required* for the conversational background to play this first role in non-literal assertion is very minimal.

The most basic examples presumably involve quantification (both universal and existential). Consider, for example, universal quantification restricted – on the semantic level – only to humans, eg of the form *Everyone is F*. There are very few predicates that apply to absolutely *everyone* and so if a speaker utters the words, say, 'Everyone is coming to the party!' it will be obvious to any competent hearer that she does not intend to assert the literal content of her remark (on the assumption that the speaker is observing the maxims governing co-operative conversation). And in order for this to be obvious, all that is required is that the speaker and hearer knowingly share the information *that no party is such that everyone is coming to it*.

This very ordinary example shows that it is not generally true that the conversational background has to be fairly rich in order for it to play its first role in non-literal assertion. In many normal cases, only minimal common ground is required for determining *that* the speaker intends to assert something other than what she says.

Next, let us turn to the second role, the role that the conversational background plays in determining *what* the speaker intends to assert. Consider again the case in which a speaker utters the words 'Everyone is coming to the party!' Assuming it is significantly more likely than not that the speaker does not intend to assert the literal content of her remark, we can proceed to ask how much it takes – vis-à-vis shared information – to determine what the speaker intended to assert instead. Now, depending on what the speaker in fact intends to assert, it presumably varies hugely how much common ground is required in order for the hearer to recognise the speaker's communicative intention. In many cases, a rich conversational background is certainly necessary, but in other – perfectly normal – cases, the speaker and hearer have to share very little information.

Say, for example, that – in addition to knowingly share the information *that no party is such that everyone is coming to it* – the speaker and hearer share the information *that the speaker has recently sent out party invitations*. In tandem with the fact that the speaker uttered the words 'Everyone is coming to the party!' these two bits of shared information give the hearer good reason to believe that the speaker intended to assert that *everyone who was invited is coming to the party*. Nothing more is strictly required.[33]

Now, although a rich conversational background is not – as a general matter – *required* for successful non-literal assertion, the conversational background will still *limit* the possibility of such assertion, by limiting the ways in which the conversational maxims can be violated and by limiting the range of plausible candidates for intended assertive content. This suggests that a rich conversational background is presumably required for *rich* pragmatic enrichment; in other words, the content of an assertion can only be as rich as the conversational background allows.

We should note, however, that there are at least two types of pragmatic enrichment for which a rich background is needed. On the one hand, there are cases in which *the material that gets added to the semantic content is relatively rich*. On the

[33] No doubt, in real-world situations similar to the one described, people frequently do share a great deal of related information (what kind of party, date and time, etc), but the fact that people often assert something other than what they literally say in circumstances in which the conversational background is relatively rich does not entail that such a rich background is *required* for such assertion. I should also note that in many real-world cases in which the conversational background is relatively rich, the hearer's warrant for concluding that the speaker is intending to assert that *p* is *overdetermined*, meaning that the context provides the hearer with multiple sufficient reasons to draw the relevant conclusion. Only one such reason, of course, is strictly required.

other hand, there are cases in which *material gets added to relatively rich semantic content*. In the next sub-section, I will argue that in the *legislative context*, questions about pragmatic enrichment are typically questions about enrichment of rich semantic content. If that is correct, then that will allow us to (i) replace Marmor's obviousness requirement with the richness requirement and, further, (ii) restrict that requirement to the legislative context.

C. Pragmatic Enrichment in the Legislative Context

Legislative texts are usually pretty complex, and even the least complex ones do not come anywhere close to the brevity of sentences like 'Everyone is coming to the party'. We should therefore, as a general matter, expect that successful non-literality in legislation – if it occurs – consists in the enrichment of already rich semantic content. If that is correct, then successful non-literality in the context of legislation will require a relatively rich conversational background.

The cases of *Holy Trinity* and *Ali*, which I described earlier in the chapter, provide good cases in point.[34] In *Holy Trinity*, as we recall, the question was whether the *Alien Contract Labor Act* of 1885,[35] which prohibited the importation of 'labor or service of any kind' except 'professional actors, artists, lecturers or singers' and 'persons employed strictly as personal or domestic servants', also prohibited the importation of people intended to serve as rectors or clergymen. According to many commentators, the Act only prohibited the importation of *manual* labour or service, and it is therefore natural to ask whether an argument can be made that the legislature asserted something other than what it literally said. (It is important to note that, at this point, I make no claims about whether or not the proposed requirements are met in the examples under discussion.)

Although the issue concerns the addition of very limited material – ie the content of the term 'manual' – the addition was allegedly made to content that is already very rich. As a result, the common ground has to be very rich in order for it to be significantly more likely than not that the legislature did not intend to assert the literal content of the text. And it has to be even richer in order for it to be significantly more likely than not that the legislature intended to assert that the prohibition concerned only manual labour.

Recall also *Ali*, in which the Supreme Court ruled that Abdus-Shahid MS Ali could not sue the government for having lost property belonging to him. The reason, the court said, was that the *Federal Tort Claims Act* preserves immunity for *all* federal law enforcement officers, since it guarantees immunity for '[a]ny claim arising in respect of … the detention of any goods, merchandize, or other property

[34] 143 US 457 (1892) and 552 US 214 (2008), respectively.

[35] 23 Stat 332 (codified as amended at 29 USC §2164 (1901)), *superseded by* Act of March 3 1903, Pub L No 162, 32 Stat 1213.

by any officer of customs or excise *or any other law enforcement officer*'.[36] Ali of course argued, and the dissent agreed, that the clause did not guarantee immunity for the government in relation to the actions of *prison* officers, but only of officers *working in customs or related domains*.

The relevant section of the Act is – like the *Alien Contract Labor Act* – very rich in content. As a result, if the proposed non-literal assertion is to be considered successful, the common ground must be rich as well, in order for the hearer both to determine that it is significantly more likely than not that the legislature was not intending to assert what it literally said and to determine what it was that it intended to assert instead.

On the assumption that neither the *Alien Contract Labor Act* nor the *Federal Tort Claims Act* are exceptional in any way, it seems safe to say that non-literal assertion in the legislative context requires that the legislature and its audience share a great deal of relevant information. In other words, if we restrict our attention to *legislative utterances*, we have a very plausible richness requirement:

RICHNESS-IN-LAW Normally, in legislation, a speaker asserts something other than what she literally says only if the speaker and hearer share a great deal of (relatively) specific background assumptions.

Now, it will vary between areas of law – and perhaps also within them – how well the restricted richness requirement is satisfied, depending on the intended audience. Criminal law, for example, is arguably to a large extent addressed to the general public, in which case the common ground between speaker and audience is relatively thin. In addition, the stakes are generally – albeit not always, as we have seen – fairly high. Overall, then, the conditions for non-literal speech do not seem to be very favourable in the area of criminal law.

In civil law, the stakes are perhaps generally lower, but – at least in the US – only a limited amount of such law comes from legislative enactment. In addition, a great deal of civil law is arguably also addressed to the general public, which makes for a rather thin common ground. I should note, though, that there is an important part of US civil law that *is* largely statute-based – namely *administrative law* – and, here, a considerable amount of relevant information is arguably shared by speaker and audience (administrative agencies and, arguably, courts). Thus, we have good reason to expect that *if* the legislature ever successfully asserts something other than what it literally says, it will primarily be in the area of administrative law, and perhaps in the area of criminal law addressed to officials.

However, even if the lawmakers do share substantial common ground with both judges and administrative officials, there is reason to believe that the relevant background is often not quite rich enough to *determinately* satisfy the relevant requirements. As I will argue in the next sub-section, there is a relevant difference in what the common ground must be like when we compare non-literal

[36] 28 USC 2680(c); my emphasis.

(descriptive) assertion and non-literal directives. And although there is no *structural* difference between the two types of context as far as the pragmatic reasoning goes, it is still the case that, *as a matter of fact*, people tend to have less access to the relevant facts when it comes to non-literal directives – including, and especially, *legal* directives. Thus, although it is indeed natural to think that the conditions for non-literal assertion are most favourable in administrative law and least favourable in criminal law addressed to the general public, with criminal law addressed to courts somewhere in between, we should nevertheless considerably temper our expectations concerning the existence of *actual, determinate* cases of such assertion.

D. The Pragmatics of Directives and the Context of Legislation

Let us, following Bach and Harnish (1979), define directives as utterances that 'express the speaker's attitude toward some prospective action by the hearer and his intention that his utterance, or the attitude it expresses, be taken as a reason for the hearer's action'.[37] Familiar pragmatic reasoning applies in the case of directives, too, and so we need some plausible reformulations of at least some of the maxims governing co-operative conversation for that particular context. In order to get at some such reformulations, let us look at a few examples.

Say that a speaker instructs a hearer to 'invite everyone to the party' and that the attitude expressed is that of desire. Clearly, it would be obvious to any competent hearer that the speaker doesn't desire that *absolutely everyone* be invited to the party. Or, to borrow and adapt an example from Manning (2003) (who borrowed and adapted it from MacCallum (1966)), say that your boss tells you to 'gather all the ashtrays you can find and bring them to the conference room'. It is obvious to you that your boss does not want you to bring *all* the ashtrays you can possibly find. Rather, she wants you to bring all the ashtrays you can find *in the building*, perhaps also assuming they belong to the company, that they are not bolted down, etc.

To take a legal example, consider the case of *Small v United States*,[38] in which the majority argued that the relevant legal directive could not – if interpreted literally – reasonably be regarded as the legislature's view of how the addressees ought to behave. In *Small*, the question was whether petitioner Gary Small, who had been convicted for smuggling in a Japanese court in 1994, had – by owning a firearm – violated the US Criminal Code, 18 USC § 922(g)(1), which makes it 'unlawful for any person … who has been *convicted in any court*, of a crime punishable by imprisonment for a term exceeding 1 year … to … possess … any firearm'.[39]

[37] Bach and Harnish (1979) 41.
[38] 544 US 385 (2005).
[39] 18 USC § 922(g)(1).

The question before the court was whether the phrase 'convicted in any court' applied 'only to convictions entered in any *domestic* court or to *foreign* convictions as well'.[40] The court held that it applied only to domestic convictions and reversed the prior court's judgment.

The majority claimed that – *as a matter of common sense* – 'Congress generally legislates with domestic concerns in mind.'[41] For our purposes here, we can characterise this 'legal presumption' as a fact about the concerns of the legislature that is – via its commonsensical nature – part of the common ground between the legislature and officials (and perhaps even between the legislature and the general public, although that claim is more difficult to defend). Read literally, then, the relevant part of the Code clashes with the common ground, prompting a non-literal interpretation. On the assumption that Congress generally legislates with domestic concerns in mind, a reasonable hearer cannot attribute to Congress the view that officials ought to convict a person for owning a firearm if she has been sentenced in a court *just anywhere*. Thus, read literally, the directive cannot be authoritatively binding. Or so the reasoning goes.

In the examples above, the hearer is prompted to reinterpret the speaker's directive because she cannot reasonably attribute to the speaker the attitude associated with the literal interpretation of the utterance. Thus, in the context of directives, the so-called *maxim of Quality* – which is normally the operative maxim in non-literal assertion – is perhaps best taken to be something like the following: *Do not direct a person to do that which you do not desire/intend/etc.*[42]

In the context of non-literal directives, then, the common ground has to contain information about the speaker's relevant *attitudes*, ie about her desires/ends/values/preferences. However, the common ground has to not only contain information about particular attitudes but also – crucially – information about their *interrelationship*. In this sense, then, the pragmatics of directives is different from – and more complex than – the pragmatics of constatives. And in many types of speech context, it is rarely the case that information about the interrelation between the speaker's desires/ends/values/preferences can be taken for granted. This includes law, or so I argue. If what I say below is correct, the context of legislation rarely determinately contains facts about the appropriate weight to be given to law's various ends, vis-à-vis the relevant legislative utterance. As a result, the common ground *relevant* for generating non-literal directives is not sufficiently rich, even if the total information knowingly shared is often substantial.

The reason that the relevant information is scarce in the legislative context, I maintain, is that law's ends compete with each other in extremely complex ways – generally, so complex that the structure of 'law's preferences', ie the relationship that holds between law's various ends, is too complex to be part of what is genuinely

[40] 18 USC § 922(g)(1).
[41] Here, the court is referring to *Smith v United States*, 507 US 197, 204, n 5 (1993).
[42] See Grice (1989) 27.

taken for granted in legislative speech contexts. In order, however, for a non-literal legal directive to succeed, it is not sufficient simply that a literal reading be at odds with just *some* end that is taken for granted in the context. It is not necessarily irrational for a speaker to express a wish or intention that is in conflict with a particular hope or a desire that she has, *even if knowledge of that hope or desire is part of the common ground between speaker and hearer*. Rather, the wish associated with the literal content of the directive has to be at odds with the *proper balance* of the relevant hopes or desires. In the case of a legal directive, then, the desire associated with its literal content has to be at odds with the proper balance of those ends of the law that can be said to be part of the common ground.[43] And it seems to me that – due in large part to the general defeasibility of aims and desires – *very* few facts about such balances can genuinely be taken for granted, although it is of course not uncommon for individual interpreters to surmise that they possess such information. If this is correct, then the common ground between the legislature and its audience rarely determinately contains facts of exactly the kind required for (successfully) issuing non-literal directives.

To fix this idea, let us revisit the case of *Small v United States*. In brief summary, the majority's reasoning was that, due to a legal presumption that 'Congress generally legislates with domestic concerns in mind', the court was invited to infer that the phrase 'any court' should be construed non-literally, its proper content being *any domestic court*. The dissent, however, argued that 'the context of [the relevant section of the federal criminal code] … suggests that there is no geographic limit on the scope of [the phrase]'. One of the central concerns of the dissent was that although it is true that that legislation of Congress is generally meant to 'apply only within the territorial jurisdiction of the United States', the specific purposes of the relevant section of the Code would be fully promoted by a literal interpretation of the phrase, ie by taking 'any courts' to include foreign courts. Thus, a literal interpretation of the legislature's utterance was perhaps in conflict with one of law's very general aims, but not with other, more specific aims. The implication of this for my argument here is that unless the common ground between legislature and courts contains unequivocal information regarding the proper balance of legislative purpose – general and specific – the legislature cannot be said to have successfully communicated something other than what it literally said. In *Small*, it seems a plain fact that such information is not available – at least not in the sense of being taken for granted. But it also seems to me that *Small* is non-exceptional, and that we can therefore generalise to say that the kind of information required for successful non-literal legislative speech is rarely available. Even if interpreters may have access to all sorts of information – including information about law's many purposes, general and specific – they are rarely warranted in taking for granted information about the proper balance of these aims. I discuss further examples in

[43] Of course, there may be some obvious facts about 'the law's preferences' that *are* part of the common ground, at least between the legislature and officials. In some legal systems, for example, *Lex Posterior*, *Lex Superior*, and *Lex Specialis* arguably each embody such a preference.

the last section of the chapter, but the idea is that – as a general matter – this lack of unequivocal information about legislative intent adversely affects the possibility of successful non-literal legislative speech.

These considerations suggest what I take to be a sound reconstruction of something akin to Marmor's original argument, albeit with significant departures from his line of thought. The requirement that is claimed to be rarely satisfied in the legislative context is now much more specific to that particular context:

RICHNESS-IN-LAW* Non-literal legislative speech is successful only if the legislature and its audience share a great deal of (relatively) specific background assumptions regarding the interrelationship between the legislature's desires/ends/values/preferences.

Thus, although it does not suffice simply to restrict Marmor's argument to the legislative context or to reconstruct it using richness, we can combine these strategies to produce a significant, but plausible, revision of the main premise. The bottom line is that despite the fact that the conversational background between lawmakers and officials often contains quite a bit of information, it rarely contains very much of exactly the kind of information required for lawmakers to issue non-literal directives.

I do not mean to suggest that lawmakers never intend to communicate something non-literal in issuing legislative directives, nor do I want to claim that they are never successful when they do. If what I have said is correct, all that has been established is that it is rarely the case that interpreters have information unequivocal enough to warrant the conclusion that the legislature intended to communicate something nonliteral, or – if it does – then to warrant a unique conclusion about what non-literal content the legislature intended to communicate.[44]

III. Testing the Argument against Experience: Ekins's Argument from Examples

Ideally, we should be able to test the kind of argument I have put forward against experience. Far from being an abstract exercise, the argument delivers – in a robust enough sense – predictions about linguistic behaviour in the legal context (broadly understood). So it is important to consider how the conclusion holds up against what we can glean from our experience of the law as it actually is.

Ekins (2012) provides a laudably thorough case against the claim that successful non-literal legislative speech is rare, offering a wealth of actual cases in which the courts have taken the content of the law to be something other than its literal

[44] Keep in mind that – as Neale (2005) points out – in order to form communicative intentions speakers do not need to believe that their audience will be likely to correctly identify them, only that it is not impossible for them to do so. See eg Neale (2005) 181.

content, seemingly based on relatively straightforward inferences about the legislature's communicative intentions.[45] Ekins takes this to falsify conclusions of the sort I reached in the last sub-section *tout court*, and identifies the second premise as the culprit; in contrast to what I argued above, Ekins holds that 'the context in which [the legislative] agent acts is not thin or opaque, but rich and complex'.[46]

First, Ekins's examples. For brevity's sake, I will only present a handful and generalise from those:[47]

A. Witnesses who attest 'any will or codicil {of real estate}' under which they are beneficiaries shall be treated as good witnesses, but the gifts made to them shall be void.[48]
B. All drug shops 'shall be closed ... at 10 pm on each and every day of the week {and shall stay closed until morning}'.[49]
C. It is an offence to 'stab, cut or wound' any person {with a weapon or instrument}.[50]
D. Every person who fraudulently harbours uncustomed goods shall forfeit a specified sum, 'and the offender {or apparent offender} may either be detained or proceeded against by summons'.

In each of these examples, the parenthetical content was unexpressed, but inferred by the court to be part of what the legislature meant to convey in using the respective sentence, on Ekins's analysis. Ekins rightly says that such examples are not out of the ordinary – rather, they constitute a large class of examples, all of which put direct pressure on my conclusion that successful non-literal legislative speech is rare. At the very least, they constitute a significant *prima facie* problem for the argument I have presented.

As Ekins presents them, these examples are all cases in which the court appropriately inferred that the legislature had clearly intended to communicate something non-literal. I take it that, on Ekins's account, this is evidenced in part by his own verdict about the quality of the court's inferences – vis-à-vis the legislature's communicative intentions – and in part by the fact that the decisions were unanimous. This, together with his assumption that such examples are pretty standard, constitutes what we can call *Ekins's argument from examples*, against the claim that successful non-literal legislative speech is rare. As I hope to show, on closer inspection, only one of the examples, case (B), is as straightforward as Ekins suggests. In the other cases, there is so much else going on that it is difficult to draw any firm conclusions about the role of language and pragmatic inference in the court's decisions. In any case, I will argue that cases (A), (C), and (D) are cases

[45] See generally Ekins (2012) ch 7. Most of the examples are offered originally in Bennion (1990).
[46] Ekins (2012) 256.
[47] See Ekins (2012) 200–01, and Bennion (1990) 233–34.
[48] *Brett v Brett* (1826).
[49] *Rex v Liggetts-Findlay Drug Stores Ltd* (1919).
[50] *Rex v Harris* (1836).

in which the legislative communication is not entirely successful. If that is correct, Ekins's argument from examples does not go through.

First, a brief general remark on drawing conclusions about genuine agreement from the fact that a decision is unanimous. Perhaps, in systems in which dissent within the higher courts is rife – such as the US and Australian systems – the fact that a decision is unanimous is some indication that the matter is fairly clear (setting aside the issue of separate, concurring opinions). In the UK, however, dissent is (and generally has been) the exception, with an extremely high rate of unanimous decisions – which is arguably just as much explained by the internal structure of the appeals process and a culture generally sceptical about the value of dissent at the appellate level, as by actual agreement about the proper legal outcome and its basis.[51] This should give us some pause in taking – as a general matter – unanimous decisions to indicate actual agreement. It seems that in systems such as the UK one, it is, at best, a highly defeasible indication thereof.

Now on to the actual examples. As I indicated above, the most straightforward case is case (B), the Canadian case of *Rex v Liggetts-Findlay Drug Stores Ltd*, in which the issue was whether closing a drug store at 10 pm and opening it a little later constituted a violation of a law requiring drug stores to close at 10 pm (without further explicit specification). In this case, I simply agree with Ekins (and other commentators) that something like 'and shall stay closed until morning' is implicated conversationally.[52] Marmor (2008), commenting on his own hypothetical example, also plainly accepts that implicatures can be successful in cases of this sort:

> Suppose that a municipal regulation requires cafés and restaurants to have 'clean and well kept indoor restrooms'. Given the context of such a requirement, surely it would be implicated by this regulation that the restrooms must be actually open for the patrons to use.

Indeed, some cases of legislative speech do seem to be so clear that interpreters can straightforwardly infer that the intention is to communicate something non-literal, and can infer pretty well what that content is.

So far, of course, this does not pose a problem. All I have argued for is the qualified claim that successful non-literal legislative speech is infrequent in comparison to successful non-literality in ordinary conversation, not that it never occurs. The pressure that Ekins's examples put on my argument is 'accumulative', and so is generated only if the rest of them go much the same way. I will argue that once we examine them closely enough, we see that they do not. In contrast to the *Liggetts-Findlay* case, examples (A), (C), and (D) merely exhibit the appearance of being straightforward.

Consider case (A), the case of *Brett v Brett*, in which the issue was whether the phrase 'any will or codicil' – occurring in the Wills Act 1752 – was being used

[51] For an interesting discussion, see eg Kerr (2012).
[52] See also Goldsworthy (2010) 234–35.

literally by the legislature or to mean 'any will or codicil {of real estate}'; if the former, the phrase included reference to personal property.[53] The judgment in the case was provided by Sir John Nicholl, who held that the phrase, viewed in 'connexion with its whole context in the statute, is not even difficult of interpretation', and that it was clearly being used to convey the more limited meaning.[54] The judgment was affirmed on appeal, by a court of nine judges, after hearing counsel for the appellant only. This all counts in favour of Ekins's argument from examples.

However, despite the fact that Sir John Nicholl in certain places presents the case as a fairly obvious one and that his judgment was affirmed on appeal, the same phrase had received the other interpretation 15 years prior. In *Lees v Summersgill*, Sir William Grant held – claiming also to interpret the phrase 'in context' – that the phrase should be interpreted generally, to apply to *any* will or codicil, whether of real estate or not.[55] Sir John Nicholl even acknowledges this in his judgment in *Brett*. So even though, historically, the statute in question was for a short while treated as fairly straightforward (in practice and in the courts), in line with Nicholl's judgment in *Brett*, things are – at least philosophically – not so simple.[56] As *Lees* attests, there is plenty of room for disagreement among competent, well-informed interpreters about what the legislature's communicative intention was in enacting the statute.

Next, case (C). In *Rex v Harris*, the issue was whether biting off the tip of someone's nose constituted 'wounding' them, for the purposes of the Offences Against the Person Act 1828.[57] As Ekins presents the case, Sir John Patteson straightforwardly held that it did not, because attending to the context revealed that use of a weapon or instrument was implied.[58] Again, this counts in favour of Ekins's argument.

In fact, however, the 'straightforwardness' of *Harris* is owed to the fact that Sir John Patteson instructed the jury that the matter had been decided in an entirely comparable case – *Rex v Stevens* – just a couple of years prior. In *Stevens*, John Stevens was held not to have wounded a policeman by biting off the end of his finger because no instrument was used. The matter, however, was controversial, and Stevens was first convicted by jury but with the sentence respited by the presiding judge, with the intention that all the judges could take up the matter and vote on it. Thirteen out of 15 judges were present for the meeting and the verdict

[53] 25 Geo 2 c 6.

[54] *Brett v Brett* (1826) 162 ER 459.

[55] *Lees v Summersgill* (1811).

[56] Sir John Nicholl's judgment in *Brett* was followed in 1827 and 1829 in the cases of *Emanuel v Constable* and *Foster v Banbury*, respectively. But that was about it – less than a decade later, the Wills Act 1752 was re-enacted in amended form as s 15 Wills Act 1837 so as to include reference to *any* will (and 'will' was defined so as to include codicils). As a further note, it is of course very hard to say what light, if any, the 1837 Act sheds on how to understand the original Act, but it seems within reason to argue that this undermines Sir John Nicholl's reasoning to the extent that he based his interpretation on what he took to be the aims reasonably attributable to the legislature.

[57] *Rex v Harris* (1836) 9 Geo 4 c31 s12.

[58] Ekins more or less follows Bennion (1990) in presenting these examples.

was close – seven held that use of a weapon or instrument was implied, six did not. The matter, therefore, is nowhere near as straightforward as the *Harris* case suggests.

Finally, let's consider case (D), which – in view of the opinions – may seem no less straightforward than *Liggetts-Findlay*, ie case (B). In *Barnard v Gorman*, the issue was whether officials had the authority to detain merely suspected offenders in virtue of the Customs Consolidation Act 1875, which provides that an 'offender may either be detained or proceeded against by summons'.[59] If not, then persons who are detained but turn out to be innocent are able to recover damages for false imprisonment. It was unanimously held that the only way to make sense of the Act was to read it to include reference to apparent offenders.

In his opinion, Lord Wright said that reading the Act so as to apply only to actual offenders would involve a manifest absurdity, as it would require a conclusive determination of guilt before action could be taken – '[t]he provision,' he said, 'is clearly intended for the purpose of bringing the charge to investigation.'[60] Accordingly, he concluded that 'offender' here meant 'One who is suspected of or charged with the offence'.[61] Viscount Simon argued that it was the duty of the court 'to take the words as they stand to give them their true construction, having regard to the language of the whole section, and as far as relevant, of the whole Act always preferring the natural meaning of the word involved, but none the less always giving the word its appropriate construction according to the context'.[62] And Lord Romer based his decision in part on the claim that 'the context in which a word is found may be, and very often is, strong enough to show that it is intended to bear other than its ordinary meaning'.[63] As before, this all counts in favour of Ekins's argument.[64]

Barnard, however, is not quite as straightforward as it seems, despite the unanimous decision. As Bennion (1990) points out, although the opinions in *Barnard* can be construed as pragmatic reasoning in response to legislative ellipsis,[65] it seems equally reasonable to analyse the case as one in which the legislative project is 'misconceived through some mistake of fact' on behalf of the drafter.[66] On Bennion's analysis, *Barnard* properly belongs to a class of cases 'where the draftsman has failed to get into his head the true nature of the factual situations with

[59] *Barnard v Gorman* (1941).
[60] *Barnard v Gorman* (1941) AC 391.
[61] *Barnard v Gorman* (1941) AC 391.
[62] *Barnard v Gorman* (1941) AC 384.
[63] *Barnard v Gorman* (1941) AC 396.
[64] On this analysis, *Barnard* is analogous to the US case of *Green v Bock Laundry Machine Co* (490 US 504 (1989)), a civil product liability case in which Justice Scalia argued that the term 'defendant' – as it occurred in Rule 609(a) of the Federal Rules of Evidence – was clearly being used to mean 'criminal defendant', and that therefore the trial court had not erred in denying Green's pre-trial motion of impeaching evidence. (The rule has since been amended to address the issue.)
[65] Although it should be noted that none of the judges wanted to read the relevant power to detain apparent offenders into the statute by implication, as Ekins's presentation suggests. Rather, they reasoned that the term 'offender' ought to be taken to mean 'apparent offender' in the relevant context.
[66] Bennion (1990) 256.

which the Act will in future have to deal'.[67] The relevant section of the Customs Consolidation Act 1876, he says, 'clearly operates upon a misunderstanding of the factual situation'.[68] If that is correct, then *Barnard* does not – after all – count in favour of Ekins's argument from examples, at least not strongly so.[69]

I hope to have shown that – *contra* Ekins – the examples he provides (following Bennion) do not, after all, amount to an accumulative empirical argument against the claim that successful non-literal legislative speech is infrequent in comparison to successful non-literality in ordinary conversation. Now, I do agree with Ekins that *as a general matter* the legislative context is not necessarily thin or opaque, and that it arguably varies both between areas of law and between legal systems how much information is shared between the legislature and its audience. However, as I have tried to show (in particular in section II.D), the problem is that the common ground *relevant* for generating non-literal directives is not sufficiently rich, even if the total information knowingly shared is often substantial. The reason, I argued, is that law's ends compete with each other in extremely complex ways – generally, so complex that the relationship that holds between law's various ends is too complex to be part of what is genuinely taken for granted in legislative speech contexts. To put the point in Ekins's terms, although the total information knowingly shared may be substantial, the context typically does not contain unequivocal enough information about the 'complex means–end package on which the legislature acts'.[70] It is *this* part of the legislative context which is generally relatively thin or opaque.

Before I go on to discuss what happens, on my account, when non-literal legislative speech is unsuccessful – vis-à-vis the content of the relevant law – I should note that there is a potentially significant difference between the frameworks that Ekins and I employ, which could help to explain to some extent our differing judgments about the cases discussed above. As I have tried to show, despite the fact that these cases may seem straightforward, there is in most of them plenty of room for

[67] Bennion (1990) 273. Bennion classifies *Wiltshire v Barrett* (1966), which relies crucially upon *Barnard*, the same way. In *Wiltshire*, the issue – like in *Barnard* – was whether officials had the authority to detain merely suspected drunk drivers in virtue of the Road Traffic Act 1960, which provides that officials may arrest 'a person committing an offence under this section'. And as in *Barnard*, the court unanimously held that the statute ought to be considered as applying to persons 'apparently committing an offence'.

[68] ibid.

[69] On this analysis, *Barnard* is analogous to the US case of *United States v Marshall* (908 F2d 1312 (7th Cir 1990)), in which the question was whether or not Mr Marshall, who had sold around 12,000 doses of LSD, should be taken to fall under a statute triggering a mandatory minimum punishment if the sold items contain 'a mixture or substance containing a detectable amount' of the relevant drug (21 USC §960). The statute has the unintended consequence that it obligates judges to impose disproportionate sentences on people who sell LSD, due to the fact that the lawmakers did not realise how the drug is sold (LSD requires a particularly heavy carrier). Because the most likely explanation of the problematic result is that it was simply not foreseen, the statute does not warrant a non-literal interpretation. As a result, the main question in *Marshall* is about how to appropriately react to a problematic result that follows from the content of the legislative utterance. Same goes for *Barnard*, on Bennion's analysis.

[70] Ekins (2012) 258.

disagreement among competent and well-informed judges about the communicative intentions of the legislature. On the framework adopted in this book, assertive content is – as we have seen – partly determined by the inferences that the hearer is warranted in making about the speaker's communicative intention and so this kind of peer disagreement has implications for how successful we ought to count the relevant legislative speech act to have been (whether the intention was to communicate something literal or non-literal).

On Ekins's view, however, '[a] successful instance of communication occurs when the hearer identifies the intended meaning by recognising the speaker's intention to this effect', and failure 'where the hearer fails to identify the speaker's intention'.[71] On this framework, the quality of the interpreter's inference does not matter – as long as she arrives at the right conclusion, success is guaranteed. Consequently, assuming – as Ekins must – that the courts correctly identified the legislature's communicative intentions in the above examples, nothing more is needed for success. Perhaps, then, the argument ultimately boils down to what the right linguistic framework is – ie to what conditions of success in communication we should adopt?

I don't think it does. The reason is that, in discussing Ekins's examples, I hope to have shown that – by and large – for each case of what on Ekins's account constitutes successful non-literal communication, there is an unsuccessful case. It is perhaps not easy maths to figure out exactly how – on Ekins's framework – success and failure stack up against each other, but if we can generalise at all from my discussion of the examples above, it seems that the successful cases of non-literal legislative speech do not outnumber the unsuccessful cases by much.

IV. Indeterminacy about Utterance Content

After the discussion in the previous sections, it is natural to ask what exactly happens – vis-à-vis the content of a legislative utterance – when the conversational background isn't rich enough to warrant a reinterpretation. And it may seem equally natural to infer that in such cases, the primary content of the relevant statutory text just is its literal content. If that is correct and if the conversational background is generally not rich enough to warrant a reinterpretation, then the primary content of a statutory text normally just is its literal content. In this section, however, I aim to show that this would be a significant overstatement. Such a result follows only if we assume a very strong version of what is often called the *presumption of literalness*, which I – along with many others – wish to deny.

On a strong version of the presumption of literalness, failure to make it sufficiently clear that one intends to communicate something non-literal entails that

[71] Ekins (2012) 210.

one is justifiably taken to have intended to communicate the literal content of one's remark. On a weaker, more plausible, version, however, there is no such entailment – rather, the priority of the literal just amounts to an assumption (of varying strength) that the speaker is intending to communicate the literal content of her remark, which can be treated like something akin to a variably high prior probability assigned to that hypothesis.[72]

I do recognise that my argument may, like Marmor's, give the impression that in case the relevant requirement isn't satisfied, then the content of the law is – by default – its literal content. There is, however, plenty of room for indeterminacy about utterance content on the framework I have adopted, assuming the weaker reading of the literalness presumption. The underlying notion is that – as a general epistemological matter – the fact that one is not warranted in inferring that *p* does not entail that one is warranted in inferring that *not-p*; sometimes, one should simply withhold belief. When this happens in communication (with respect to the speaker's communicative intention), then the primary content of the relevant utterance will be indeterminate between the literal content of the sentence uttered and some non-literal enrichment thereof. That is, if it is – all things considered – neither significantly more nor significantly less likely than not that the speaker is intending to assert what she literally said, then the hearer is justified only in withholding belief about the speaker's communicative intention. Consequently, since – on the view expounded here – assertive content is partly determined by the inferences that the hearer is warranted in making about the speaker's communicative intention, the assertive content in such cases is to some extent indeterminate.

Moreover, I take the indeterminacy discussed in this chapter to be a type of vagueness, since – on the face of it – indeterminacy about utterance content seems rather removed from, say, borderline cases of 'blue', 'crowd', 'vehicle', etc. I think it can be shown that it comes from the vagueness of speech act terms like 'say', 'assert', 'command', etc. To see this, recall that assertion was partly defined in terms of epistemic warrant: a speaker asserts *p* only if a rational hearer, knowing the conversational background and context, is warranted in taking her to be intending to assert *p*. And epistemic warrant, in this context, was defined partly in terms of a vague probabilistic concept: a rational hearer, knowing the conversational background and context, is warranted in taking a speaker to be intending to assert *p* only if it is *significantly more likely than not* that the speaker is intending to assert *p*. The phrase 'it is significantly more likely than not that' is obviously vague – it both admits of borderline cases and is Sorites-susceptible. Imagine, for example, a case in which it is clearly significantly more likely than not that *S* intended to assert *p* and let's then say that there is a small change in the context with the result that it is now trivially less likely that S intended to assert *p*. Such a small change doesn't make a difference for whether it is appropriate to say that it is significantly more

[72] This reading is subscribed to, for example, by Bach and Harnish (1979).

likely than not that *S* intended to assert *p*. If we introduce enough minute changes into the context, however, we end up with a full-fledged Sorites-series.

A. Indeterminacy and Levels of Pragmatic Reasoning

It is important to note that indeterminacy can enter into the picture at two different levels, given the two roles that the common ground plays in pragmatic reasoning: it can either be indeterminate *that* the speaker asserted something other than what she literally said or indeterminate *what* pragmatically enriched proposition the speaker asserted. As discussed in section II.B, these notions are – although closely related – analytically distinct.

Let's first revisit two significant legal cases that I believe are best analysed as cases in which it is indeterminate that the legislature asserted something other than what it literally said: *Church of the Holy Trinity v US* and *Ali v Federal Bureau of Prisons*. In the context of *Holy Trinity* and the *Alien Contract Labor Act*, it was presumably pretty clear to all parties that what Congress wished to accomplish was to prevent the importation of cheap unskilled labour. Further, as Vermeule (1998) notes, the court later argued that 'in no event could [the Act] be construed as applying to a contract for the services of a rector or a pastor of a religious corporation',[73] suggesting that it took it to be common knowledge that Congress did not wish to 'prohibit the immigration under contract of a Christian minister'.[74] This is all significant evidence that Congress did not intend to enact the literal content of the Act. Still, the Act did include a number of specific exceptions that cannot count as exceptions on a pragmatically enriched reading of the Act. An exception for professional artists, for example, cannot be an exception to a law that prohibits the importation of manual labour or service. This significantly undercuts the evidence mentioned so far (at this point, I wish to remain silent about whether or not the explicit exceptions provide evidence that Congress did intend the relevant part of the Act to be taken literally).[75]

In this case, it seems to me reasonable to say that the common ground between Congress and the courts was neither rich enough to make it significantly more likely than not that Congress did not intend to prohibit the importation of all types of labour or service, including those of rectors and clergymen, nor rich enough to make it significantly more likely than not that they positively did intend to do so. Taking everything into account, the evidence seems to favour neither claim over the other. If that is correct, the content of the *Alien Contract Labor Act* was to some

[73] *US v Laws*, 163 US 258, 264. Cited by Vermeule (1998) 1842, fn 41.

[74] Vermeule (1998) 1842.

[75] As it turns out, there was also significant debate about the issue in Congress, but since the legislative history was not part of the common ground, it did not – on my view – play a part in determining the content of the law.

extent indeterminate. There is simply no answer to the question 'Does the Act apply to people intended to serve as pastors?'

Similar reasoning applies in *Ali*, I believe. It seems safe to say that it was part of what was (reasonably) taken for granted both by Congress and the Supreme Court that, in enacting the *Federal Tort Claims Act*, Congress wished – as Justice Kennedy of the dissent put it – to '[allow] those who allege injury from governmental actions over a vast sphere to seek damages for tortious conduct'.[76] Citing the case of *Kosak v United States*, Justice Kennedy also pointed out – rightly, I think – that 'unduly generous interpretations of the exceptions [established by the *Federal Tort Claims Act*] run the risk of defeating the central purpose of the statute'.[77] The majority, however, further pointed out that since the exception relevant to *Ali* concerned the detention of property, it was far from obvious that interpreting the exception to apply to absolutely all law enforcement officers would go against the wishes of Congress. Thus, given the fact that Congress uttered the relevant text in the relevant context, it is arguably neither significantly more likely than not that Congress intended federal immunity from the relevant type of tort claims to extend only to officers working in customs or related domains nor that it intended such immunity to extend to officers of all kinds. If that is correct, then the *Federal Torts Claim Act* is indeterminate *in that respect*.[78]

In addition to cases in which it is indeterminate whether or not the speaker asserts something other than what she literally says, there are also cases in which it is significantly more likely than not that the speaker did not intend to assert what she literally said but indeterminate what enriched proposition she asserted instead. Consider for example a case in which a speaker utters the following: 'Everyone is coming to the party!' And let us say that the hearer is in charge of supplying chips and salsa for said party. Now, let us further stipulate that – given the context – it is indeterminate whether the speaker intended to assert that *everyone in the department* is coming to the party or that *everyone in the group of students* is coming to the party. In this case, what the speaker asserted is indeterminate, but it is still determinate that she did not assert the literal content of her remark.

To take an analogous legal example, consider the case of *United States v Gonzales*.[79] In *Gonzales*, the question was whether or not the court could order that a federal prison sentence could run concurrently with a state-imposed sentence, despite the fact that a section of 18 USC §924 states that a sentence imposed under it 'shall [not] … run concurrently with any other term of imprisonment'. The majority held that it could, but Justice Stevens of the dissent argued

[76] 552 US 214 (2008).

[77] 465 US 848, 854 (1984).

[78] There were of course a number of other issues that were relevant to *deciding* the case, but since questions about non-literal statutory content turn just on the language used and the common ground, these issues concerned the proper *development* of the Act, given that it was indeterminate what the exact content of it was.

[79] 520 US 1 (1997).

that the statute could not 'reasonably be interpreted as containing any command to state sentencing judges or as requiring the suspension of any federal sentences when concurrent state sentences are later imposed'.[80] '[C]ommon sense,' he said, 'requires us to reject a purely literal reading of the text.'[81] I take this to indicate that Justice Stevens thought that it was obvious that – taken literally – the code has certain legal consequences and that it was obvious that these consequences clashed with Congress's wishes.

If – for the sake of argument – we concede that Justice Stevens is correct, then it is indeed significantly more likely than not that Congress did not intend the statute to be understood literally. However, as he rightly notes, it still remains to be determined what non-literal content was intended, and this may well make a difference to the outcome of the case. According to Justice Stevens, there were two plausible candidates. Either Congress intended to use the phrase 'any other term of imprisonment' to mean *any other term of imprisonment {that has already been imposed}* or to mean *any other {federal} term of imprisonment*. Only the latter was in favour of the respondent.

Justice Stevens cited three reasons why he thought that it was more likely than not that Congress intended to use the phrase to mean *any other {federal} term of imprisonment*. However, he did not go so far as to claim that it was obvious that Congress could not have intended to use the phrase in the former way. Since *Gonzales* was a criminal case, and the epistemic constraint is therefore arguably high, this arguably means that it was *not* significantly more likely than not that Congress intended to say that a sentence imposed under the relevant code 'shall [not] ... run concurrently with any other {federal} term of imprisonment'. But it certainly does not mean that it was *significantly* more likely than not that Congress intended to say that a sentence imposed under the relevant code 'shall [not] ... run concurrently with any other federal term of imprisonment {that has already been imposed}'. As a result, it is determinate that the content of the statute is not its literal content but indeterminate what exactly the content of the statute is (on the assumption that Justice Stevens is right).

B. Indeterminacy about Content and the Notion of a Well-functioning Legal System

There is a prima facie worry here. Neither the *Alien Contract Labor Act*, the *Federal Torts Claim Act*, nor 18 USC §924 seem like unique – or exceptional – cases. If that is correct, then indeterminacy about the content of the law appears to be rampant. If such indeterminacy is seen as a failure – eg as a failure on behalf of lawmakers to communicate to subjects what their legal rights and obligations are – then this would

[80] 520 US 1 (1997).
[81] 520 US 1 (1997).

indicate a widespread failure in the legal system. Hasn't something gone seriously wrong if it is the normal state of affairs that the persons to whom the law is addressed are not able to fully determine what the lawmakers intended to communicate?

The answer, I think, is no. Scenarios like the ones we have been considering do not necessarily indicate a general pragmatic failure – neither in ordinary conversation nor in law. In the 'salsa case', for example, the reason for the speaker's assertion – the knowledge of which we stipulate to be shared by speaker and hearer – is that she wants the hearer to be able to bring enough chips and salsa to the party. In case the difference between the two sets of people is immaterial, vis-à-vis the relevant purpose, nothing has really gone wrong. And although the speaker presumably had in mind one of the two candidate propositions, the student-to-faculty ratio in the department may be high enough so that it does not matter that the hearer has insufficient evidence about which enriched proposition the speaker intended to communicate.[82]

Similarly, despite being indeterminate to some extent, the *Alien Contract Labor Act* still determinately applies to manual labour. And the immunity established by the *Federal Torts Claim Act* still determinately extends to officers working in customs or related domains. Finally, the section of 18 USC §924 that states that a sentence imposed under it 'shall [not] … run concurrently with any other term of imprisonment' still determinately prohibits that a sentence imposed under it run concurrently with any other federal term of imprisonment that has already been imposed. The general principle here is that even if it may be indeterminate what the content of a particular statute is, the statute still determinately applies to those cases to which it applies *on any reasonable enrichment*.

Ultimately, then, it is the practical context that determines if, and to what extent, something has gone wrong, and cases like the salsa case appear to be a regular – and relatively unproblematic – feature of successful human communication. Similarly, partially indeterminate legal directives like the *Alien Contract Labor Act*, the *Federal Torts Claim Act*, and 18 USC §924 are regular features of any legal system. Insofar as the number of actual cases of indeterminacy resulting from such directives is manageable, such indeterminacy is also relatively unproblematic. Although the law is often to some extent indeterminate, due to the fact the common ground between the legislature and its audience rarely contains sufficiently specific information about legislative intent, this will not necessarily prevent it from functioning reasonably well. As a general principle applying both to the case of ordinary conversation and to the legislative context, we can perhaps say that as long as a rational hearer, knowing the conversational background and context, is able to extract sufficient information from the speaker's utterance, relative to the purpose(s) of the conversation, the relevant speech act counts as reasonably successful.

[82] I'm assuming in this case – safely, I think – that it has no non-instrumental value for the speaker to have her communicative intention fully recognised.

6

Textualism, Content and Interpretation

Relying, as I have, on the communicative content-thesis, argued for in chapter one, my view may seem to imply a version of textualism. And in one sense it does, at least insofar as textualism is taken to be a theory of legal *content* rather than legal *interpretation* (on the understanding that legal interpretation is the act of developing the law in the face of indeterminate/inconsistent legal content or a particularly problematic result).

But textualism is more than just a theory about legal content – it is primarily a normative theory of adjudication of which such a theory is a part. And as I will try to make clear, my view differs significantly from full-fledged textualism. Part of the reason is that I think that legal content is often less determinate than textualist rhetoric suggests. Mainly, however, the difference is that I don't think that the standard textualist considerations support their limited view of the judge's role in all cases in which interpretation is called for.

I begin the chapter by explaining what textualists think that judges shouldn't do and why. This will give us a sense of what textualists think is at stake in the debate. Next, I argue that the pragmatic framework underlying (my version of) the communicative-content thesis confers a non-negligible amount of plausibility on what Perry (2011) calls *conception-textualism* – a view that he has pronounced 'confused, implausible, and unworkable'.[1] But I also note that the willingness of contemporary textualists to recognise pragmatic factors as contributors to legal content appears to get them into a certain amount of trouble. In particular, the way they conceive of the context and conversational background of legislative utterances indicates that – despite their rhetoric – they do not care only about the actual communicative content of statutory enactments. Finally, I argue that when it comes to judicial decision making in cases in which the legal content is vague (whether semantically or pragmatically), the standard textualist considerations against judicial lawmaking do not apply. As a result, judges will have to look elsewhere for guidance about how to resolve such cases.

I. Textualism and Legislative Intentions

Textualism, as a normative theory of adjudication, has both a critical aspect and a constructive aspect. The critical aspect of the theory tells us what judges

[1] Perry (2011) 106.

shouldn't do and why, while the constructive aspect tells us what judges *should* do and why. As for the critical aspect, textualism holds that there are primarily two things that judges shouldn't do: they should neither (i) attempt to attribute purpose and meaning to a statute by putting themselves 'in imagination in the position of the legislature which enacted the measure',[2] nor (ii) consult legislative history in the hope of finding evidence of the lawmakers' actual communicative (ie illocutionary) intentions or actual further intentions (ie their perlocutionary intentions) in enacting the statute.

There are several reasons why textualists maintain that judges should not attempt to attribute purpose and meaning to a statute by putting themselves in the shoes of the enacting legislature, but the weightiest one is presumably that they think that the more judges engage in the 'imaginative reconstruction' of legislative intent, the more they are assuming authority that they do not possess, insofar as their speculations lead to binding judicial decisions. That is, in doing so – and to the extent that they do it – they are making assumptions that are not theirs to make, since they are neither democratically elected representatives of the people nor authorised by Article 1, section 7 of the Constitution to make law. Thus, says the textualist, both respect for democracy and for legislative supremacy requires that judges refrain from engaging in imaginative reconstruction of legislative intent. The argument has also been made that judges shouldn't allow such reconstruction to influence their judicial decisions because that would diminish the separation of powers (legislative and judicial). Finally, some have argued that it lessens predictability, vis-à-vis application of the law in question, and thereby significantly frustrates the ideal of the Rule of Law.

According to the textualist, then, judges should – for important political reasons – not attempt to attribute purpose and meaning to a statute by putting themselves in the shoes of the enacting legislature. But why are judges not permitted to look for concrete evidence of *actual* legislative intentions by consulting legislative history, given the fact that inference on the basis of concrete evidence seems like a much more constrained activity than imaginative reconstruction?

There are two primary reasons why textualists don't think judges should consult legislative history in the hope of finding evidence of the legislature's intentions (whether illocutionary or perlocutionary). First, they think that there are – due in significant part to the adversarial nature of legislative institutions in modern democratic societies – very few intentions that can in good faith be attributed to the legislature as a collective. Legislative history is, according to the textualist, not a window into the coherent, collective mind of Congress; on the contrary, it usually contains evidence of several competing viewpoints and the danger is that judges will pick and choose those viewpoints that support the legal outcome they prefer. Thus, judges tend to (consciously or unconsciously) select evidence from legislative history according to their own preferences and, in doing so – the

[2] Hart and Sacks (1958) 1414.

textualist thinks – their actions frustrate the aforementioned ideals: democratic legitimacy, legislative supremacy, separation of powers, and the Rule of Law.

Second, legislative history not only contains evidence of several competing viewpoints open to cherry-picking, it also contains strategically placed statements intended to influence the decisions of judges who choose to consult legislative history. Politicians have become very good at manipulating legislative history in their favour and it therefore provides, according to the textualist, too little reliable evidence of the legislature's intentions to be worth consulting.

II. Textualism, Communicative Content and Legal Content

As for the constructive aspect of the theory, textualists hold that judges should – in the first instance – determine the *content* of the relevant statute, which in their view amounts to determining the meaning of the statutory text. And the meaning of a statutory text, according to contemporary textualists, is the linguistic content that a rational and competent speaker of the English language would, knowing the relevant context and conversational background, have associated with relevant text at the time of enactment.[3] That is, they think that legal content is determined by the *objective content of the legislative utterance*, which – in turn – is partly determined by *contextual* factors. As Scalia (1997) puts it, 'the import of language depends upon its context, which includes the occasion for, and hence the evident purpose of, its utterance'.[4]

As it turns out, however, there is a remarkable dearth of direct argument for the textualist claim that the legal content of a statute is the objective content of the respective utterance (ie the enactment). And although some rather obscure hints at arguments can be found in the literature,[5] many textualists seem content to focus primarily on arguing against the alternatives (for example that legal content is determined by the intentions of the lawmakers) and then more or less simply propose that judges should instead focus on determining the content that a rational hearer would, knowing the relevant conversational background and context, associate with the statutory text.[6] Nevertheless, I think that the textualist thesis of legal content is basically correct and in chapter one I outlined a jurisprudential framework on which it – or something sufficiently close to it, anyway – comes out as necessarily true: the legal content of a statute or constitutional clause corresponds directly to its communicative content (determined by reference to what a competent, rational hearer would take the speaker to be intending to communicate

[3] See eg Easterbrook (1990) 443; see also Manning (2005) 434.
[4] Scalia (1997) 144.
[5] See eg Manning (2006) 79.
[6] See eg Easterbrook (1988).

in uttering the relevant words). I have been calling this the communicative-content thesis, but depending on the context we could also choose to call this a variant of the *new-textualist thesis* or *public-meaning originalist thesis of legal content*.[7]

Below, I use this thesis to elucidate the important role that contextual enrichment plays in textualist and originalist legal reasoning. The aim is to show how the linguistic framework underlying sophisticated versions of the communicative-content theory of law can help to shed important light on the plausibility of what John Perry calls *conception textualism* – the (by his lights deeply mistaken) view that 'the conceptions that the enactors had of the states, conditions, phenomena, and the like referred to by their words, used in the operative senses, are determinative [of statutory content]'.[8]

Conception textualism, as defined by Perry, is arguably best classified as a version of what has come to be known in the legal literature as *expected-applications originalism*, which is often contrasted with public-meaning originalism.[9] Following Jack Balkin, we can say that expected-applications originalism is the view that the expectations that lawmakers have about the application of a statute or constitutional clause are legally binding on judges and other officials.[10] Such expectations, as Mark Greenberg and Harry Litman discuss in laudable detail, in turn often crucially depend on beliefs about the application of the terms used.[11] According to Justice Scalia, for example, even if the death penalty were in fact cruel and unusual, the Eighth Amendment of the US Constitution would not prohibit it, since it is clear that the framers believed that it was not in the extension of the term 'cruel and unusual', and so they did not expect the amendment to be applied to that particular form of punishment.[12]

During the past three decades or so, expected-applications originalism has fallen increasingly out of favour.[13] Some oppose it on normative grounds, while others accuse it of being linguistically confused.[14] Perry is one of the most recent additions to the latter group of critics, arguing that the view is – from the perspective of philosophy of language and linguistics – 'confused, implausible, and unworkable'.[15] His main argument is that the view clearly fails to satisfy a requirement necessary for the adequacy of any theory of legal interpretation – that its

[7] See eg Scalia (1987), Scalia (1997), Lawson (1992), Goldsworthy (1997), Barnett (1999), Whittington (2004) and Solum (2008).

[8] Perry (2011) 106. Similar attitudes are expressed in Goldsworthy (1997) and in Greenberg and Litman (1998).

[9] See eg Balkin (2007) and Solum (2011); though, as Solum points out, the earliest – and probably still most thorough – discussion of the concepts at play is found in Greenberg and Litman (1998).

[10] See Balkin (2007) 292–93 and Solum (2011) 24–26.

[11] See Greenberg and Litman (1998) 586–91, esp 588–89.

[12] See Scalia (1997).

[13] See Balkin (2007) 293, fn 4 and Solum (2011) 22 ff.

[14] The former include Greenberg and Litman (1998) and Balkin (2007); the latter include Greenberg and Litman (1998), Balkin (2007), Goldsworthy (1997) and most recently Perry (2011).

[15] Perry (2011) 106.

claims about the content of an enactment can be supported using the tools of contemporary philosophy of language and linguistics.

Contra Perry, I do not think that conception textualism is such an implausible view. In fact, a moderate version of it seems to fall quite naturally out of the linguistic framework underlying sophisticated public-meaning originalism. As I hope to show – at least in the case of speech acts with a world-to-mind direction of fit, such as legislation – once we fully appreciate the role of contextual enrichment in communication, it becomes plausible to think that when a speaker's (mutually known) false beliefs about that to which she wishes to refer or quantify over clash with the literal content of her remark, these beliefs manage to affect utterance content by making that content to some extent indeterminate. This has potential implications for a range of important and controversial legal cases, including *FDA v Brown & Williamson Tobacco Corp.*[16]

III. Textualism/Originalism and Contextual Enrichment

I should begin this section by noting that – as indicated in the previous chapter – there are two main theories or notions of communicative content in the contemporary literature in philosophy of language and linguistics; we can call them the *objective theory* and the *subjective theory*. According to the objective theory, to which I subscribe, the content that a speaker counts as having communicated is determined by the inferences that a rational hearer, knowing the context and conversational background, is warranted in making about the speaker's communicative intentions.[17] In contrast, on the subjective theory, the communicative content of a speaker's remark is simply the content that she intended to communicate.[18] A speaker – in uttering a sentence – means, says, asserts, and so on what she intends to mean, say, assert, and so on. For many purposes, the choice between these two notions of communicative content does not matter at all. As shown below, however, the difference between them is crucial when it comes to assessing the plausibility of conception textualism. We will proceed, however, on the basis of the objective theory.

The objective theory, of course, does not by itself say anything about what sort of content can, according to the new-textualist/public-meaning originalist, form part of the objective content of a legislative utterance. However, as shown

[16] *FDA v Brown & Williamson Tobacco Corp*, 529 US 120 (2000).

[17] See eg Goldsworthy (2005), Soames (2011) and Marmor (2013).

[18] See eg Grice (1989), Schiffer (1972), Neale (2005) and Bach (2006). Note that on most sophisticated subjective theories, the formation of the relevant intentions is subject to certain constraints, which safeguards them from the so-called 'Humpty-Dumpty' objection. Although a speaker simply says, asserts, etc. what she intends to say, assert, etc, it is *not* the case that she can intend to say, assert, etc whatever she likes.

below, standard textualist reasoning in prominent legal cases suggests that new textualists/public-meaning originalists are at least willing to concede that insofar as such content forms part of the primary content of the relevant utterance, contextually enriched content can form part of the content of the law.[19]

This is just as well, since it is by now commonplace to recognise that linguistic intuitions – that is, the 'data' by which we determine what content a rational hearer, knowing the relevant conversational background and context, would be warranted in taking the speaker to be intending to assert – do not track literal content but rather utterance content, which is often contextually enriched. Generally, competent speakers of language have reliable intuitions about the content communicated via an utterance without having reliable intuitions about the exact literal content of the words used and the details of how such content is affected by context to produce the content communicated.[20] Thus, if new textualism/public-meaning originalism is to have a sound linguistic basis, it must concern utterance content rather than literal content.

The examples I discuss below are well-worn by now, but they are worth recalling, along with some linguistic commentary, in order for us to see just how natural it might be for new textualists/public-meaning originalists to acknowledge the relevance of application beliefs for legal content. In briefly rehearsing these examples through the lens of philosophy of language, we will be reminded both of the role of contextual enrichment in communication and of the extent to which contemporary textualists embrace its contribution to legal content. This, in turn, helps us evaluate the plausibility of conception textualism, which is one of the main purposes of the chapter. As I hope to make clear, the view's plausibility lies to a significant extent in the fact that – *contra* Greenberg and Litman – what needs to be established in order to demonstrate the relevance of application beliefs to new textualism and public-meaning originalism is a relation not between application beliefs and literal meaning but between such beliefs and the broader notion of utterance content.[21]

Let us first consider Scalia's famous dissent in the case of *Smith v United States*.[22] During a drug-trafficking crime, Mr Smith had exchanged a firearm for drugs, and the question was whether he had thereby violated 18 USC §924(c)(1) of the *United States Code*, which mandates certain penalties if the defendant 'during and in relation to … [a] drug trafficking crime[,] uses … a firearm'.[23] In the case of a

[19] In addition, Scalia (1997) explicitly states that 'the good textualist is not a literalist' (24); rather, 'the import of language depends upon its context, which includes the occasion for, and hence the evident purpose of, its utterance' (144). See also Manning (2005) 434. I should note that I will not on this occasion be concerned with the question of whether presuppositions or implicatures can form part of the content of the law. For a discussion, see Marmor (2011).

[20] See Neale (2005) 183–84, Bach (2002), 29–32 and Soames (2008) 460–62.

[21] See Greenberg and Litman (1998) 601–02.

[22] *Smith v United States*, 507 US 197 (1993).

[23] 18 USC §924(c)(1).

firearm of the sort used for bartering by Mr Smith (a MAC-10), the mandatory sentence is 30 years.

The majority held that Smith had indeed violated the statute, arguing that its content did not specify any particular way in which the firearm in question had to be used. All that was required was that Smith used it in *some way or other*. And if the legal content of a statute is confined to its literal content – perhaps including semantic presuppositions – then the majority's position appears to be correct.

Scalia, on the other hand, argued that the communicative content of the statute was a specific contextual enrichment of its literal content and that in order to violate the code, Smith would have had to use the firearm *as a weapon*. 'When someone asks "Do you use a cane?"', Scalia said, 'he is not inquiring whether you have your grandfather's silver-handled walking stick on display in the hall; he wants to know whether you *walk* with a cane.'[24] 'Similarly,' he continued, 'to speak of "using a firearm" is to speak of using it for its distinctive purpose, ie, as a weapon.'[25]

In linguistic terms, *Smith* was a case of *required enrichment* – a case in which the literal content of the sentence uttered has to be contextually enriched in order for the speaker to count as having successfully conveyed a complete proposition.[26] A verb like 'use', for example, may occur in a sentence with a *purpose parameter* but may also occur without one; compare, for example, 'He used a hammer to pound in the nails' and 'He used a hammer'. In the latter case, the literal content of the sentence does not express a complete (ie, truth-evaluable) proposition, and contextual enrichment is therefore required. The general explanation for this systematic necessity of contextual enrichment is that speakers routinely compress intended communicative content into linguistic structures, or forms, which subsequently require contextual enrichment in order to be expanded.[27]

With a term like 'use', there will of course be a range of possible enrichments, corresponding (at a minimum) to the range of possible parameters: he used a hammer {to pound in the nail/as a door prop/as a weapon to fight off the burglar/etc}. In all these cases, we look to context and the norms of conversation in order to determine the speaker's communicative intention. Some enrichments, of course, may be more 'natural' than others, due, perhaps, to the way in which an object is typically used. For example, if someone says to me that a person needs to use a hammer, I will probably infer that she needs to use it in the way that people normally use hammers – to pound in nails. Similarly, if someone tells me that a person used a firearm during a crime, I will take the speaker to be saying that the person used the firearm as a weapon. And although we cannot really say that 'use'

[24] *Smith v United States*, 507 US 197 (1993) (Scalia J dissenting).

[25] *Smith v United States*, 507 US 197 (1993) (Scalia J dissenting).

[26] Bach (1994) calls this *completion*; Recanati (2004) calls it *saturation*. For a helpful discussion of contextual enrichment in general and of the difference between required and optional enrichment in particular, see Recanati (2012).

[27] For similar discussions of *Smith*, see eg Neale (2007) 251–61 and Geis (1995) 1136.

by itself, unaccompanied by any noun phrase, has a 'default' enrichment of this sort, it is still sensible to say that in cases in which a speaker uses a verb phrase of the form '[use] an *F*', the hearer is justified in taking the speaker to have in mind the normal use of an *F* (if there is one), unless, of course, the context provides significant evidence to the contrary.[28]

I should note that it may seem reasonable to ask whether we are talking about *ambiguity*, or even *polysemy*, rather than contextual enrichment.[29] The significance of settling this issue is that if what is going on in *Smith* has to do with ambiguity or polysemy, then Scalia's reasoning in the case is simply a matter of disambiguation, in which case *Smith* does not count as evidence that contemporary textualists are willing to count anything beyond literal meaning as contributing to legal content. That is, if *Smith* is really a case of ambiguity or polysemy, then the function of contextual inference is in this case to give us the relevant literal meaning of the phrase 'use a firearm' rather than to provide us with a contextual completion of such content.

There are two good reasons, however, to believe that the relevant issue in *Smith* does in fact concern pragmatic enrichment rather than ambiguity or polysemy.[30] The first rests on the fact that semantics is in the business of describing those features of expressions that are invariant between contexts of use. And considering the various uses of the verb 'use', there really is a feeling of invariance present. This invariance can be exemplified, for example, by paraphrasing simple sentences containing the verb so that the purpose parameter is made explicit: 'He used a hammer' might, for example, be paraphrased as 'He used a hammer to pound in the nails'. But if the (here, stereotypical) 'sense' of the verb has been given by the infinitive clause 'to pound in the nails', then, since the sentence still contains the verb 'use', the meaning of 'use' must be neutral between various types of purposes, or else what is said by the infinitive clause would be redundant – and it clearly is not. This strongly suggests that the verb 'use' is not ambiguous; rather, it is 'skeletal' and requires a piece of information to be provided by the context of use, information comparable to the infinitive clause.

The second reason for thinking that we are dealing with contextual enrichment rather than polysemy comes from the fact that we do not want to postulate *indefinite polysemy*. Given the uncountable variety of uses to which we can put a verb like 'use' (no pun intended), a proper linguistic account of the expression would require an indefinite number of lexical entries plus an explanation of the relation between all of them. Further, since we have already established that 'use'

[28] This notion of *default enrichment* is perhaps sufficiently captured by Grice's notion of *generalised conversational implicature* if we allow the relevant considerations to affect the *primary* content of the utterance. The idea is that a default enrichment is an enrichment *e* of the literal content *q* of a sentence *s* uttered such that *e* would *normally* – ie, in the absence of special circumstances – be associated with utterances of *s*.

[29] See eg Marmor (2014) 120–25.

[30] Similar considerations, for example, motivate Kratzer (2012) to provide a monosemic account of modals and arguably also motivate Grice (1989) to postulate a unified semantics for 'or'.

has a neutral sense, a lexical entry would also be required for that. But then the other (indefinitely many) entries become redundant. A single lexical entry for the neutral 'use' provides a much more plausible semantics.[31]

Getting back to textualism, it appears, then, that Scalia's reasoning in *Smith* allows us to conclude that contemporary textualists think that required contextual enrichment can form part the content of the law. But there seems to be clear evidence that they want to allow for (at least) the possibility that legal content also includes *optional enrichment*, that is, contextual enrichment of literal content that already constitutes a complete proposition prior to enrichment.[32] In his concurring opinion in *Green v Bock Laundry Machine Co*,[33] for example, Scalia argued for such a conclusion.

Bock Laundry was a civil product-liability case in which petitioner Paul Green sued Bock Laundry Machine Company after having been injured by one of its machines while he was on work-release from a county prison. He testified that he had received inadequate information about the machine's operation and risks of use. Bock, however, impeached Green's testimony on the basis that he was a convicted felon. Green had filed a pre-trial motion for the exclusion of impeaching evidence, which was denied, and on appeal Green argued that the trial court had erred in denying his pre-trial motion, citing Rule 609(a) of the Federal Rules of Evidence, which – at the time – stated the following:

> For the purpose of attacking the credibility of a witness, evidence that the witness has been convicted of a crime shall be admitted if elicited from the witness or established by public record during cross-examination but only if the crime (1) was punishable by death or imprisonment in excess of one year under the law under which the witness was convicted, and the court determines that the probative value of admitting this evidence outweighs its prejudicial effect *to the defendant*, or (2) involved dishonesty or false statement, regardless of the punishment.[34]

Green claimed that the probative value of admitting the testimony of his prior convictions did *not* outweigh its prejudicial effect. The problem with Green's argument was that Rule 609, read literally, does not apply to him, since he was a plaintiff and not a defendant. So the question was whether or not it was reasonable to read the rule non-literally, so as to refer not just to civil and criminal defendants but also to civil plaintiffs. If so, then the trial court did in fact err in allowing testimony regarding Green's prior convictions.

[31] The general principle underlying this second part of my argument is generally known as the *modified Occam's razor*: senses are not to be multiplied beyond necessity; see Grice (1989) 47.

[32] Bach (1994) calls this *expansion*; Recanati (2004) calls it *strengthening*; others have called it *free enrichment*. Implicit quantifier domain restriction is a good example of such enrichment: a speaker may, for example, utter the sentence 'Everyone is coming to the party', which expresses a complete proposition, intending to communicate that everyone *in the department* is coming to the party.

[33] *Green v Bock Laundry Machine Co*, 490 US 504 (1989).

[34] Federal Rule of Evidence 609(a); emphasis added. The rule has since been amended to address the issue that arose in *Bock Laundry*.

The Supreme Court majority – led by Justice Stevens – held that Rule 609 could indeed not be interpreted literally. The reason was that on a literal interpretation, the rule would establish an odd asymmetry between the rights of the disputing parties in civil cases: the defendant, but not the plaintiff, would have special protection from impeaching evidence. But neither party in a civil case, the court said, enjoys any protection over the other party, and so the rule 'can't mean what it says'. We can say that given the common ground between lawmakers and the courts (concerning the proper way in which to treat parties to a civil case), it would be unreasonable for the court to attribute to the legislature the intention to establish special protection against impeaching evidence for civil defendants but not for plaintiffs. To use Scalia's phrase, such an intention would constitute an 'unthinkable disposition'.[35] Assuming that the legislature did not just make a mistake, it must therefore have intended to communicate something other than what it literally said.

If this is all correct, what has been shown is of course just that it is very unlikely that the legislature intended to enact the literal content of the legislative text. It remains to be seen what inference, if any, can be legitimately drawn about what content the legislature *did* intend to enact. In order to determine the proper non-literal content of Rule 609, the majority turned to a close examination of legislative history, concluding that it did not provide sufficient evidence that the lawmakers intended the protection provided by the rule to extend to parties other than criminal defendants. The court therefore held that Rule 609 did not apply to Green, thereby affirming the court of appeal's decision that the trial court had not erred in admitting evidence regarding Green's prior convictions.

Scalia, in his concurring opinion, agreed with the majority's conclusion and with certain aspects of its reasoning.[36] He disagreed, however, with the majority's use of legislative history in determining the non-literal content of the rule, arguing that there was only one relevant non-literal interpretation that the language of the rule could bear; the term 'defendant' as it occurs in Rule 609, he said, was *obviously* being used to mean *criminal defendant*. As Scalia rightly notes, it makes sense to say that speakers sometimes use 'defendant' to mean *criminal defendant*, but makes little sense to say that speakers sometimes use 'defendant' to mean *civil plaintiff, civil defendant, prosecutor*, and *criminal defendant* or *civil plaintiff and defendant and criminal defendant*. To quote his dissent in *Johnson v United States*, a word or phrase will bear a suggested meaning only if 'you could use the word in that sense at a cocktail party without having people look at you funny'.[37]

Scalia's reasoning in *Bock Laundry*, then, is easy enough to model on the linguistic framework underlying the objective-communicative-content theory of law. And note that it does not really make a difference whether the word 'defendant'

[35] *Green v Bock Laundry Machine Co*, 490 US 504 (1989) 527.
[36] *Green v Bock Laundry Machine Co*, 490 US 504 (1989) 529–30.
[37] *Johnson v United States*, 529 US 694, 718 (2000).

was being used intentionally to mean *criminal defendant* or whether it was a 'scrivener's error' (an inadvertent omission of the word 'criminal'). As a general matter, there is often no way to tell when it comes to the suspected omission of words and phrases – due simply to the way in which we use language. But the reasoning is the same – in both cases, the primary question is whether or not there is sufficient evidence that the speaker intended to communicate something other than what she literally said.

The point of the preceding examples is not to show anything new but rather to highlight the role that contextual enrichment plays in textualist legal reasoning. In the next section, the aim is to show how a good understanding of this important aspect of new textualism and public-meaning originalism can help to shed light on the plausibility of what John Perry dubs *conception textualism*. If what I say is correct, then it is, *contra* Perry, far from clear that this view is 'confused, implausible, and unworkable'.[38]

IV. On the Plausibility of Conception Textualism

Perry distinguishes between two types of textualism that can be extracted from Scalia: *meaning textualism* and *conception textualism*. Meaning textualism, says Perry, is the view that 'the content of a statute is determined by the words in the text of the statute, given the meaning that those words had at the time of enactment or ratification'.[39] Conception textualism, on the other hand, is the view that 'the conceptions that the enactors had of the states, conditions, phenomena, and the like referred to by their words, used in the operative senses, are determinative [of statutory content]'.[40] Although formulated as theories of statutory interpretation, Perry takes these views to extend to constitutional clauses as well.[41]

According to Perry, what makes it the case that meaning textualism is a sensible philosophy of legal interpretation while conception textualism is 'totally implausible' is the fact that the former – but not the latter – applies to statutes and constitutional clauses 'the same apparatus we use to determine what some individual says when they are talking to us'.[42] As I understand him, Perry thinks that it is a necessary requirement for the adequacy of any theory of legal interpretation that its claims about the content of an enactment can be supported using the tools of contemporary philosophy of language and linguistics. And he obviously thinks that conception textualism does not satisfy this requirement. Call this Perry's *foundational argument* against conception textualism.[43]

[38] Perry (2011) 106.
[39] ibid.
[40] ibid.
[41] One of the main examples that Perry discusses is the constitutionality of the death penalty.
[42] Perry (2011) 106.
[43] Perry has at least one other argument against the view, one that we can call the *argument from convergence*; see Perry (2011) 108–09. The worry driving this argument is that conception textualism

I think that Perry's requirement is a reasonable one – at the very least insofar as we are concerned with new textualism/public-meaning originalism. My aim in this section, therefore, is to show that it is far from obvious that conception textualism fails to satisfy his requirement. Although I am not necessarily convinced that the view can ultimately be made to work or that the best case for it is a linguistic one, I do think that once we have recognised the contribution that contextual factors make to utterance content, a very decent case can be made that conception textualism does in fact apply to legal texts the same apparatus we use to determine what a person says when she is talking to us. It seems to me that in at least some cases of linguistic communication, it is not implausible to argue that a speaker's (mutually known) beliefs about that to which she wishes to refer or quantify over manage to affect utterance content.[44] If what I say is correct, these cases put significant pressure on Perry's assessment of conception textualism.

The points I make below are for the most part general, but in the specific context of legislation, the cases I have in mind are ones in which (1) lawmakers enact a statute the literal content of which covers, among other things, a certain class of 'objects' (broadly construed); (2) they clearly believe that the relevant predicate of the statutory or constitutional text does not apply to the class; and (3) they do not have a positive intention that the statute not cover the relevant class. The main question, then, to which the discussion here is meant to supply an answer, is whether in this kind of case the resulting law covers the relevant class of objects. Unlike Perry, I think it is far from obvious what the answer is. If what I say below is correct, then beliefs about the application of a term sometimes do manage to affect utterance content by making that content to some extent indeterminate.

It is important to stress that the examples I discuss are cases in which there is no positive intention to exclude the relevant class of objects, but rather there is a clear (false) belief that the predicate does not cover the relevant class of objects. I take it that if it is possible to show that false beliefs about the application of a term sometimes manage to affect utterance content even in the absence of clear intention to exclude the relevant set of things, then presumably clear intention to exclude most certainly manages to do so, too. And although I discuss only

cannot explain 'how people of diverse opinions about matters can nevertheless agree on principles, rules, policies, and laws, and expect the principles, rules, policies, and laws to be followed by others with different conceptions about things'. Owing to limitations of space, I cannot address this argument here. For the time being, suffice it to say that I do not think this is too much of a worry. First, the version of conception textualism that I am trying to motivate in this chapter requires the relevant speaker beliefs to be part of the common ground between the speaker and hearer and so to be publicly available. Second, there will often be sufficient overlap between the conceptions that people have of the relevant things, which in turn produces sufficient agreement, or convergence, vis-à-vis the matter at hand. Third, conception textualism should not raise any more worries about convergence than should context-sensitive accounts of, say, gradable adjectives or modals. If we do not think that such accounts have a general 'convergence problem', then we probably should not take conception textualism to have one either.

[44] For an argument in a similar vein, see Ostertag (2018).

cases that concern exclusion, I take what I say to apply equally to cases that concern inclusion.[45]

It is also important to emphasise that it is crucial to what follows that we adopt the objective notion of communicative content rather than the subjective one. The reason is that if we adopt the subjective notion – according to which speakers say, assert, and so on what they intend to say, assert, and so on – conception textualism never even gets off the ground, at least not insofar as it is supposed to have a linguistic basis. The content of an utterance – on the subjective theory – is determined by the actual communicative intentions of the speaker, and since it is part of the description of the cases we are interested in that the lawmakers lack a positive intention that the statute in question not cover the relevant class of objects, it follows that the content of the respective utterance is unaffected by the lawmakers' false beliefs about the extension of the relevant predicate. On the subjective theory, a speaker's false beliefs about things – or any mental state of the speaker, for that matter – affect utterance content only insofar as they affect her actual communicative intentions. Thus the choice between the objective and the subjective notion of communicative content is crucial for assessing the plausibility of conception textualism.

Getting back to the relevant type of scenarios, say, for example, that Congress enacts a statute according to which 'All *F*s ought to φ' and that Congress also *falsely* believes that *F* does not apply to a certain subset *X* of objects. Accordingly, in uttering the sentence, Congress neither intends *F* to cover *X* nor intends *F* not to cover *X*. Given its false belief, it simply has no intention regarding the relationship between *F* and *X* vis-à-vis this particular utterance. But if Congress's *belief* that the members of *X* are not within the extension of the predicate *F* is part of the conversational background, it becomes difficult to say whether or not this can affect the communicative content of the relevant speech act.

Consider, for example, the case of *FDA v Brown & Williamson Tobacco Corp*,[46] in which the central question was whether the Food, Drug, and Cosmetic Act gives the FDA authority to regulate tobacco products.[47] In the first instance, the Food, Drug, and Cosmetic Act gives the FDA authority to regulate *drugs*; and 'drugs', according to the Act, means, among other things, 'articles (other than food)

[45] I do not rely on this literature here, but there is a great deal of similarity between my concerns in this chapter and the subject matter of recent work on so-called *ad hoc concepts*; in describing the general features of such a concept, Carston (2010) says that it is a:

> pragmatically derived concept [that] may be more specific or more general than the encoded concept; that is, its denotation may be either a proper subset or a superset of the denotation of the linguistically encoded concept, or it may be a combination, both extending the lexical denotation and excluding some part of it. (242)

[46] *FDA v Brown & Williamson Tobacco Corp*, 529 US 120 (2000). Other relevant cases arguably include the controversial case of *Boutilier v INS*, 387 US 118 (1967), in which the question was whether a 1952 immigration act applied to homosexuals in virtue of the fact that the lawmakers clearly but falsely believed that the term 'afflicted with psychopathic personality' applied to them.

[47] Food, Drug, and Cosmetic Act, 21 USC §301–399(a) (1938).

intended to affect the structure or any function of the body of man'.[48] So the literal meaning of the Act *does* cover nicotine. However, it is not implausible to claim that the legislature lacked a positive intention to exclude nicotine with its particular use of the term 'drugs'[49] because the lawmakers believed that nicotine was not in the extension of that term, as defined in the Act. The question, then, is whether this (false) belief affects the content of the legislature's utterance in such a way that the Food, Drug, and Cosmetic Act does not count as giving the FDA the authority to regulate tobacco. As we see below, I do not have an entirely firm opinion either way, but I think that we should at least not be too hasty in ruling out the possibility that it does affect the utterance content in some relevant way.

Generally speaking, my intuition is that while it may be implausible to think that a speaker's false belief about the extension of a predicate affects the content of speech acts with a *mind-to-world fit* (such as assertions), it is not so implausible to think that they sometimes play a part in determining the content of speech acts with a *world-to-mind fit* (such as directives). What seems to make the difference is that a speaker's beliefs may well have special relevance when it comes to interpreting utterances in which the speaker represents the world not as she thinks it is but rather as she would like it to be. As mentioned above, one reason I am interested in these kinds of case is that Perry thinks it is a 'rather bizarre and hopeless' idea that the conception that a speaker has about that to which he wishes to refer or quantify over can affect the primary content of the speech act. *Contra* Perry, I think it is possible to make a decent case for this position, at least in the case of speech acts with a world-to-mind fit – including enactments.

First, consider the difference between assertions and directives, with respect to intuitions about how information about speaker beliefs may affect what gets communicated. Say that S utters the following: 'All *F*s are *G*.' Say also that it is part of the common ground that S believes that a class of objects, *C*, is not within the extension of the predicate *F*. Finally, say that *C* is in fact within the extension of *F*. The question, then, is this: In uttering 'All *F*s are *G*', did S predicate *G*-hood of the objects in *C*? The answer is not entirely clear, but it seems more reasonable to say that the erroneous belief does *not* affect the communicative content in such cases.

Say, for example, that someone utters the following: 'No mammal weighs more than 15,000 pounds.' And that it is part of the common ground that the speaker believes that whales are not mammals. Does it follow from the communicative content of the speaker's utterance that she attributed the property of not-weighing-more-than-15,000-pounds to whales (among other things)? My intuition is that it does, since I am inclined to judge the speaker as having asserted something false. And if that is correct, then the speaker's false belief did not affect what was communicated. Assuming that the scenario is unexceptional, it is reasonable to

[48] ibid, §321.

[49] That is, it is *not* the case that the lawmakers thought that the term 'drug' actually covered nicotine and that they just intended implicitly to exclude nicotine from the relevant domain of quantification.

generalise from the case and say that in the case of assertion, it does not make a difference to the communicative content of a speaker's utterance of '… *F* …' that the speaker falsely believes of a class of objects that they are, or are not, within the extension of *F*. And I think it is not unreasonable to explain the intuition in part by reference to the fact that the speaker *misrepresented the world*. If that is correct, then I would like to generalise further and claim that *in the case of speech acts with mind-to-world fit*, false beliefs that a speaker has about that to which she wishes to refer or quantify over do *not* affect utterance content.

Next, consider a case in which a speaker utters these words: 'Get me all the *Fs*!' Say also that it is part of the common ground that S believes that a class of objects, *C*, is not within the extension of *F*. Finally, say that *C* is in fact within the extension of *F*. The question, as before, is this: In uttering 'Get me all the *Fs*!', did S direct the addressee to get her (among other things) the objects in *C*? Again, the answer is not entirely clear, but it does not seem totally unreasonable to say that the erroneous belief manages to affect the communicative content.

Say, for example, that a boss utters the following to her assistant: 'Get me all the ashtrays you can find in the building!' Now, one issue concerns what further restrictions – if any – the speaker intends on the quantifier 'all the ashtrays in the building'.[50] This is a relevant issue but it is not the one I am interested in here. The issue I am concerned with is whether it would affect the communicative content of the speaker's utterance if it were part of the common ground between speaker and hearer, for example, that the speaker believes that the ashtrays that were ordered only last week are not in the building, when in fact they have just arrived.

Here I am not so inclined to say that it follows from the communicative content of the boss's utterance that the new ashtrays belong to the set of things that the assistant was directed to collect. However, I do not have a robust intuition that they do not belong to that set either. Nevertheless, what this indicates is that – *contra* Perry – it is not entirely implausible to think that the conception that a speaker has about that to which she wishes to refer or quantify over can affect the primary content of the speech act – at least, not in the case of directives. And since it is not unreasonable to think that this judgment is explained in part by reference to the fact that the speaker's utterance represented the world as she would (in some sense) like it to be, I think it is sensible to suggest that in the case of speech acts with world-to-mind fit, false beliefs that a speaker has about that to which she wishes to refer or quantify over can affect utterance content.

I do, of course, have to say something a bit more specific both about how and about in what way utterance content is supposed to be affected by a speaker's false beliefs about, say, the extension of a predicate. As I say above regarding the 'ashtray directive', I do not have – putting myself in the hearer's shoes – a robust intuition that it follows from the communicative content of the boss's utterance that the new ashtrays belong to the set of things that the assistant was told to collect.

[50] For a discussion, see eg MacCallum (1966) and Manning (2003).

But I do not have a robust intuition to the contrary either. If these intuitions are reliable, and thus reflect the hearer's epistemic situation with respect to the content of the speaker's utterance, then it seems warranted – given that we are operating with the objective notion of communicative content – to say that it is *indeterminate* whether it follows from the communicative content of the boss's utterance that the new ashtrays belong to the set of things that the assistant was told to collect.

If the example is not an exceptional one, we can generalise and say that – at least in normal cases of speech acts with world-to-mind fit – the fact that a speaker falsely believes of a subset *X* of objects that they are (or are not) within the extension of *F* makes it the case that the content of the speaker's utterance of '… *F* …' is indeterminate with respect to the inclusion/exclusion of *X* (assuming that it is mutual knowledge between speaker and hearer that the speaker has this belief). This provides, I think, a reasonable and empirically testable explanation of *in what way* utterance content may be affected by a speaker's false beliefs about that to which she wishes to refer or quantify over.

In explaining *how* utterance content comes to be affected in this way, it is crucial to make sure that we are evaluating the situation from the perspective of the hearer. Unlike you and me, the hearer does not know that the speaker lacks a positive intention to include/exclude *X* in her utterance of '… *F* …' After all, it is the hearer's task to figure out what the speaker's communicative intentions are in uttering it. It is my hypothesis that in the relevant scenarios, the reason the hearer has for believing that the speaker intended her utterance to cover *X* – provided by the fact that the speaker uttered '… *F* …' – is defeated (but undercut, rather than outweighed) by the (mutually known) fact that the speaker believes that *F* does not apply to *X*. Assuming absence of other decisive evidence, this leaves the hearer in a state of partial uncertainty vis-à-vis the speaker's utterance of '… *F* …', that is, uncertainty regarding the inclusion or exclusion of *X*. Since communicative content is – on the objective notion – determined by the inferences that the hearer is warranted in making about the speaker's communicative intentions, this uncertainty makes the content of the relevant utterance to some extent indeterminate.[51]

Coming back to *Brown & Williamson*, it seems, then, that it is not out of the question to argue that the communicative content of the Food, Drug, and Cosmetic Act does not entail that the FDA has authority to regulate nicotine – at least not determinately so – and this despite the fact that nicotine is in the extension of the term 'drug' as it is defined in the Act itself. This cautious conclusion also has significant counterparts in the domain of constitutional interpretation. On one reading of Scalia's argument about the legal content of the Eighth Amendment, for example, he can be taken to claim that, indeed, the conception that the

[51] There are other reasons – also having to do with contextual enrichment – for thinking that the content of legislative utterances is often to some extent indeterminate; see ch 5.

framers had about the extension of the term 'cruel and unusual punishment' somehow affects the content of the amendment.[52] In particular, Scalia thinks that the death penalty – which may in fact be within the extension of the term 'cruel and unusual punishment' – is not among the punishments that are prohibited by the amendment because it is clear that the framers believed that it was not in the extension of that term.

I should point out that in his discussion, Perry does not really distinguish between statutory interpretation and constitutional interpretation. This is significant, since Scalia endorses meaning textualism for statutes but conception textualism for constitutions. And although it may be possible to show that some form of conception textualism is defensible from a linguistic perspective, Scalia provides in his reply to Dworkin the ingredients to a non-linguistic argument for the claim that the framers' beliefs about those things to which they intended to refer or quantify over affect the content of the Constitution.[53] According to Scalia, it is among the essential functions of constitutions that they 'freeze' contemporary conceptions of morality; this is one of the things that make a constitution what it is. If Scalia is right, then he may have a non-linguistic explanation of why the content of, say, the Eighth Amendment is affected by the beliefs that the framers had about cruel and unusual punishment; it is *their* beliefs about right and wrong that the Constitution – in virtue of being a constitution – 'freezes' (insofar as these beliefs can be taken to have been representative of popular morality).

A fuller discussion is beyond the scope of this chapter, but one of the distinct benefits that this functional argument for the legal relevance of the framers' mental states has over the linguistic argument for conception textualism is that if it works out, its conclusion appears to be decisive. Another benefit is that Perry's linguistic worries about conception textualism would have little or no bite. In contrast, my above linguistic case for the relevance of application beliefs for anyone committed to the objective-communicative-content theory of law guarantees only that we should not be too hasty to rule the view out as implausible. One of the major advantages of the linguistic argument, however, is that it does not rely on any controversial claims about the constitutive functions of constitutions.[54]

To sum up the discussion of conception textualism, according to Perry's foundational argument against the view, it clearly fails to satisfy a requirement necessary for the adequacy of any theory of legal interpretation: that its claims about the content of a statute or constitutional clause can be supported using the tools of contemporary philosophy of language and linguistics. The requirement, I think, is a reasonable one, at least insofar as we are concerned with new textualism/public-meaning originalism, given their adherence to the objective communicative-content theory of law. But, as I hope to have shown, once we

[52] Scalia (1997) 144–49.
[53] ibid.
[54] For a thorough critique of Scalia's normative argument, see Greenberg and Litman (1998) 604–05.

fully appreciate the role of contextual enrichment in communication, it becomes plausible to think – at least in the case of speech acts with a world-to-mind direction of fit, such as legislation – that when a speaker's (mutually known) false beliefs about that to which she wishes to refer or quantify over clash with the literal content of her remark, these beliefs manage to affect utterance content by making that content to some extent indeterminate. If that is correct, then conception textualism – at least the moderate version presented here – does in fact satisfy Perry's requirement.

Although I am not necessarily convinced that conception textualism can ultimately be made to work or that the best case for it is a linguistic one, I do think that a decent case has been made that the view is, *contra* Perry, far from being confused, implausible and unworkable from the perspective of philosophy of language and linguistics. Perry, it seems, has been much too hasty in ruling conception textualism out on such grounds.

V. Contemporary Textualism and the Problem of Legislative Context

From what I have said so far, it might seem that – at least from the perspective of someone holding the communicative-content thesis – contemporary textualists have a pretty plausible view regarding the legal content of statutes and constitutional clauses. As many have pointed out,[55] however, the textualist's insistence on the legal relevance of pragmatic inference about utterance content has the potential to get her into trouble. One reason is that the context and conversational background presumably matter to utterance interpretation only insofar as these provide evidence of the speaker's communicative intention. But, as I explained above, textualists think that very few intentions can in good faith be attributed to the legislature as a collective. So although textualists don't hesitate to say that the legal content of a statute is determined by its meaning and that 'meaning depends on the way speakers use words in context',[56] the fact that the speaker's illocutionary intentions determine how she is using the relevant words seems to present an obvious problem: it follows that the speaker's illocutionary intentions determine legal content – a very bad result for the textualist.

The standard textualist response to this problem, embraced in one form or another by the main champions of contemporary textualism (Scalia, Easterbrook, and Manning), is to say that the meaning of an utterance is determined not by how the words are actually being used (by the speaker) but rather – as we have seen – by the inferences that a rational hearer, knowing the context and conversational

[55] See eg Soames (2011) and Marmor (2013).

[56] Manning (2003) 2461; Scalia (1997) 23–25, 37, 135, 144.

background, would be warranted in making regarding the way in which the relevant words are being used. If the objective theory of communicative content is correct, this makes good sense, philosophically.

It seems, then, that – much of their rhetoric notwithstanding – textualists are perhaps best construed to be claiming not that intentions are irrelevant *tout court* but that the only intentions that judges should be concerned with are intentions of the *illocutionary* kind; and – further – that they should be concerned not with the *actual* illocutionary intentions of the lawmakers but rather with those illocutionary intentions that a rational hearer would, knowing the context and conversational background, be warranted in ascribing to the legislature, vis-à-vis the relevant enactment. This position, however, seems to get the textualist into at least one of two problems, depending on *what* – and *how much* – a person knows when she knows the context and conversational background of an enactment.

According to Easterbrook (1990), for example, '[t]extualists … want to know [the] context [statutory language], including assumptions shared by the speakers and the intended audience'.[57] And, he continues, 'it may be essential to mine the context of the utterance out of the debates [recorded in legislative history]', which 'may be useful in showing the scope of an enactment'.[58] On Easterbrook's view, then, the common ground between the legislature and its intended audience may include information found in legislative history. In particular, information about bargains made by the lawmakers is supposed to be able to shed light on the communicative content of the resulting enactment.[59]

I think, however, that it would be a significant stretch to say that the information contained in legislative history generally forms part of the actual conversational background of enactments, since such information is – as a matter of fact – not generally 'shared by the speakers and the intended audience', especially when it comes to law addressed to ordinary citizens. But more importantly, perhaps, if information about *actual* bargains made in the legislative process is supposed to be able to shed light on the communicative content of legislative utterances, then Easterbrook must after all care about the *actual* illocutionary intentions of lawmakers. But this seems inconsistent with the critical aspect of textualism outlined in the first section of this chapter.

If, on the other hand, legislative history does not form part of the conversational background – as Scalia, for example, appears to think – then the common ground between the legislature and its intended audiences seems to become quite thin, although its richness may of course vary significantly depending on the audience. As a result, the content that a rational hearer, knowing the context and conversational background, would associate with a particular enactment will presumably rarely go beyond its literal content. This, as we saw, was indeed my own conclusion

[57] Easterbrook (1990) 443.
[58] Easterbrook (1990) 443.
[59] Easterbrook (1990) 443–45.

in chapter five. But this seems to significantly undermine the contemporary textualist's proud rejection of literalism. In addition, as Marmor (2008, 2011a) notes, other aspects of the conversational context are often fairly indeterminate. There seems to be significant indeterminacy, for example, about what members of Congress are actually parties to the relevant conversation (bill initiators/sponsors, indifferent supporters, opponents, everyone?).[60] In general, Marmor thinks, '[t]he conversational situation of an act of legislation is often much more open-ended [than in ordinary conversation], without clear boundaries'.[61]

Manning (2001, 2003), however, believes that worries like these should not be exaggerated; due attention to the contemporary textualist's notion of conversational context, he thinks, shows that even if legislative history does not form part of the common ground between the legislature and its intended audience, the context is often rich – and determinate – enough to facilitate pragmatic enrichment. Two aspects of the common ground make the difference, he says. First, a nuanced competence with the English language is assumed (or whatever language is relevant). Such competence, for example, includes knowledge of how words are normally used; as Manning notes, the term 'vehicle', for example, is normally used to refer to (something like) '[t]hat in or on which a person or thing is or may be carried', although it can also be used to refer to '[a]n art form or device used to convey an effect'.[62] Similarly, people normally use phrases of the form '[use] an F' to communicate that the F is/was/will be used for its intended purpose (if it has one); for example, people normally use the phrase '[use] a gun' to communicate that a gun is/was/will be used *as a weapon*. In addition, Manning says, if the intended audience is a specialised subcommunity – such as lawyers, scientists, or people working in the financial or commercial industry – competence with the technical terms particular to those communities is assumed.

Second, the common ground includes *firmly established common law doctrines* – that is, the audience is supposed to be 'conversant with [substantive] legal conventions'.[63] Criminal statutes, for example, that, per their language, do not contain any *mens rea* requirements are nevertheless taken to contain *implicit* requirements (as part of their communicative content). And according to Easterbrook (1999), 'the legal system's accepted procedures, evidentiary rules, burdens of persuasion – and defenses' also form part of the common ground.[64] And given the 'abundance of such conventions in a legal system as old as [the US system]', Manning says, 'textualists have at their disposal a *collection* of well-settled background norms'.[65] This rich collection of norms, then, forms part of the 'background ... against which Congress presumptively legislates'.[66] What

[60] See Marmor (2008) 434–35 and Marmor (2011a) 98.
[61] Marmor (2011a) 435.
[62] Manning (2003) 2458, citing *Webster's New Collegiate Dictionary* 953 (1953).
[63] Manning (2003) 2467.
[64] Easterbrook (1999) 1913.
[65] Manning (2003) 2468; my emphasis.
[66] Manning (2003) 2468.

this means for the textualist is that established legal conventions do not kick in *after* the communicative content of the law has been determined, but can actually affect the communicative content of relevant legislative utterances, for example by adding the equivalent of an implicit *unless*-clause to the literal content of a statute.[67]

Now, I have no problem with the first element of the supposed common ground. Presumably, for example, any competent speaker will have good intuitions about the normal uses of words (assuming they have one). And if such uses are default enrichments rather than just relatively frequently occurring 'senses' of certain ambiguous or polysemic terms, then the context may indeed sometimes be rich enough to facilitate pragmatic enrichment of the required kind. I should also note that although Manning does not discuss the so-called *linguistic canons of construction*,[68] it is not implausible to assume that these principles attempt to make explicit certain general pragmatic rules of thumb, competence with which can be ascribed to any sufficiently skilled language user.

I think, however, that the second element is more problematic. A great deal of law – criminal law in particular – is arguably addressed to ordinary citizens, who are by no means 'conversant with legal conventions'. As a result, knowledge of substantive legal doctrines on behalf of the hearer cannot always be assumed. This variation between contexts regarding what can reasonably be taken for granted has significant consequences for the contemporary textualist's position. Consider for example the majority's reasoning in *Staples v United States* (Scalia joining).[69] In *Staples*, the question was whether or not Mr Staples had – by possessing an unregistered machine gun – violated the National Firearms Act, 26 USC § 5861(d), which states that 'It shall be unlawful for any person … to receive or possess a firearm which is not registered to him in the National Firearms Registration and Transfer Record'. It was an undisputed fact that Mr Staples *did not know* that the firearm he possessed required registration, due to the fact that the weapon was a semiautomatic model inconspicuously modified to operate as an automatic one.

Now, the literal content of the Act does not stipulate any requirements regarding the epistemic state of the 'possessor', and the district court therefore concluded that the Act *did* cover Staples's situation and he was sentenced to probation and a fine; the court of appeals affirmed. The Supreme Court majority, however, argued that the relevant part of the Act had to be construed 'in light of the background rules of the common law … in which the requirement of some *mens rea* for a crime is firmly embedded'.[70] For the textualists on the court (Justices Thomas and Scalia), this meant that the *communicative content* of the legislative utterance

[67] For a view similar to this, but expressed in more nuanced linguistic terms, see Goldsworthy (2010) 238–43.
[68] See eg Scalia (1997) 25–29; see also Sunstein (1989) 454–60.
[69] 522 US 398 (1998).
[70] 511 US 600, 605 (1994).

was something roughly equivalent to the following: it shall be unlawful for any person … to receive or possess a firearm which is not registered to him in the National Firearms Registration and Transfer Record, *unless the person does not know that the object in question belongs to a type of firearm that requires such registration*. In other words, due crucially to the background assumptions shared by the legislature and its intended audience, the actual communicative content of § 5861(d) is a pragmatic enrichment of its literal content. Or so contemporary textualists maintain.

The problem with this line of reasoning, however, is that if ordinary citizens are generally the intended audience of criminal law, then the doctrine of *mens rea* cannot reasonably be taken to form part of the actual common ground and, consequently, there is no linguistic basis for claiming that the communicative content of § 5861(d) is a corresponding pragmatic enrichment of its literal content. This means that if the textualist wants to avoid a conviction for Mr Staples without stepping outside the boundaries of the law, then she will have to concede that the *mens rea* doctrine is a source of law *in virtue of* its continued and widespread application by the courts – something that textualists do not particularly like to do, evidenced by their reference to common law doctrines as 'judicial power-grabs'.[71]

What *Staples* and similar cases indicate, I think, is that textualists are – despite their rhetoric – *not* simply concerned with the actual communicative content of legislative utterances. If they were, they would be more sensitive to the significant variation in the common ground between the legislature and its various audiences. To be sure, the textualist framework is heavily constrained by highly plausible ideas about language and communication, but to some extent their notion of context and conversational background appears to be designed or constructed in order to obtain certain legal results and block others. I suspect that one reason for this stems from the textualist's desire to ultimately ground the authority of established legal doctrine in the authority of Congress. If established common law doctrines form part of the background of legislative utterances, and thereby affect their communicative content, then such utterances arguably count as *implicit recognition* of the relevant doctrines; as a result, judges still act as faithful agents of Congress when they recognise established doctrine, despite the fact that doctrine originates with the courts.

As we have seen, this may well be the case when the relevant audience is in fact 'conversant with legal conventions' – such as in the case of law addressed to courts or administrative agencies. But there will also be a significant set of cases in which the textualist – on pain of having to permit a severely problematic result – will *have to* recognise that the authority of established legal doctrine is grounded in its having been established by judicial practice. In those cases, as discussed more fully in chapter one, doctrine does not affect the communicative content of the law,

[71] Scalia (1997) 29.

but rather kicks in after that content has been established. *Staples*, I think, was an example of such a case.

VI. Textualism and Legal Interpretation

The preceding discussion has concerned textualism as a theory of legal content. In this final section, I want to briefly explain my main reasons for rejecting the textualist approach to legal *interpretation*, on the understanding that such interpretation is the act of developing the law in the face of indeterminate/inconsistent legal content or a particularly problematic result.

At the level of interpretation, textualism tells us that judges should play a very limited role. In case the communicative content of a statute yields a result that is undesirable without being unconstitutional, the court is obligated to follow the law in its decision. To illustrate, consider the case of *United States v Marshall*.[72] In *Marshall*, Mr Marshall, who had sold what constituted relatively few doses of LSD (around 12,000), was taken to fall under a statute triggering a mandatory minimum punishment if the sold items contain 'a mixture or substance containing a detectable amount' of the relevant drug. In order to receive a similar sentence in the case of heroin, Marshall would have had to sell around 10 kilograms of it, so it makes sense to say that, on a literal reading, the statute has the unintended consequence that it obligates judges to impose disproportionate sentences on people who sell LSD, due to the fact that the lawmakers did not realise how the drug is sold. Despite this problematic result, however, the majority, headed by textualist champion Judge Easterbrook, held that the content of the relevant statute was in fact its literal content, and that it was not the court's job to rectify legislative mistakes.

In case the content of the law is indeterminate with respect to the case before the court, textualists – in the first instance – take the court to be bound by precedent. Have similar enough cases been settled in the past? If so, then the court should treat the current case in the same way. If not, the court should decide in favour of the defendant. So, basically, a judicial decision against a (criminal or civil) defendant is legitimate only if the case falls determinately under the relevant statute or if there is precedent for applying the statute to sufficiently similar cases.[73] In all other cases, the court's decision should be in favour of the defendant.

It is beyond the scope of the present discussion to discern under what conditions courts should or should not follow clear law, and so I will not venture to critically analyse the textualist position on the authority of judges in cases in which the content of the relevant statute yields a result that is undesirable but

[72] 908 F2d 1312 (7th Cir 1990).
[73] See eg Easterbrook (1983) 549–50.

not unconstitutional, or in which clear precedent does. Perhaps the standard textualist considerations – democratic legitimacy, legislative supremacy, separation of powers, and the Rule of Law – support their position, and perhaps not. Instead, I will focus on the question whether or not these considerations support the textualist's view that the role of the judiciary should also be so limited when it comes to cases of vagueness, specifically.

The answer to this question, I think, is no. Owing to the nature of borderline cases, none of the traditional textualist considerations suffice to support a universal rule to favour the defendant in borderline cases. The short answer is that these considerations count against judicial lawmaking *only insofar as the courts have a choice between following the law and changing the law* (as the court did in *Marshall*, for example). Borderline cases, however, necessitate a change in the relevant law – the courts usually have no choice but to precisify the law, and in doing so they are engaged in a limited form of lawmaking. But if there is no choice but to make law, then the considerations that otherwise count against judicial lawmaking have no bite. Even the Rule of Law virtue of predictability is promoted equally well by making it a rule to decide against defendants in borderline cases.

Appealing to considerations of fairness (such as fair notice) will not do the trick either, since such appeal presupposes that somehow the defendant's legitimate expectations would be frustrated by a decision against her. But – as many have pointed out[74] – it does not make much sense to claim that the resolution of a borderline case frustrates legitimate expectations, since it is partly constitutive of such cases that it is impossible to justifiably form the beliefs that are necessary for having such expectations (although I don't want to exclude the possibility of excusably forming such beliefs). Thus, since it is impossible to have legitimate expectations regarding borderline cases, it is also impossible that legitimate expectations are frustrated in the resolution of such cases. If this is correct, then fairness is not a concern in borderline cases and cannot ground a rule in favour of the defendant (or the plaintiff, for that matter).

What seems left for the textualist, then, is to argue that limiting government is independently desirable. In fact, Marmor (2007) argues that this is the real motivation behind contemporary textualism.[75] Of course, if what matters – with respect to borderline cases – is primarily to 'move' these cases determinately outside law's reach, and hence outside the reach of the government, then the intentions of lawmakers don't matter for resolving such cases. It might therefore seem that the neo-conservative agenda of contemporary textualism can rationalise their view about how to settle borderline cases.

Now, although I am not sympathetic to using the judiciary to rein in the government, I will not argue against the claim that limiting government is desirable. Instead, I will suggest that even if it were desirable, respect for legislative

[74] See eg Hart (1994) 276 and Marmor (2007) 23.
[75] See Marmor (2007) ch 8.

bargaining/compromise is *more* desirable (the latter is discussed more fully in chapter seven). And if that is correct, then the intentions of lawmakers do in fact matter, vis-à-vis legal interpretation. Sometimes, the intentions of lawmakers ought to dictate which way borderline cases are decided.

The reason that respect for legislative bargaining matters more than the judicial limitation of government is that such bargaining is fundamental to our legislative system. If it is not respected, the incentive to bargain is lost and legislation is severely impeded. So when it comes to borderline cases, respect for legislative bargaining directs the courts to find out if a relevant bargain was made and if so, what it was.

Now, the way in which the courts find this out would presumably be by consulting legislative history, which of course raises the worry that legislative history is an unreliable source for determining the intentions of lawmakers, due to the fact that many recorded statements have been strategically placed in order to sway judges in favour of a desired result. However, while this is indeed a worry worth taking seriously, legislative history is not entirely unreliable, as we will see in chapter seven. In fact, it contains a fair amount of reliable evidence of the intentions of lawmakers relevant to legislative bargaining. And if it can be shown that there exists some efficient method of discerning when statements indicating legislative intentions can be taken to be credible, then there is – at least in borderline cases – no reason for the courts not to consult legislative history in the aim of finding evidence of the lawmakers' intentions. As I argue in chapter seven, such a method is indeed available.

7

Resolving Cases of Vagueness

In chapter three, I introduced Roy Sorensen's epistemic account of vagueness and his distinction between absolute and relative borderline cases, and explained his argument that vagueness, understood as the possession of absolute borderline cases, does not have a constructive power-delegating function in law.[1] I summarised his argument in the following way:

> P1. Delegation of decision-making authority, vis-à-vis borderline cases, is valuable only if the relevant delegates are in a better position to answer the question whether *x* is *F* than those delegating the power.
>
> P2. When *x* is an absolute borderline case of 'F', it is not the case that the relevant delegates are in a better position to answer the question whether *x* is *F* than those delegating the power.
>
> C. Therefore, when *x* is an absolute borderline case of 'F', it is not the case that delegation of decision-making authority, vis-à-vis *x*, is valuable.

My reply was to argue that P1 is false. Delegation of decision-making authority can be valuable even if the relevant delegates are not in a better position to answer the question whether *x* is *F* than those delegating the power. The key to seeing why is to acknowledge that when faced with absolute borderline cases, the courts must engage with a related *normative* question – whether *x* *ought*, relative to the purposes of the law, to *count* as an *F*.

In my discussion of Sorensen's argument, however, I was not discriminating regarding what sort of legislative purposes can settle the normative question. I assumed, for the sake of simplicity, that it is settled if *any* background justification of the law dictates a decision either way. I assumed this because there is no need to discriminate between types of legislative rationale in order to reply to Sorensen's argument. In the current chapter, however, I want to consider what restrictions, if any, there may be on appealing to background justifications in order to appropriately settle the normative question. To be more specific, I want – in the first instance – to examine some of the conditions under which such deference can reasonably be said to *maximise fidelity to law*. I think a good case can be made that, insofar as the aim is to maximise fidelity to law, the resources for answering

[1] See Sorensen (2001a).

the normative question are – at least normally – restricted to rationale expressed by lawmakers during the legislative process under conditions that deter so-called *cheap talk*.

It is one thing, however, to say that borderline cases *can* be settled by reference to legislative purposes and quite another to say that they *should*. I want, therefore, also to consider what normative reasons judges might have to resolve cases of vagueness on the basis of the relevant statute's background justification. As we will see, I think that there are at least two types of reason for judges to defer to the intentions of lawmakers – one general and one dependent on the legal system in place. As Marmor (2005) argues, judges can – irrespective of the legal system in place – have authority-based reasons to defer to legislative intentions, if the legislature can be expected to possess expertise regarding the relevant domain of conduct. In fact, Marmor thinks that expertise-based reasons exhaust the kinds of reason for which judges ought to defer to legislative intentions. But, as I will argue, judges in legal systems in which the legislative process depends crucially on legislative bargaining – like the US – may also have non-expertise-based reasons for such deference. As I indicated at the end of chapter six, I think that when it comes to legal systems that rely on legislative bargaining, one of the strongest reasons in favour of settling the normative question by reference to legislative rationale is that doing so respects such bargaining and thereby helps preserve a fundamental feature of the legislative institution.

To sum up, then, there are two primary questions with which I will be concerned in this chapter. First, appeal to what sort of legislative rationale can reasonably be said to maximise fidelity to law, vis-à-vis judicial decision-making in borderline cases? And, second, under what conditions *should* judges aim to maximise fidelity to law in deciding such cases? I should emphasise that the aim is not to propose a complete decision procedure for resolving vagueness in the law. Far from it. The goal is simply to show that, under a modest set of circumstances, judges have strong reasons to appeal to legislative intentions in settling borderline cases. If that is correct, then a constrained form of *intentionalism* will sometimes be the best theory of legal interpretation (on the understanding that legal interpretation is the act of developing the law in the face of indeterminate/inconsistent legal content or a particularly problematic result).

I should also note that what I say in this chapter applies not only to the resolution of borderlines cases associated with vagueness *of* content (discussed in chapters two to four), but also to the resolution of borderline cases associated with vagueness *about* content (discussed primarily in chapter five).

I. Expressly Offered Rationale and the Notion of Commitment

It seems clear enough that legislative purposes can sometimes help settle a verdict in borderline cases. It is less clear, however, what restrictions there are on appeal to legislative purposes if such appeal is to reasonably count as appeal to *law's* purposes. I hope to show that insofar as appeal to legislative purposes in borderline cases is to count as maximising fidelity to law, such appeal is – at least within the US legal system – normally restricted to rationale that certain lawmakers have in their official capacity expressly offered, 'on record'.

At a very general level, the argument is a relatively simple two-premise argument. The first premise is that *what it is* for judges to decide a borderline case in accordance with fidelity to law is for them to decide the case in accordance with (the proper balance of) those purposes to which the 'legislatively relevant' actors have – in their official capacity – *incurred a commitment*. The second premise is that the primary way in which such actors incur the relevant kind of commitment is through the express offering of legislative rationale.

The process by which many UK laws get enacted naturally suggests this simple picture, for example. In most cases, the government will outline proposals for new laws in so-called *White Papers*, official documents that – among other things – contain statements regarding the ends that the government hopes to achieve by the relevant piece of legislation. The government itself – rather than Members of Parliament – will normally introduce the bills outlined and justified in the White Papers, and on many occasions the bills pass more or less unamended; that is, the legislative process in Parliament is – more or less – a matter of voting 'yes' or 'no' on a bill introduced by the government. In these cases, it seems to make particularly good sense both to talk about expressly offered rationale (the rationale offered in the government White Papers) and to say that this rationale counts as the *law's* purposes, since (in these cases) the government reasonably counts as a legislatively relevant actor.

A lot depends, however, on the contingent structure of the lawmaking process in the relevant system. In the US, for example, bills are introduced by members of the legislature, rather than the government, and the legislative process is very rarely just a matter of voting 'yes' or 'no'; conflicts of interest are prominent and legislative bargaining is a fundamental feature of the system. These considerations complicate the picture outlined above a great deal. One reason is that there are usually no official documents that can count as clear equivalents of White Papers, and it will be fairly contingent whether – during the legislative process – lawmakers offer any statements of what they take to be the purpose of the relevant piece of legislation.

Consider, for example, the companion cases of *Curran v Mount Diablo Boy Scouts* and *Randall v Orange County Council*,[2] in which the question was whether or not the Boy Scouts should count as a business establishment under California's *Unruh Civil Rights Act*.[3] On the reasonable assumption that the Boy Scouts share enough characteristics with paradigm business establishments to count as a borderline case of the term 'business establishment', the question is

[2] 17 Cal 4th 670 (1998) and 17 Cal 4th 736 (1998), respectively.
[3] Cal Civ Code §51.

whether the courts could have settled these cases by appealing to the rationale for the Act offered by lawmakers in the legislative process. As it happens, however, there simply is no legislative history for the relevant piece of legislation, except for different versions of the bill that ultimately passed as the *Unruh Civil Rights Act*. As a result, there were no official statements of legislative purpose to which the courts could have appealed in settling these cases. On the assumption that the remedial purpose of the Act wasn't sufficiently obvious so as to not need explicit expression (more on such cases below), the court's decision in *Curran* and *Randall* therefore arguably had to be justified by considerations beyond fidelity to law (in my sense of the term).

The main complication for the simple picture, however, comes from the prominence of strategic factors in systems of the relevant sort. The reason is that in order for speakers – in this case lawmakers – to genuinely incur commitments via utterances, a certain amount of co-operation is normally needed. In a game of Bullshit, for example, speakers are not taken to be committed to the truth of the statements that they make, because it is mutually known that the speech context is not a co-operative one; in particular, speakers cannot be relied on to assert a proposition only if they believe it and have adequate evidence for their belief. Or, for those familiar with Gricean jargon, the strategic nature of the game makes it the case that the Maxim of Quality is suspended.[4]

It is interesting – and relevant – to note that the US legal system appears to recognise that strategic factors have this undercutting effect on linguistic commitment. Under federal perjury law, for example, witnesses are not taken to be committed to the implied content of their testimony, due to the adversarial nature of cross-examination. Consider the case of *Bronston v United States*,[5] in which the question was whether Mr Bronston had correctly been found guilty of perjury, in virtue of having provided an 'unresponsive' reply to a question that in ordinary conversation would be taken to trigger a so-called *relevance implicature* (the content of which would be false). Mr Bronston, who for a five-year period had a personal bank account in Switzerland, was asked the following question: 'Have you ever [had a bank account in Switzerland]?' His reply was this: 'The company had an account there for about six months.' Now, if the purpose of the relevant conversation had been the co-operative exchange of information, Mr Bronston would have counted as having – *via implication* – incurred commitment to the false proposition that he himself had *not* had an account in Switzerland. The Supreme Court, however, unanimously argued that – for the purposes of the federal perjury statute – Mr Bronston was *not* committed to this proposition, and that he should therefore not have been convicted of perjury. And although the court's decision was not framed in linguistic terms, the decision nevertheless has a good linguistic

[4] On the suspension of conversational maxims, see eg Martinich (1984) 33.

[5] 409 US 352 (1973). Although, for reservations about such an analysis, see ch 8, section III.B.

justification; in the context of cross-examination, the conflict of interest between speaker and hearer makes it the case that speakers cannot be relied on to assert a proposition only if it is relevant. Or, again for those familiar with Gricean jargon, in the context of cross-examination, the Maxim of Relevance is suspended. Assuming otherwise would be a mistake on behalf of the examining lawyer.

The relevance of these examples to the discussion here is that when it comes to legal systems in which strategic factors are as prominent as they are in the US and similar systems, it is a legitimate concern whether lawmakers *ever* incur the right kind of commitment via their statements regarding legislative rationale (assuming they sometimes offer such statements). The concern is that we get information regarding the relevant statements primarily from legislative history, ie from bills, committee reports, floor debates etc. As I mentioned earlier, some of the problems concern the availability and/or relevance of legislative documents. Do we have any statements regarding legislative purpose 'on record'? Do all official legislative documents count? And do those that count all count equally? However, the most critical issue is due to the strategic nature of lawmaking and concerns the frequent manipulation of official documents by lawmakers in order to increase the likelihood of certain outcomes in high-level court cases.

As Rodriguez and Weingast (2003) note, the incentive to influence or manipulate legislative history can be great; ardent supporters of a bill, for example, might be moved to influence legislative history in such a way that future interpretation fails to acknowledge significant compromise made in the legislative process (more on this below). This means that even if we have clear statements regarding legislative purpose, there is a good chance that these statements are not sincere. In addition to all this, it is usually also far from clear – unlike in the standard UK lawmaking case – *whose* statements are most relevant. That is, in the US and similar systems, it is very often not clear which members of Congress count as the *most* legislatively relevant actors (in my sense of the term).

Taking all these issues into account, there seems, then, to be a significant tension between my claim that borderline cases can be settled by deference to law's purposes, understood as the rationale to which lawmakers have expressly incurred commitment, and the strategic nature of the legislative environment. It is important to point out, however, that this tension is not a theoretical one; that is, the tension is not evidence of a problem internal to the model that I am arguing for. Rather, the tension concerns the *application* of the model – it is an indication of a limitation on the number of cases in which it might be possible to resolve vagueness in such a way as to maximise fidelity to law.

This sort of limitation, however, should be expected. In fact, as I will argue below, there is actually a further limitation on the applicability of the model, due to the fact that it is not always the case that judges *ought* to maximise fidelity to law (even if they *can*). But, as I said at the beginning of the chapter, the aim here is not to propose a complete decision procedure for resolving vagueness in the law. It is simply to show that, under a modest set of circumstances, judges have strong reasons to appeal to legislative intentions in settling borderline cases.

Before I go on to talk about this further limitation on (all things considered) appeal to legislative rationale, however, I want to consider a number of ways in which the limitations discussed so far can be mitigated. Interestingly, the most important way in which these limitations can be mitigated turns out to be grounded in the legislative system itself, in that certain parts of the institutional design manage to remedy the incentives that lawmakers have to engage in cheap talk.

II. Institutional Remedies to Non-co-operation

One of the most significant limitations of the model I have been discussing is that even if we have statements about legislative rationale on record, legal systems with an adversarial legislative process and widespread conflict of interest among lawmakers typically offer more opportunity and incentive for cheap talk than for sincere utterances. Since insincerity undercuts the relevant kind of commitment, the question is whether or not we can identify any conditions in the legislative process that remedy these incentives. Taking a lead from Boudreau et al (2007), I think we can, which – if correct – means that lawmakers sometimes do in fact manage incur the right kind of commitment in offering legislative rationale. In addition, the resulting framework – at least in some cases – offers a plausible answer to the question *whose* utterances count, as far as fidelity to law is concerned.

The primary issue here is that since legislators may have significant incentive, for example, to exaggerate or misdescribe the content and/or purposes of a bill, interpreters must be wary of indiscriminate appeal to legislative history. Given the strategic environment in which bills (if lucky) become laws, sincerity is presumably only guaranteed when these incentives are somehow remedied. And they are remedied, say Boudreau et al, when it is sufficiently costly to make a statement or when the product of the penalty of insincerity and the subjective probability of verification is sufficiently great. In general, legislative history may be taken to be reliable, or credible, to the extent that the likelihood of cheap talk is minimised.

Based on the empirical work of Lupia and McCubbins (1998), the idea is that, under certain conditions, the non-co-operative nature of the legislative conversation can be remedied by 'institutional intervention'. That is, the design of the legislative process (in the US and similar systems) is such that, sometimes, the institutional structure substitutes for common interests, which are assumed in co-operative conversational settings. As I said above, the relevant institutional structures are those that generally make it costly to make statements or, as I will focus on here, make the product of the probability of verification and the penalty of lying sufficiently weighty.[6]

[6] See Lupia and McCubbins (1998) 17–96.

Boudreau et al point out that the legislative process is structured in such a way that it yields certain benefits to the majority party (especially since the late nineteenth century) and that it rewards and punishes certain behaviour on behalf of officials.[7] These rules, the authors argue, affect the communicative incentives that lawmakers have. In particular, these rules give members of the minority party an incentive, for example, to grandstand and to describe proposed statutes and their rationale in ways that do not reflect their genuine understanding of it (typically, exaggeration and misdescription are common). But these rules also give some actors, especially members of the majority party, incentive to 'speak their mind' or describe things how they genuinely understand them. If a committee's proposal, for example, is not representative of the majority party's collective interest, then it is highly probable that the proposal will be killed by either the Speaker or by the Rules Committee (ie it is highly probable that it will not advance to the floor).[8] Given these different incentives, we ought generally to take communication among majority members as significantly more credible than those of the minority.

This does not mean that we should simply ignore the minority and take everything produced by the majority as credible sources of justification. We have to discriminate between records of majority communications as well. In examining majority communication – such as committee reports – we must, then, look for two things: penalties for lying and probability of verification. Boudreau et al only roughly point out what kinds of situation in the legislative process count as providing penalties for lying; a more detailed identification is presumably further work for positive political theory. But they do identify some, such as the possibility of loss of leadership.[9] In the case of legislative rationale, I take it that, for example, exaggeration or significant misdescription of the justification behind a proposed statute might lead to losing a position as committee chair or as party whip etc. But only under certain circumstances is the probability of such a loss sufficient. If, for example, remarks about justificatory aims are made during open floor time while the House is in recess, there are no penalties to speak of.[10] Hence, such remarks should be ignored – as they frequently are, if Boudreau et al are correct. Other obvious penalties for misdescription might be loss of necessary support for passing the relevant bill. Such penalties are prominent, for example, in cases in which significant legislative bargaining is required in order to pass a bill. These sorts of penalty, as we will see, have a special sort of relevance to the discussion in this chapter.

Matters of verification are a little trickier here, since I am concerned with justifications rather than factual statements (as I take to be the main focus of Boudreau et al). Still, we can make relevant sense of the concept of verification by

[7] Boudreau et al (2007) 959–60.
[8] ibid, 979.
[9] ibid, 978.
[10] ibid, 978.

focusing on situations in which a possible statement grossly misrepresents what is commonly taken to be the justifying goals of a proposed law, that is, the ends for which the legislation is intended to be a means. If the audience of the relevant remark does not include anyone who is able to verify whether the justification is misrepresented or not, or if there is little chance that a third party later checks the records, then conditions for sincerity are not met and the statement should be ignored.

In general, whether or not the conditions for sincerity hold will be determined by whether the penalties for lying are sufficiently high given certain likelihood of verification and whether the likelihood of verification is sufficiently high given certain penalties for lying – that is, by whether or not the product of penalties for lying and probability of verification is sufficiently weighty. In addition, it is important to privilege only statements that are made relatively late in the legislative process, or else the statements – although sincere – may not reflect the ultimate bargains that actually facilitated the legislation. Thus, there are *three* main aspects to look for, vis-à-vis statements made by lawmakers in the legislative process: (i) the type of speaker (majority member or pivotal minority member), (ii) the expected utility of cheap talk, and (iii) when the statement is made.

Now, as I have mentioned already, it complicates matters even further that not only do we need to know under what conditions lawmakers' utterances in general count as sincere, we also need to know *whose* utterances – if sincere – count, vis-à-vis fidelity to law. Boudreau et al appear to assume that – as a general matter – it is the majority party that counts and that certain utterances by certain majority members can be taken as representative of the party's view of the purposes of a particular piece of legislation. Perhaps this is true, and perhaps not. However, at least in cases in which significant legislative bargaining between the majority and moderate members of the minority is required in order for a bill to pass, the context of bargaining provides incentive for sincerity and the need for bargaining determines *whose* utterances count.

To fix this last idea, let us consider the following scenario, borrowed and adapted from Marmor (2008).[11] Say that there are 100 members in a parliament. And that a bill has been initiated with the ardent support of 20 legislators. They need 31 additional votes, then, in order for the bill to pass. Assume that these 31 legislators are not ardent supporters of the bill, but that they have negotiated certain amendments to the initial bill in return for their support. Further, assume that the 20 ardent supporters have expressed an intention that would count in favour of extending the law to cover some borderline case *x* and that the 31 non-ardent supporters have expressed an intention that would count in favour of *not* extending the law to cover *x*. Given the fact that the commitments that the lawmakers have incurred recommend different decisions, vis-à-vis *x*, *whose* commitments should be taken to represent the commitments of the *law*? That is,

[11] See Marmor (2008) 436–37.

insofar as the aim is to maximise fidelity to law, whose expressed rationale should guide judicial decisions in possible legal cases concerning *x*?

This is not an easy question. As Marmor points out, giving effect to the expressed intentions of the 20 ardent supporters would be giving effect to a clear minority, which seems problematic. Not only are they a minority, they are the *smallest* minority with respect to this particular bill, with 31 moderate supporters and 49 that do not support it. Giving effect to the expressed intentions of the 31 moderate supporters also seems problematic, since they presumably know and care less about the relevant issues and also form a minority. Lastly, giving effect to some aggregate intention won't help at all since what created the problem in the first place were conflicting intentions between members of the majority. The lesson that Marmor draws from cases of this sort is that in many circumstances involving borderline cases, the legislature should not be seen to have *any* particular intention that could settle whether or not *x* ought to be included in the relevant rule's domain of application. If that is correct, then that points to another significant limitation of the model that I am proposing.

In cases that involve significant legislative bargaining, however, the model is able to avoid Marmor's problem and may lead to slightly different conclusions (although this will vary from case to case). The reason, explained above, is that when such bargaining is involved, the need for bargaining determines whose utterances count and the context of bargaining guarantees sincerity in those utterances, which in turn guarantees commitment to their content. The utterances that count are those made by the bargaining parties (in the context of bargaining) and these utterances can be taken to be sincere due to the presence of severe penalties for insincerity (here, loss of necessary support for passing the relevant bill). In the hypothetical case above, then, it seems clear – from the perspective of the present model – that, insofar as the aim is to maximise fidelity to law, judges ought to consult records of conversations between the 20 and the 31, since the hypothetical law is taken to be the result of significant legislative compromise. And it seems equally clear that both statements of the 49 (the minority) and the ardent supporters – when not made under conditions of sincerity – should be ignored. The model thus gives certain priority to the moderate 31 and, in particular, to statements by ardent supporters addressed to the moderates (in the context of bargaining).

To fix these ideas even further with an actual example, let me describe very briefly an analysis, by Rodriguez and Weingast, of the use of legislative history in interpreting the *Civil Rights Act of 1964*.[12] Very long story short, significant compromise was needed in order to have the bill pass, both in the House and Senate, mainly because of a Southern Democrats' filibuster. In particular, this required gaining the support of moderate Republicans, which generated a number of accepted amendments, mainly fashioned to protect the interests of American

[12] 42 USC §1981–2000(h).

businesses (especially in the North).[13] This resulted in a somewhat weakened bill, although the basic framework was unaltered, Rodriguez and Weingast argue.

Litigations following the final bill's enactment were numerous, and the courts often looked to legislative history as an aid in their decision-making process. History shows that, in the 1960s, 1970s and 1980s, judges frequently disregarded the compromises made at the later stages of the legislative process, relying primarily on statements made by ardent supporters, like the bill's manager (and Democratic whip) Senator Humphrey and Senator Clark.[14] The result was a string of expansive interpretations of certain portions of the Act. In *Griggs v Duke Power Co*,[15] for example, the court disregarded a crucial non-cheap statement made by ardent supporters aimed at Republicans in order to secure their support. The so-called *Clark-Case* memorandum includes a statement of one of the aims of Title VII of the Act: it is meant to '[protect] the employer's right to insist that any prospective applicant, Negro or white, must meet the applicable job qualifications. Indeed, the very purpose of Title VII is to promote hiring on the basis of job qualifications, rather than on the basis of race or color.'[16] In *Griggs*, the issue was whether or not Duke Power Co had violated the Civil Rights Act by requiring a high school diploma and an IQ test for the higher paying jobs in the company. Since the statement quoted from the Clark-Case memorandum presumably qualifies as rationale offered publicly under sincerity-inducing conditions, it is arguable that in *Griggs*, the court should – *insofar as its aim was to maximise fidelity to law* – have decided for the defendants, although it is an open question whether or not fidelity to law should have been maximised in this case.

If what I have said so far is correct, then judges should – insofar as the aim is to maximise fidelity to law – sometimes appeal to rationale expressed by lawmakers under sincerity-inducing conditions in order to settle borderline cases. One of the obvious limitations of this model is that it is limited to rationale that has actually been expressed, and so it makes sense to ask if there is any way in which to reasonably expand the model. In the next two sections, I will therefore consider two ways in which the model might be expanded to include rationale that is unexpressed but to which lawmakers are nevertheless committed (in the right way).

III. Is Expression Required?

In this section, I want to address a worry regarding the requirement that the relevant rationale be explicitly offered by lawmakers. The worry is that in some cases, the purpose of an enactment may be quite obvious, and in that sense publicly available. If that is correct, then there seem to be cases in which appeal could

[13] Rodriguez and Weingast (2003) 1472–73.
[14] See also Rodriguez and Weingast (2007) 1210.
[15] 401 US 424 (1971).
[16] 110 Cong Rec 7247 (1964).

reasonably be made to rationale that has not been explicitly offered, which may seem to indicate a problem for my view. If what I say below is correct, however, then one of the upshots of addressing this worry is that although expression is still the normal means by which lawmakers incur commitment to legislative rationale, the applicability of the model is significantly expanded by allowing for the possibility that lawmakers are committed to such rationale in virtue of its being obvious.

On the assumption that there really are cases in which there is an obvious and non-vacuous remedial purpose (that is, a sufficiently specific description of the mischief sought to be remedied), I think such cases are, on my account, best dealt with by saying that *if* the relevant rationale can in fact be legitimately appealed to, then that is because the legislature's commitment to it has been incurred in a way that is sufficiently similar to the way in which commitment is incurred in cases of expressly offered justification. Or, to put it more concisely, I think that the way in which commitment to a rationale is incurred in virtue of its being obvious is simply a special case of the way in which commitment is incurrent by expression.

On the account of assertion assumed throughout this book, assertions are made (in part) against a set of background propositions that may be called the *common ground* between the speaker and hearer. Assertions are seen as attempts to add propositions to the common ground, which accurately predicts that in ordinary situations speakers will *not* assert propositions that are already part of it. The participants in the relevant conversation, however, still count as being *committed* to the propositions that form the common ground. This can be fairly well explained by looking at cases of *presupposition accommodation* – cases in which the speaker will utter a sentence the assertive content of which presupposes something that is not yet part of the common ground.

Imagine, for example, that you don't know much about your co-worker and that she tells you that she has to pick up her sister at the airport. Her utterance *presupposes* that she has a sister, yet this information is not part of the common ground between the two of you. In order for the conversation to continue smoothly, you must therefore 'accommodate' the presupposition, by adding the relevant information to the conversational background without objection. If you do not object, you (and, of course, the speaker) will now count as being committed to the truth of the proposition that she has a sister – and you will do so *in virtue of* the fact that this information has become part of the common ground.

Presuppositions, then, are propositions *taken for granted* in a conversation. Moreover, it is *mutually recognised* that every participant in the conversation takes those propositions for granted. The relevance of this to my discussion here is that *if* a proposition is in fact genuinely obvious (and sufficiently salient), then it will be part of the common ground and thus the object of mutual commitment. Thus, although lawmakers can indeed be committed to genuinely obvious – but unexpressed – legislative rationale, such commitment will have been incurred in virtue of the rules of conversation, the same set of rules that explain expressly incurred commitment.

It might be objected that the commitment I am talking about here is the wrong kind of commitment – that it is a special sort of linguistic commitment that falls short of the kind of commitment required for my reply to the worry to work. I don't think that this is the case. The reason is that the obviousness of the relevant propositions gives participants to the conversation a warrant for treating each other in a certain way, namely as being committed to the truth of these propositions, unless otherwise indicated. Linguistic commitment is *no less normative* than any other form of commitment, or so I submit.

Moreover, to see that there is nothing uniquely linguistic about this phenomenon, imagine that Bobbi and Clive form a joint plan to rob a bank. Among the things that form part of the common ground between Bobbi and Clive are the following propositions: *Bobbi intends to rob a bank with Clive*, *Clive intends to rob a bank with Bobbi*, *Bobbi recognises that Clive intends to rob a bank with her*, and so on. Usually, several further propositions go into the common ground – some general and some specific. In Bobbi and Clive's case, the following propositions might for example be part of it: *Banks have security measures*, *This particular bank stands on a narrow one-way street*, etc. Bobbi and Clive are each committed to these propositions. Further, this commitment is mutually recognised and they are therefore warranted in treating each other accordingly. If so, then each is, for example, entitled to expect the other not to spend part of the preparation budget on a wide and unwieldy getaway vehicle – exactly *because* their commitment to the proposition that the bank stands on a narrow one-way street is mutually recognised. There is nothing linguistic about this explanation, yet the phenomenon seems to be essentially the same, which suggests that the linguistic case is simply a special case of a more general practical phenomenon. If that is correct, then the relevant commitment is no less normative than the practical commitment described in the bank robbery case.[17]

Although perhaps not decisive, this reply offers a plausible explanation for why genuinely obvious, but unexpressed, rationale *can* be appealed to in settling borderline cases (again, assuming the aim is to maximise fidelity to law). It may be appealed to *in virtue of being presupposed*, ie of being mutually accepted as part of the common ground in the 'legislative conversation'. However, it is still the case that, *normally*, commitment to the relevant legislative rationale is incurred via explicit statements made by lawmakers.

IV. Commitment and Counterfactuals

There is another way in which we might expand the model. The idea is that in cases in which commitments expressly incurred by (the appropriate set of) lawmakers

[17] This example is inspired by Lewis (1979), who also suggests a close connection between linguistic presupposition and joint plans, although his concern is with the analogy between the *accommodation* of presuppositions and of (sub)plans.

do not suffice to settle the normative question ('Ought *x* count as an *F*?'), the notion of commitment may be flexible enough to include *counterfactual* expression of intention, which *may* dictate a verdict. If that is correct, then perhaps it makes sense to expand the model in such a way that a court also counts as deciding in accordance with fidelity to law if the decision is in accordance with the rationale that (the appropriate set of) lawmakers *would be* willing to offer under sincerity-inducing conditions.

As far as the notion of commitment is concerned, I think that this is a reasonable expansion of the model. There are some significant limitations, however, on the scope of the resulting expansion. First, counterfactual propositions are themselves significantly vague. As Stoljar (2001) points out, standard theories of counterfactuals, such as those proposed, for example, by Lewis (1973) and Stalnaker (1968), analyse such propositions partly in terms of the *comparative overall similarity* of possible worlds.[18] The relation of comparative overall similarity, however, is vague, as Lewis himself points out.[19] This means that many counterfactuals that might be relevant with respect to settling borderline cases in courts are simply indeterminate (or false, depending on the theory).[20]

A second limitation on this possible expansion of the model is that it is often very difficult to answer questions about counterfactuals, not least when they concern human action. To be sure, there will probably be certain highly general counterfactuals that can be considered plausible descriptions of the relevant lawmakers' commitments, but the more abstract such descriptions are, the less likely they are to bring anything to bear on verdicts in particular borderline cases. In other words, in the case of counterfactuals relevant to settling borderline cases, the likelihoods of truth and practical application seem to be *inversely related*. Thus, although I think it does make sense to expand the model by including commitment analysable in terms of counterfactual claims about the willingness of lawmakers to provide express rationale under sincerity-inducing conditions, we have good reason not to overestimate the extent of the resulting expansion.

V. Legislative Rationale and Levels of Abstraction

This brings me to another significant issue left open by the present model, that that legislative rationale can be more or less general or specific, depending on how lawmakers choose to describe it. Which invites the following question: if a specific rationale recommends a different decision than a general one, do we have reason to believe that lawmakers are – as a rule – more committed to one than to the other? This answer, I think, is 'no'; it will vary hugely with circumstances whether

[18] See Stoljar (2001) 457–58.

[19] Lewis (1973) 94.

[20] For a good discussion of these issues as they relate to intentionalism in general, see Stoljar (2001) 457–63.

lawmakers are more committed to one than to the other, or equally committed to both.

To see why, consider the well-worn 'No vehicles in the park' example, in relation to which we can imagine the following plausible hierarchy of rationales:

Statute: No vehicles in the park.

Specific rationale: Reduction of noise, pollution, danger, etc in the park.

Intermediate rationale: Making the park a pleasant place to spend time.

General rationale: Promote the well-being of the public.

For the sake of argument, let us assume that lawmakers have – in one way or other – incurred commitment to each of these rationales.

Say that a case turns on whether or not an electric wheelchair ought to count as a vehicle for the purposes of the law. Each of the three rationales above arguably recommend the same decision, since counting electric wheelchairs as vehicles seems to help satisfy *none* of them. This invites at least two important questions. The first question is whether a court would – insofar as the aim is to maximise fidelity to law – be warranted in appealing to any one of these rationales in order to justify its decision that wheelchairs should not count as vehicles. The second question is whether the answer to the first question generalises to all borderline cases.

In the fictional example above, I think the answer to the first question is probably 'yes', on the assumption that the lawmakers are genuinely committed to each aim and regard the relatively specific aims as means to achieve the relatively general aims. But not all cases are so straightforward, which means that the answer to the second question is 'no'. In some cases, the different rationales may recommend *different* decisions, in which case it makes sense to ask whether the lawmakers can be taken to be *more* committed to the specific rationale than to the general one, or vice versa.

One way to go about answering this question is to ask *which* aims the lawmakers would be willing to give up if it turned out that the specific aims did not really promote the general ones. As Marmor (2005) notes, it would – as a matter of pure instrumental rationality – be incoherent to stick to the means if those means are inappropriate for achieving the ends, and so he holds that lawmakers' specific aims should be taken into account 'only if, and to the extent that, their realization is likely to enhance [the legislature's general aims]'.[21] If that is correct, then considerations of instrumental rationality seem to indicate that lawmakers are more committed to their general aims than to their specific aims.

However, not all questions regarding lawmakers' commitment to general vs specific legislative rationale can be answered by appeal to considerations of instrumental rationality. In some cases, the relationship between the general aims and

[21] Marmor (2005) 131.

the specific aims is not fundamentally a means–ends relationship at all. Rather, the general aim is a more abstract *redescription* of the specific aim. Since the commitment on behalf of the lawmakers is – in these cases – arguably just commitment to a single aim described in more or less abstract terms, it would make little sense to say that they are *more* committed to one aim than to the other.

In other cases, the relationship between the general aims and the specific aims is indeed a means–ends relationship, but a *complex* one. At the very general level, lawmakers often have several aims that need to be balanced. These general aims will typically move them to draft bills, but as the proposed legislation is worked on, more specific aims usually emerge. *Subaims* are adopted, which are taken to be the best available means by which to attain the original aim while taking into account other relevant aims. Thus, the more specific aims work somewhat like complex subplans, intended to promote certain general aims while minimising the danger of frustrating other general aims. In these cases, it becomes very difficult to determine whether the lawmakers can be regarded as more committed to the general aims (taken individually) than to the specific aims, or vice versa.

In yet other cases, the relationship between the general aims and the specific aims is also a means–ends relationship, but the lawmakers' commitment to the specific aims is affected by considerations *beyond* instrumental rationality. In many cases, the specific aims will be the result of legislative bargaining, in which case the moderate members of the minority may have 'signed off' on the general aim of the relevant bill (proposed by the majority) but not *entirely* on the means by which to achieve this end (also proposed by the majority). Thus, the moderates may negotiate a *qualification* on the means, for example by securing exceptions for certain things etc. In these cases, it also becomes difficult to determine whether it makes sense to say that the relevant lawmakers are more committed to the general aims than to the specific ones (or vice versa).

The above considerations are admittedly very abstract, but their role is just to illustrate a limited but important point: it will vary hugely with the circumstances whether considerations of instrumental rationality warrant that we take lawmakers to be more committed to their general aims than to their specific aims. We should be careful, therefore, in claiming that – insofar as fidelity to law is concerned – general aims trump specific ones (or vice versa for that matter). As a result, fidelity to law *alone* will often not suffice to settle a borderline case if two or more of the relevant aims (at different levels of generality) recommend different decisions.

To illustrate this point further with a concrete – albeit fictional – example, let us borrow one from Soames (2011). Imagine a community – Plainsboro – whose legislature enacts the following statute: 'It shall be a misdemeanor in the Township of Plainsboro for children on their way to or from school to accept rides in automobiles from strangers.'[22] The background rationale of the statute is to 'reduce

[22] Soames (2011) 36.

the danger of sexual assaults against the town's children'.[23] But, as we have seen, justifications come in different levels of abstraction, one of which can appropriately be characterised as the aim of 'reducing the danger of harm to [the town's] residents'.[24] Let us, for the sake of argument, say that the lawmakers are committed to both rationales.

To illustrate how the two rationales may recommend different decisions in borderline cases, Soames invites us to imagine that Susan – to whom the statute applies – works after school in a dangerous part of Plainsboro and that working there makes her a likely target of robbery. If Susan accepts a ride to work from a borderline stranger who is clearly not dangerous (and so the more specific background rationale would not warrant a conviction), appealing to the more general aim could be used to justify convicting Susan. The reason being that doing so would discourage people from getting rides to dangerous parts of town, thereby reducing the danger of harm to the town's residents.

Soames argues that this example shows that whereas appeal to the more specific aim can be appropriately used in determining borderline cases, the more general one cannot. If what I have said so far is correct, however, this is not guaranteed by fidelity to law considerations alone. In particular, Soames's case seems to be one in which the relationship between the general and the specific aim is not fundamentally an instrumental one. Rather, the general aim is a redescription of the specific aim, in which case I have said that it does not really make sense to say that the lawmakers are more committed to one than to the other. As a result, the judgment that judges *ought* to decide the case by appeal to the more specific aim has to be grounded in substantive considerations beyond fidelity to law.

VI. Authority, Legislative Bargaining and Maximising Fidelity to Law

To sum up the preceding discussion, I have proposed that *insofar as the aim is to maximise fidelity to law* in settling a borderline case, judges ought to decide in accordance with those legislative purposes to which lawmakers have incurred a commitment, and that the primary way in which lawmakers incur the relevant kind of commitment is via the express offering of legislative rationale under conditions that deter cheap talk. I also argued, however, that lawmakers may be committed to certain legislative rationale in virtue either of the fact that it is just obvious what that rationale is, and so there is no need to express it, or in virtue of the fact that they *would be* willing to offer the relevant rationale under sincerity-inducing conditions. And although such rationale may not always be available or,

[23] ibid, 55.
[24] ibid, 55.

if it is, it may not always suffice to settle the relevant case, we should nevertheless expect that in a significant number of cases, borderline cases *can* be settled in accordance with fidelity to law.

Now, even if what I have said so far is correct, all that this establishes is that in order to maximise fidelity to law, judges sometimes ought to defer to a law's operative rationale, ie the rationale to which the (relevant set of) lawmakers have incurred commitment. Since this is an instrumental claim, it doesn't tell us anything about the value of the relevant end, ie of maximising fidelity to law. Next, therefore, I want to turn to the second main question of the chapter, the question whether judges have reason to maximise fidelity to law, and if so, then under what conditions?

I think there are primarily two types of reason for judges to defer to the operative rationale of a statute. First, as Marmor (2005) has argued, judges can have *authority-based* reasons for such deference if, in doing so, they are more likely to comply with right reason than if they try to figure out the best course of action on their own. Second, judges can have *function-preserving* reasons to do so. In legal systems in which there is an adversarial legislative process and widespread conflict of interest – such as the US legal system – *legislative bargaining* is a fundamental feature of the system; without compromise among lawmakers, the system is not able to do what it is supposed to do, which is to produce legislation. On the safe assumption that the system is a valuable thing to have, there will therefore in many cases be a need to respect compromises reached in the legislative process, which in turn gives rise to reasons on behalf of judges to decide in accordance with the operative rationale of the relevant statute.

Marmor (2005) argues that 'generally, the primary way of justifying reasons for complying with the intentions of the legislator involves the very same considerations which are taken to vindicate compliance with an authority's directives in the first place'.[25] On the assumption that Joseph Raz's 'service conception' of authority captures the nature of legitimate authority – in particular, what he calls the *normal justification thesis* – it follows that deference to legislative intentions must be justified in one of the two following ways:[26] such deference is justified if the lawmakers can be expected either to have *expertise* with respect to the relevant domain of conduct or, in case the matter at hand is a collective action problem, if they can be expected to be in a superior position to solve the relevant problem. Following Marmor, call these the *expertise justification thesis* and *collective action justification thesis*, respectively.

Marmor further argues that there is rarely reason to believe that lawmakers are in a superior position to judges with respect to solving collective action problems. 'When the legitimacy of the legislator's authority … derives from the collective action justification thesis,' he says, 'judges have no particular reason to defer to

[25] Marmor (2005) 134.
[26] See Raz (1986) 53, for the basic idea.

the legislators.'[27] Thus, if deference to operative rationale is *ever* justified, according to Marmor, this justification must be grounded in the expertise justification thesis. If what I say below is correct, then this conclusion is too strong – respect for legislative bargaining can also give judges a reason to defer to a statute's operative rationale. Moreover, if such reasons conflict with authority-based reasons, then – as I will argue – the former often outweigh the latter.

As Marmor acknowledges, it is presumably often sensible – on the basis of the expertise justification thesis – to defer to a law's operative rationale (consider, for example, FDA and EPA regulations). But if expertise (with respect to a certain domain of conduct) is lacking, then judges do *not* have an authority-based reason to defer to the expressed intentions of the lawmakers. Further, if a particular judge would do better to try to figure out the best course of action on her own, then she would actually have a positive reason to *refrain* from such deference.

It is important, however, to note that there may be factors *beyond* considerations of instrumental rationality that are relevant to determining reasonable deference to a law's operative rationale. Although instrumental considerations play a major role in determining the extent to which the aims of lawmakers ought to be taken into account, there are certain *institutional* factors that may be crucially relevant as well. In fact, Marmor (2011b) argues that we cannot fully understand the concept of legitimate authority unless we give due consideration to the institutional setting in question. Most importantly, the reasons for complying with the directives of an authority are intimately connected to the reasons for *having* the institution in virtue of which the relevant authority possesses its normative power. That is, whether or not an authority is legitimate cannot, à la Raz's service conception, be determined *solely* by whether or not the subject, on average, does better – vis-à-vis conformity with right reason – by following the authority's directives (ie better than she would do on her own). Legitimacy, says Marmor, must *also* involve good reasons to have the kind of institution in virtue of which the relevant normative power exists.[28]

Something similar, I think, can be said with respect to a significant subset of cases in which judges lack authority-based reasons to defer to operative rationale, including cases in which they actually have authority-based reasons to *refrain* from doing so. On the assumption that there is good reason to have the relevant legislative institution, in particular some particular aspect of it, there may often be good reason to respect the aims expressed by lawmakers, *even when* the recommendations of those aims conflict with the recommendations of the expertise justification thesis. As I will illustrate with an example in the next paragraph, a very strong case can be made that operative rationale should often prevail *even if* adopting the relevant aims is – strictly speaking – not the best course of action (from the perspective of the expertise justification thesis). The primary reason is that if courts do not, as a rule, respect the essential compromises made in the legislative

[27] Marmor (2005) 136.
[28] This line of thought is further developed in Marmor (2011c).

process, then similar agreements will be harder to reach in the future, and the valuable institution of legislative bargaining is thereby undermined. Since such compromise is at the *foundation* of the institutional setting of many contemporary legal systems, it seems plausible to say that there are often weighty institutional reasons to defer to operative rationale, weighty enough to sometimes outweigh competing instrumental reasons.

Recall, for example, the case of *Griggs v Duke Power Co*, in which the question was whether or not Duke Power Co had violated the Civil Rights Act by requiring a high school diploma and an IQ test for the higher paying jobs in the company. One strong reason for thinking that the court should – *all things considered* – have decided for the defendants is, as Rodriguez and Weingast (2003) point out, that ignoring essential compromise and thus important parts of the operative rationale of a law will result in subsequent difficulties in reaching important agreements. Why would legislators have any incentive to offer support on moderate premises if the courts will interpret the law expansively according to the cheap talk of ardent supporters? Broad and expansive interpretations are sure to make subsequent legislative compromise very difficult. Since legislative compromise is an essential part of an institution that is good to have, courts therefore have a weighty reason to respect legislative bargaining in their decisions. And they respect such bargaining by deferring to the operative rationale of the law (if it is available).

Granted, *Griggs* was not a case of vagueness, or was in any case not treated as one. It seems safe enough, however, to say that if the judges in this case had a strong bargaining-based reason to defer to the operative rationale of Title VII of the Civil Rights Act, then surely judges can have such reasons in borderline cases too. If that is correct, then the normative argument offered in the preceding couple of paragraphs suffices for the philosophical purposes of this chapter. There is of course plenty of work to do in identifying the exact conditions under which the need to respect legislative bargaining provides the most weighty reasons. This, however, is presumably work for positive political theory and related fields, most notably behavioural law and economics.

As a last remark, I should note that bargaining-based considerations provide judges with a strong reason to defer to *specific* rationale rather than *general* rationale (in case they conflict). To see this, consider again cases in which the legislature's specific aims fail to promote its general aims. As I explained above, it would – as a matter of pure instrumental rationality – be incoherent to stick to the means if those means are inappropriate for achieving the ends. Respect for legislative bargaining, however, sometimes requires that deference be made to the legislature's specific aims *even if* they do not sufficiently promote its general aims. The reason is that in some cases the primary concern is not rational coherence on behalf of lawmakers, but rather whether or not ignoring their subplans – ie their own views about how to achieve their general legislative goals – runs the risk of impeding future legislative compromise. Insofar, then, as respect for legislative bargaining gives judges a reason to defer to the operative rationale of a law, it gives them a reason to privilege rationale that is relatively specific.

Let's, then, briefly sum up the most significant similarities and differences between authority-based considerations and considerations based on respect for legislative bargaining, vis-à-vis deference to such rationale. The chief difference, of course, is that authority-based reasons are – unlike bargaining-based reasons – not dependent on a particular legal system being in place. A second important difference is that whereas – as we saw – respect for legislative bargaining privileges specific rationale, authority-based considerations, as Marmor notes, privilege general rationale.[29] As for the main similarities, both types of consideration provide *non-absolute* reasons to defer to legislative intent and in both cases the weight of the relevant reasons is significantly affected by the dimension of time. As Marmor also notes, expertise changes over time and thus the weight of an expertise-based reason tends to decrease as time goes by.[30] Similarly, the importance of respect for legislative bargaining lessens as the bargains get older, since the negative 'feedback effect' on the legislature arguably decreases over time.

VII. Expressly Acknowledged Compromise vs Tacitly Acknowledged Compromise

I have claimed – and spent a significant portion of this chapter arguing – that one of the main reasons that judicial appeal to background justification is (all things considered) appropriately limited to operative rationale is that it respects, and thus helps to preserve, a fundamental feature of our legislative system – the valuable institution of legislative compromise. I want, therefore, to conclude the chapter by addressing the worry that the prescriptive account that I have been arguing for might actually *undermine* the ability to reach such compromise. The worry is worthwhile addressing because it illustrates something significant about the different kinds of strategic compromise at play in the legislative environment.

In order to see why this worry is worth taking seriously, consider the following argument about the strategic mechanics of legislative compromise, presented by Marmor (2011a):

> Consider ... two legislators striving to achieve a compromise on a particular legislative act ... Part of what enables opposing parties to reach a compromise consists in their ability to conceal, or at least not make very explicit, the overall implications of their collective speech. ... Had the conversational maxims that govern a strategic conversation been as clear and determinate as they are in the case of an ordinary conversation, it would have been very difficult to make strategic moves in the conversation. Precisely because there is some degree of uncertainty about the norms that govern the conversation, parties can exploit implications of what they say in ways which they would not be willing to make very explicit ex ante.[31]

[29] See Marmor (2005) 139.
[30] Marmor (2005) 138.
[31] Marmor (2011a) 94.

The thought behind this passage is, I take it, something like the following. Lawmakers are often able to reach compromises in virtue of the fact that it is uncertain how the courts will interpret certain bits of the legal text. Each party to the compromise hopes – and usually does what it can, in and out of Congress, to ensure – that its favoured interpretation will prevail. That is, a compromise may seem like a good bargain if each party has a reasonable chance to fight for their interests on another front. The worry that I have in mind, then, is this: if the courts were to follow my recommendation that appeal to legislative purpose be limited to operative rationale, legislators might lose a great deal of the incentive that they have to compromise, since it will in many (reasonably foreseeable) cases be evident which way the operative rationale leans. In other words, it would seem that certainty at once facilitates and impedes compromise! Something appears to be amiss.

I think that the context of the Civil Rights Act can help to dispel this worry, because it highlights a *general* feature of legislative compromise, a feature that may have been abstracted away from in Marmor's example. The feature is this: the bargaining positions of the two legislators in Marmor's example cannot – if the example is to reflect the legislative situations that *I* have been discussing – be seen to be equal. That is, we must recognise that the moderate legislator has the upper hand. Thus, although it is, I believe, correct that legislators in an *equal* bargaining position would lose their incentive to compromise if the interpretive principles employed by courts were clear and determinate, what matters in normal cases of the sort of legislative compromise I have been discussing is that the moderates, whose support is required in order to pass the relevant bill, believe that it is sufficiently likely that any compromises will be respected by the courts.

Now, this is not to say that it cannot happen, with respect to some parts of a bill, that ardent supporters and moderates are in roughly equal positions. In some cases, the parties will both be sufficiently eager to not let some issue, irresolvable by explicit agreement, sink the legislative effort. If so, uncertainty regarding judicial interpretation *would* offer a way to resolve the matter 'tacitly', as Marmor calls it, by leaving 'some of the implications of their collective expression undetermined or deliberately vague or ambiguous'.[32] And here it really is a pressing question whether the account I have been espousing undermines the possibility of such a resolution.

While I do recognise that there is potential trouble here for my view, I think there is a fairly natural strategy that lawmakers can, and probably *would*, employ in order to retain mutual incentives to compromise in the way suggested by Marmor, *even if* the courts were to consider operative rationale the only authoritative rationale. The strategic norm would be something like this: in order to ensure sufficient uncertainty regarding outcomes in the relevant types of case, take care

[32] Marmor (2011a) 94.

not to reveal any compromissory legislative purpose that might settle the matter. In fact, it is unlikely that lawmakers will even need any strategic instruction of this sort, since it is highly unlikely that any such explicit rationale will emerge, exactly because of the strategic considerations that Marmor identifies. Lawmakers will indeed have an incentive to *not* make explicit anything that might dictate a decision either way.

It seems, then, that the tension between the certainty required for the sort of compromise I discussed and the uncertainty required for the sort of compromise discussed by Marmor is only superficial, or in any case can be – and typically is – avoided by giving due attention to what the operative rationale does and does not contain. Thus, the notion of operative rationale does after all allow both for Marmor's 'tacitly acknowledged' type of compromise and for the sort of compromise highlighted by laws like the Civil Rights Act, which we can call *expressly acknowledged compromise*, both of which seem centrally important to the strategic practice of democratic lawmaking.

VIII. Conclusion

In this chapter, I have discussed some plausible restrictions on what can count as an answer to the question whether – from the perspective of the *law* – *x* ought to count as an *F*. If *x* is an absolute borderline case of 'F', I argued, *x* ought to count as an *F* only if this is dictated by the *operative rationale* of the relevant law, at least insofar as the aim is to maximise fidelity to law. The operative rationale of a law, I said, is normally the legislative rationale to which lawmakers have incurred commitment by *expressly* offering it during the legislative process under sincerity-inducing conditions, although they may also count as being committed to such rationale either in virtue of the fact that they *would be* willing to offer it under such conditions or in virtue of the fact that the relevant rationale is just *obvious*.

I also acknowledged, however, that there are significant limitations to this model. In many borderline cases, appeal to legislative rationale will not dictate a decision, either because the relevant kind of rationale isn't available or because, if available, it doesn't suffice to pull the decision one way rather than the other. These sorts of limitations on decision procedures, however, are to be expected, especially if such procedures depend heavily on contingent matters, as they do in this case.

I also argued that although appeal to operative rationale *can* help settle a verdict in a borderline case, it is not always the case that it *should*, which suggests a further significant limitation on the model. That is, it is one thing to determine what fidelity to law requires and quite another to determine whether or not fidelity to law should prevail over other competing considerations relevant to legal interpretation. I argued that judges can have at least two kinds of reason to maximise fidelity to law in borderline cases, ie to defer to operative rationale. They may have expertise-based reasons to do so, as discussed by Marmor (2005), or they may have reasons grounded in the need to respect legislative bargaining.

What we get from all this is the following, rather complex, generalisation about legal interpretation in borderline cases (for the sake of relative simplicity, I'm ignoring obvious commitment and counterfactual commitment in the following statement): in cases of vagueness, judges (*pro tanto*) ought – if the relevant legislation pertains to a domain of conduct with respect to which lawmakers possess relative expertise or if the legislation was reached through significant legislative bargaining – to settle the question whether *x* ought to count as an *F* by reference to the rationale (general or specific, depending on the type of legislation involved) offered expressly under sincerity-inducing conditions late in the legislative process by majority members or by members of the minority pivotal to the legislation. As I have stressed, this does not describe a complete decision procedure for resolving vagueness in the law. Nor should it. What it *does* describe is a modest but significant set of circumstances under which (a constrained form of) *intentionalism* is the most appropriate approach to legal interpretation in cases of vagueness.

8

Legal Practice and Theories of Vagueness

Scott Soames has recently argued that the fact that lawmakers and other legal practitioners regard vagueness as having a valuable power-delegating function in the law, evidenced by actual legislative practice, gives us good reason to favour one theory of vagueness – the *partial-definition/context-sensitive theory* – over another – the *epistemic theory*.[1] The reason, Soames says, is that for a significant set of cases, the former helps explain this function, whereas the latter does not. If Soames is right, then facts about legal practice can in an important sense adjudicate between rival theories of vagueness, which is an exciting conclusion, both from the point of view of philosophy of law and philosophy of language. The argument is also likely to generate considerable optimism about what else we might expect to learn about language by looking at the law.

The purpose of this chapter – which in some sense functions more like an appendix to the main discussion – is to significantly temper any such expectations, by arguing that – for reasons explained in chapter one – we have to give up the one premise of Soames's argument that he seems to take to be uncontroversial: that the legal content of a statute or constitutional clause is identical with its communicative content. Following Mark Greenberg, as before, we can call this a version of the *communicative-content theory of law*.[2]

As we saw in chapter one, the communicative-content theory has recently come under serious pressure from several philosophers of law and legal scholars, who point out that legal textbooks are full of examples in which there appears to be some clear difference between the communicative content of a statute or constitutional clause and its legal content. In response to this problem – which I called the *Gappiness Problem* – I proposed my own version of the communicative-content theory, on which the legal content of a (valid) statute or constitutional clause directly corresponds to (but is not identical with) its communicative content (determined by reference to what a competent, rational hearer would take the speaker to be intending to communicate in uttering the relevant words). By providing a specific account of how individual legal contents interact to produce the overall legal content of a given system, the picture I presented manages to explain away the apparent gaps in a principled and unified way, I maintained.

[1] See Soames (2012).
[2] See Greenberg (2011b) 217 ff.

Despite being a version of the communicative-content theory of law, however, the view presented in chapter one does not suffice to vindicate Soames's argument for the partial-definition/context-sensitive theory of vagueness. Since legal content is not identical with communicative content, facts about legal practice do not, after all, seem to be able to adjudicate between rival theories of vagueness – at least not in the way envisioned by Soames. Discussing, briefly, the cases of *Maurice v Judd* and *Bronston v United States*, I conclude by arguing that my point about Soames's argument is generalisable: owing to the fairly complex relationship between language and law, we should be quite cautious about drawing general conclusions about language on the basis of facts about legal practice.

I. Explaining the Value of Vagueness in the Law

In outline, Soames's argument for the partial-definition/context-sensitive theory of vagueness (hereinafter the 'PD/CS theory') runs as follows. His starting point is the observation that we seem to have good reason to believe that the value of vagueness in the law consists – in large part – in the fact that, under certain circumstances, it is a good idea for lawmakers to formulate laws in vague terms and thereby facilitate their incremental, case-by-case precisification, resulting from the adjudication of borderline cases aimed at furthering their rationale. Thus, one of the main functions of vagueness in the law, according to Soames, is to appropriately delegate a limited kind of lawmaking power to judges. For a significant set of cases, he says, the PD/CS theory entails this function, given certain basic suppositions about the US legal system and about legal practitioners, whereas its main competitor – the epistemic theory – does not. On the assumption that some version of hypothetico-deductive reasoning is appropriate in this case, legal practice therefore gives us good reason to favour the former theory over the latter, on Soames's view.

In the remainder of this section, I explain in brief the relevant features of the two rival theories of linguistic vagueness and the way in which they are supposed to generate different predictions about the value of vague language in the law – at least for a significant set of cases. I also explain how the predictions of the epistemic theory, but not the PD/CS theory, are supposed to conflict with our firm intuitions about that value.

A. Two Rival Theories of Vagueness

It is standard to define vagueness with reference to borderline cases, in the sense that most writers on the topic hold that a term is vague either *only if* or *if, and only if*, it has possible borderline cases.[3] It is possible, for example, for someone

[3] Sorensen (2001), for example, accepts the stronger claim that a term is vague *if, and only if*, it has possible borderline cases, but several authors on vagueness take the existence of borderline cases alone

to be borderline bald, for things to be borderline blue, for causes to be borderline probable, and so on. The nature of borderline cases is controversial, but most theorists would accept the characterisation that these are cases in which there is inherent uncertainty regarding whether or not the relevant term applies. They will vary, however, in how they think this uncertainty ought to be understood.

As the name suggests, the PD/CS theory, espoused, for example, by Soames himself, holds that vague predicates – such as 'tall', 'bald', 'blue', 'cruel', 'unusual', 'excessive', 'reasonable' and the like – are both partially defined and context-sensitive.[4] Such predicates are partially defined because the semantic rules governing them provide sufficient conditions for application and non-application that are mutually exclusive, but not disjunctively exhaustive. This is to say that in addition to the set of objects to which they apply – their *default extensions* – and the set of objects to which they do not apply – their *default anti-extensions* – there is also a set of objects to which they neither apply nor do not apply. For each vague predicate, then, there is a set of objects for which it is defined and a set of objects for which it is undefined.

Vague predicates are, on this view, also context-sensitive, because they have parameters that allow speakers to contextually adjust their extension and anti-extension, although their *default* extension and *default* anti-extension remain constant. Speakers have a certain amount of discretion, then, to adjust the extension or anti-extension so as to cover objects for which the predicate is undefined, to suit the needs of the relevant conversation. On this account, genuine borderline cases are cases in which the objects in question are neither in the default extension or default anti-extension of the relevant predicate, nor in the contextually adjusted extension or anti-extension. That is, borderline cases involve objects for which the predicate is undefined and which have not been 'contextually' included or excluded. For these objects, there is – on the PD/CS theory – *no fact of the matter* whether or not the relevant predicate applies to them.

On the PD/CS theory, genuine borderline cases can be included in the relevant predicate's extension or anti-extension further on in the conversation. If, for example, *o* is a borderline case of *P* and a speaker nevertheless predicates *P* of *o*, the audience may – instead of considering it an improper assertion – take this as an invitation to accommodate the speaker by adjusting the extension of the predicate to include *o*. Typically, such accommodation is successful only if the relevant adjustment suits the purpose of the conversation. But if accommodation is successful, *P* will then count as true of *o in that context* and *by stipulation*.

Unlike the PD/CS theory, the epistemic theory regards vague predicates as totally defined – they either (determinately) apply or do not apply to any given object. On this view, borderline cases arise when we cannot – in principle – know

to be insufficient for vagueness (see eg Soames (1999)). It is also important to distinguish between *intensional* vagueness – the possibility of having borderline cases – and *extensional* vagueness – actual borderline cases. Vagueness is properly characterised in terms of the *possibility* of borderline cases.

[4] See eg Soames (1999) ch 7.

whether or not a predicate applies to an object.[5] The issue, according to the epistemic theory, is therefore not that vague predicates are undefined, but rather that for a range of objects we simply don't know – and cannot know – *how* they are defined. The reason we cannot know this, on this view, is that knowledge requires a 'margin for error' – in effect, this ensures that knowledge never depends on 'epistemic luck'. In non-borderline cases, this margin is satisfied – it is known that if *P* determinately applies to *o*, then *P* applies to all objects relevantly similar to *o*. We know, for example, that if three grains of sand are not a heap, then neither are two grains of sand, nor four. In other words, we know that for the purposes of applying *P*, two, three, and four grains of sand are relevantly similar, which is required in order to be justified in believing, on any given occasion, that three grains of sand are not a heap.

According to the epistemic theory, this condition is – as a general matter – not satisfied in borderline cases. Vague predicates have sharp cut-off points the exact location of which we cannot know and so, for any object *o* in the borderline region of a predicate *P*, it is always possible that *P* does not apply to some objects relevantly similar to *o*. Thus, although *P* may in fact apply to *o*, we can never be justified in believing that it so applies, and so – as a principle – we cannot know that it does.

On the epistemic theory, speakers do not – semantically speaking – have discretion to contextually adjust the extensions and anti-extensions of vague predicates, since the relevant semantic rules provide sufficient conditions for application and non-application that are mutually exclusive *as well as* disjunctively exhaustive. Insofar as the primary concern in a given speech context is assertion – ie to state facts – there is thus no room, on this account, for scenarios in which a speaker predicates *P* of *o* in an attempt to stipulate that *o* is *P* (for the purposes of the conversation), unless the speaker's evidence is genuinely indifferent. Instead, every sincere utterance must be taken to presuppose that the speaker has sufficient evidence for believing that *o* is *P*. It follows from this that predicating *P* of a borderline object *o* is strictly speaking always improper, since borderline cases are cases in which we cannot possibly have sufficient evidence for believing that *o* is *P*, or that *o* is not *P*. It is important to note, however, that in some borderline cases, the evidence may slightly favour one over the other, in which case predicating *P* of *o* may be the right thing to do in scenarios in which a determinate verdict is for some reason required.

B. Inconsistent Predictions Regarding the Value of Vagueness in the Law

Recall that, according to Soames, we have good reason to believe that the value of vagueness in the law consists – in large part – in the fact that, under certain

[5] See eg Williamson (1994). For Soames's account of this view, see Soames (2012).

circumstances, it is a good idea for lawmakers to formulate laws in vague terms and thereby facilitate their incremental, case-by-case precisification, resulting from adjudication of borderline cases aimed at furthering their rationale. The basic idea is that actual legislative practice gives us good reason to believe that lawmakers and other legal practitioners themselves think that 'legislation sometimes involves broad agreement about central objectives, combined with disagreement or ignorance at the margins, plus a confidence that those who implement the law and adjudicate disputes arising from it will, through acquaintance with the facts of particular cases and the benefit of an incremental procedure, be in a better position than the lawmakers to further the law's rationale'.[6] In this way, facts about legal practice are supposed to generate solid intuitions about the value of vagueness in the law.

For the purposes of this chapter, I have no problems with Soames's claim about legal practice. It might, of course, be objected that legal practitioners in general do not – and should not – expect those who implement the law and adjudicate borderline cases to be concerned with furthering the law's rationale. Legal practice may seem equally to give us reason to believe that the value of vagueness lies in the fact that it allows legislators with conflicting intentions to reach a compromise and to fight for their interests on another front, ie in the courts. We can call this the *strategic-compromise function* of vagueness in the law. Soames is careful enough, however, to claim only that vagueness *sometimes* has the (more co-operative) power-delegating function he is concerned with. And this is all he needs to get the argument going.

According to Soames, the two theories of vagueness – the PD/CS theory and the epistemic theory – differ significantly in the extent to which they are able to explain our intuition about the power-delegating function of vagueness in the law. The difference, he says, lies in the fact that for a significant subset of borderline cases, the PD/CS theory allows judges and administrative officials – in line with our intuition about this function – to declare a borderline case *o* of *P* to be *P* for the purposes of one legal provision and not-*P* for the purposes of another, while the epistemic theory does not. On the PD/CS theory, it is perfectly permissible for speakers to adjust the extension of a predicate to include a borderline case in one context and to exclude it in another, depending on the purpose of the communication. If the purpose of a provision prohibiting vehicles in the park were to minimise noise pollution, for example, then it would make sense to count skateboards as vehicles. If, instead, the purpose were to reduce exhaust pollution and/or risk of serious accidents, then it would make sense not to do so. In this way, the PD/CS theory provides a 'smooth' and uniform explanation of how the judicial resolution of borderline cases is able to vary with the relevant provision's

[6] Soames (2012) 102.

rationale and the theory thereby straightforwardly helps explain what facilitates the value of vagueness in the law, according to Soames.

On the epistemic theory, however, things are different, Soames says. For any borderline object *o* of *P*, *o* already is or is not *P* and, insofar as the primary concern of judges in such cases is to report legal facts, their task is to figure out whether *o* is more like those objects that are clearly *P* (in which case *o* is probably *P*) or more like those that are clearly not-*P* (in which case *o* is probably not-*P*). In many borderline cases, of course, the evidence may be genuinely indifferent, in which case the judges must base their verdict on other grounds. This is to be expected, for example, when the objects in question are well into the borderline region. However, Soames says, in a significant set of cases, the evidence will provide some pull in one direction rather than the other, in which case the judge is typically required to reach a verdict accordingly, unless she has very weighty reasons against doing so. This is one way, then, in which the epistemic theory is supposed to generate different predictions than the PD/CS theory and conflict with our intuitions about the value of vagueness in the law.

More importantly, however, once it has been settled whether the evidence favours counting *o* as *P* or as not-*P*, the legal system is in an important sense stuck with that verdict. Insofar as the primary concern of judges in the cases under discussion is to report legal facts and the evidence favours, say, counting *o* as *P*, it would not be permissible to count *o* as *P* in the case at hand and as not-*P* in another (a difference in evidence relating to *o*'s being *P* notwithstanding). If, for example, a skateboard is judged to be more like things that clearly count as vehicles than things that don't, then – coupling Soames's account of the epistemic theory with his view of the role of judges – officials simply ought to consistently count skateboards as vehicles, no matter what the purpose of the relevant 'vehicle-related' provision is. According to Soames, then, the epistemic theory further predicts that there is a significant set of borderline cases the judicial resolution of which cannot vary with the relevant provision's rationale. This provides what is perhaps the strongest conflict with our firm intuitions about the power-delegating function of vagueness in the law, in Soames's view. As a result of all this, he concludes that we have a significant reason to favour the PD/CS theory over the epistemic theory. If Soames is right, then facts about legal practice can in an important sense adjudicate between rival theories of vagueness, which is an exciting conclusion, both from the point of view of philosophy of law and philosophy of language. It would also encourage investigation into further ways in which legal practice might be relevant to theorising about language. A good deal, therefore, is at stake.

In section II, we will take a closer look at the overall structure of Soames's argument, in order to see more clearly what work the communicative-content theory is doing. Before I go on, however, let me say that it seems to me that Soames significantly overstates the result of the argument. The reason is that – at least to a large extent – the weight of the reason in favour of the PD/CS theory is a function of the size of the set of cases for which the epistemic theory produces 'bad' predictions, vis-à-vis our intuitions about the value of vagueness in the law; and I think this set is significantly smaller than Soames suggests.

As we saw above, Soames does point out that the two theories make the same predictions with respect to borderline cases that are well into the borderline region. The set of cases with respect to which the theories make different predictions, however, is only a subset of the remaining set of borderline cases, definable – on the epistemic view – by the following four characteristics: (i) elements can be partially ordered along dimensions that determine the applicability of the relevant predicate; (ii) evidence for where an item falls on these dimensions is evidence for the claim that the predicate applies, or does not apply, to it; (iii) evidence that an item is closer to things that are known to be in the predicate's extension than to things known not to be in it provides justification for the claim that the item is in the predicate's extension; and (iv) the same holds for evidence that an item is closer to things known not to be in the predicate's extension than to things known to be in it.[7]

My concern about Soames's apparent conclusion regarding the weight of the resulting reason to favour the PD/CS theory is that very few legal provisions contain predicates that satisfy these conditions to a robust degree. The reason is twofold. First, it seems to me that the number of predicates that robustly satisfy these conditions is rather low – unidimensionally vague predicates (such as 'heavy', 'old', 'slow', and 'tall') are, of course, good cases in point, but once we move to multidimensional ones it quickly becomes very difficult to determine both where an item falls on the relevant dimensions and – perhaps more importantly – whether an item is closer to things that are known to be in the predicate's extension than to things known not to be in it; the set of things known to be, or to not be, in the extension of such multidimensional terms is simply too heterogeneous. As Soames himself points out, using the term 'neglect' as an example, 'the variation in behavior exhibited by a range of obvious, non-borderline cases, is enormous'.[8] As a result, I think Soames is wrong to claim that '*surely* many [vague predicates satisfy the relevant conditions to a robust degree]'.[9]

Second, in addition to these purely linguistic considerations, the predicates that seem to most robustly satisfy Soames's conditions are typically avoided in law. And rather easily so: the easier it is for a predicate to satisfy these conditions, the easier it is to replace them with a cut-off point somewhere along a sufficiently relevant dimension. The easiest cases involve unidimensional predicates and multidimensional predicates that have – or are significantly correlated with – at least one totally ordered dimension; instead of using 'young' and 'child', for example, legislators will typically specify an age, and safe driving can be regulated using a precise speed limit (along with a host of other more or less precise rules).

[7] ibid.
[8] ibid.
[9] ibid.

As the number of dimensions increases, the more difficult it tends to get to find an adequate, more precise replacement for the term in question. Consequently, we are more likely to see such predicates in legal provisions. However, it also becomes less likely that the relevant predicates robustly satisfy the conditions that define the set of 'test cases', the size of which determines the weight of the reason to favour the PD/CS theory. The likelihoods of a vague predicate satisfying Soames's 'test case' conditions and of it appearing in actual legal provisions seem to be inversely related.

As a result of all this, I think that even if we were to agree that the epistemic theory makes predictions that are not neatly in line with our intuitions about the value of vagueness in the law, those predictions concern a set the actual size of which is fairly limited. Thus, even if Soames's argument were unaffected by the problems facing his version of the communicative-content theory of law, the resulting reason to favour the PD/CS theory would be significantly less weighty than seems implied by his conclusion.

II. A Closer Look at Soames's Argument

Below, I provide what I hope is a reasonable breakdown of Soames's central argument. Basically, the idea is that the power-delegating function of vagueness in the law follows deductively from the PD/CS theory plus a few basic suppositions about the US legal system and about legal practitioners (referred to below as 'S1', 'S2', and 'S3'). If these suppositions are true and we have good reason to believe that one of the main functions of vagueness in the law is to appropriately delegate a limited kind of law-making power to judges, then – assuming that some version of hypothetico-deductive reasoning is appropriate in this case – we have good reason to believe that the PD/CS theory is correct. Or, in any case, good reason to favour that theory over those theories of vagueness that cannot explain this function – such as, and perhaps most notably, the epistemic theory.

We begin by assuming that the PD/CS theory of vagueness is correct. This is the hypothesis, then, which entails, among other things, that vagueness leaves borderline cases semantically undefined (assuming they have not been contextually included or excluded) and that the resolution of such cases modifies the linguistic content of the relevant statement (via the adjustment of the relevant predicate's extension). On the supposition that the legal content of a statute or constitutional clause is identical with, or constituted by, its communicative content – call this S1 – this further entails that vagueness *in the law* leaves borderline cases *legally* unsettled and that the judicial resolution of such cases modifies the legal content of the relevant statute or constitutional clause. If, moreover, we suppose that legal practitioners more or less understand these facts about vagueness – call this S2 – and that lawmakers can expect officials (on the basis of their obligations, qua officials) to maximise fidelity to legislative rationale in the resolution of borderline cases – call this S3 – then vagueness can, at least under certain conditions, be valuable as a tool for appropriately delegating limited rule-making authority to officials.[10]

This, then, is how we are supposed to get from the PD/CS theory to the power-delegating value of vagueness in the law. Insofar as our choice stands between the PD/CS theory and the epistemic theory, we therefore have good reason to favour the former over the latter, according to Soames.

A. Soames's Three Suppositions

Soames's argument is deductively valid (when laid out completely), and the methodology seems sound enough to me, although it does require, of course, that our intuitions about the value of vagueness in the law properly count as evidence. This might, of course, be objected to, perhaps as a general matter or specifically on the grounds that this particular issue is too complex to allow for reliable intuitions. And even if we accept that intuitions count as evidence, a committed epistemicist might simply argue that if the epistemic theory of vagueness is not consistent with our intuitions about the value of vagueness in the law, then so much the worse for those intuitions. They may give us reasons to believe in their content, but these reasons are easily outweighed by good theory, she might say.

Obviously, then, there is already plenty to disagree about. Here, however, I will question neither the intuition-based methodology nor the claimed deliverance of our intuitions, vis-à-vis the value of vagueness in the law. This, then, leaves only Soames's three suppositions about the US legal system and legal practitioners:[11]

S1 The legal content of a statute or constitutional clause is identical with, or constituted by, its communicative content.
S2 Legal practitioners more or less understand what vagueness is.
S3 Lawmakers can expect officials (on the basis of their obligations, qua officials) to maximise fidelity to legislative rationale in the resolution of borderline cases.

In his paper, Soames recognises that S2 and S3 might be considered controversial. Even if the PD/CS theory of vagueness were true, legal practitioners might not recognise this. That is, they might fail to recognise that vagueness leaves borderline cases semantically undefined and that the resolution of such cases modifies the linguistic content of the relevant statement. Consequently, assuming S1, they might also fail to recognise that vagueness in the law leaves borderline cases legally unsettled and that the judicial resolution of such cases modifies the legal content of the relevant statute or constitutional clause. In that case, S2 would be false, which would undercut our reasons to believe the hypothesis. Soames, however, thinks

[10] ibid.
[11] ibid.

that the way in which legal practitioners seem to think and behave gives us reason to believe that they more or less understand that vagueness is what the PD/CS theory says it is.[12]

It might also not be the case that lawmakers can expect officials to maximise fidelity to legislative rationale in the resolution of borderline cases. Perhaps officials have an obligation to do so, but do not reliably act in accordance with it. Or perhaps they have no such obligation. In this case, S3 would be false. It is Soames's contention, however, that actual legal practice indicates that officials do have such an obligation, and for good reason.[13]

On this occasion, we will not be further concerned with S2 and S3, although there is, of course, much to be discussed, as Soames himself points out. The remaining thesis, then, is S1 – ie Soames's version of the communicative-content theory of law – which, as I argued in chapter one, we have reason to give up in favour of a more complex version of the theory, on which the legal content of a (valid) statute or constitutional clause directly corresponds to (but is not identical with) its communicative content (determined by reference to what a competent, rational hearer would take the speaker to be intending to communicate in uttering the relevant words). This view, however, does not suffice to vindicate Soames's argument for the PD/CS theory. The reason is that the explanation it provides for our intuitions about the value of vagueness in the law is rather different from the one favoured by Soames.

Recall that, on Soames's view, vagueness in the law leaves borderline cases legally unsettled and the judicial resolution of such cases – by precisification – modifies the legal content of the relevant statute or constitutional clause. Given S1, ie an identity- or constitution-based version of the communicative-content theory of law, this entails that such resolutions (thereby) also modify their communicative content. In contrast, on the Pro Tanto account – as I called it – presented in chapter one, adjudication modifies neither the legal content of vague provisions nor their communicative content. Rather, adjudication provides (or constitutes) a reason to treat cases that are sufficiently similar to the resolved case in a certain way, a reason that the statute or constitutional clause itself does not furnish. Thus, although the law – broadly understood – has been precisified, perhaps in the aim of furthering the relevant provision's rationale, the provision itself remains just as vague.

This has significant implications for Soames's argument. Granted, facts about legal practice do seem to count against the epistemic theory to some degree, assuming that one agrees with Soames that the primary concern of judges is to report legal facts, but in order to explain the power-delegating role of vagueness in the law the Pro Tanto view only has to assume *some* theory on which vagueness leaves borderline cases semantically undefined. Nothing more is required of a

[12] ibid.
[13] ibid.

theory of vagueness in that respect. Thus, although the view is consistent with the PD/CS theory, it is ultimately indifferent with respect to it. As a result, facts about legal practice do not, after all, seem to be able to adjudicate between rival theories of vagueness – at least not in the way envisioned by Soames.

III. Generalising the Argument: Other Cautionary Tales

As I have indicated, I think that – in important respects – my point about Soames's argument is generalisable: since legal content is not identical with communicative content, we should – as a general matter – be quite cautious about drawing general conclusions about language on the basis of facts about legal practice. I want to conclude the chapter, therefore, by illustrating this generality with a brief discussion of the cases of *Maurice v Judd* and *Bronston v United States*.[14]

A. *Maurice v Judd*: Does Legal Practice Show a Need for 'Carefully Formulated Metasemantic Principles'?

As it is commonly presented, the main question in the curious case of *Maurice v Judd* was whether whales were fish, for the purposes of an 1818 New York statute 'authorizing the appointment of guagers [sic] and inspectors of fish oils'.[15] James Maurice sued Samuel Judd for unpaid fees for 'gauging, inspecting, and branding' three casks of fish oil, but since the casks inspected contained whale oil, Judd's primary line of defence was that whales were not fish. Both parties presented a number of people from various professions (anatomists, merchants, seamen, etc), testifying either that whales were indeed fish or that they were most certainly not. At the time, of course, people generally used the term 'fish' to include whales. The jury decided in favour of Maurice.

Sainsbury (2014) takes the jury's verdict in *Maurice v Judd* to tell us something important about language: by generating a dilemma, he says, it teases out the need for 'carefully formulated metasemantic principles', at least regarding creature-kind terms like 'fish'.[16] The dilemma, according to Sainsbury, is that either we take the jury's verdict to have been wrong, which upsets the idea that 'the meaning of a word in a community is determined by how it is used in that community',[17] or we take it to have been correct, which makes the disagreement between the disputing

[14] Mayor's Court of New York (1818) and 409 US 352 (1973), respectively.

[15] New York (State) Legislature 1819.

[16] Sainsbury (2014) 5. I avoid using the term 'zoological-kind term', since that seems to beg the question against outdated 'ordinary' understandings of the term.

[17] ibid.

parties a merely verbal one, rather than a substantive one.[18] He does not go on to tell us what these principles are, but it is clear that, by Sainsbury's lights, facts about legal practice allow us to draw significant general conclusions about language.

Now, on the assumption that legal content is identical with, or constituted by, communicative content, it makes sense – given some of the most prominent rhetoric in the case – to take the *Maurice* case to be about the meaning of the term 'fish', as used in the 1818 statute, and, thus, to view the jury's verdict from a linguistic perspective. However, once we give up this assumption in favour of the Pro Tanto view and remind ourselves that various kinds of legal content interact to determine the proper all-things-considered legal result of a case, both prongs of Sainsbury's dilemma go away. As we will see below, taking the jury's verdict to be incorrect does not require giving up the idea that the meaning of a word in a community is determined by how it is used in that community, and we can take it to be correct without reducing the dispute to a merely verbal one.[19]

To see this, consider Judge Riker's instructions to the jury. As he made clear, there were several ways to think about the case and it was the jury's job to decide on which of them to base the verdict.[20] And not all of them concerned the meaning of the term 'fish' (or 'fish oil'). One way to go, for example, was to take into consideration the fact that the common law treated whales as fish. If this was the controlling factor in the jury's decision, then taking the decision to have been incorrect is not inconsistent with the idea that the meaning of a word in a community is determined by how it is used in that community. Rather, the problem – on this analysis – is that the jury incorrectly gave controlling weight to what it thought was legal content provided by common law. And taking the decision to have been correct does not render the disagreement between the parties insubstantial, let alone merely verbal. As we see from the records, there was plenty of disagreement about what weight should be given to the common law in deciding the matter.[21]

Another way to reason about the case was to take into consideration not the actual meaning of the term 'fish' but the expected or intended application of the term 'fish oil'. That is, to place controlling weight on the fact that (most likely) the term was intended to include whale oil, not by virtue of this intention being a determinant, or evidence, of the actual meaning of the term 'fish', but rather by virtue of it being such an intention. If this was the controlling factor in the jury's decision, then taking the decision to have been incorrect does not conflict with the idea that meaning is determined by use. Rather, the error would have involved a misidentification of the legal content of the statute, or that unwarranted weight was given to the expected application of the term 'fish' (or 'fish oil'). And – as

[18] ibid.

[19] In addition, recent work on the semantics and pragmatics of disagreement shows that we have significant reason to doubt the idea that 'substantive disagreement requires agreement in meaning'. See eg Plunkett and Sundell (2013).

[20] See Sampson (1819).

[21] ibid.

Philips (2014) draws our attention to in his reply to Sainsbury – taking the decision to have been correct does not conflict with our intuition that the debate was substantive.[22] There was plenty of disagreement both about whether to give weight to the application intentions of the lawmakers and about the extent to which such intentions could be established.[23]

Maurice v Judd is an interesting case, to be sure, but, as the preceding discussion shows, Sainsbury is too optimistic about what we can learn about language by looking at the law. In order to generate the dilemma that motivates his conclusion that carefully formulated metasemantic principles are needed in order to account for creature-kind terms like 'fish', Sainsbury has to assume that the jury's verdict is to be evaluated exclusively from a linguistic perspective, which is correct only if the matter turns solely on whether or not the meaning of the term 'fish' includes whales. This makes sense on an identity- or constitution-based version of the communicative-content theory, but the dilemma goes away once we adopt an account on which the relationship between legal content and communicative content is more complex. *Contra* Sainsbury, legal practice does not show that there is anything 'paradoxical about fish'.[24]

B. *Bronston v United States*: Does Legal Practice Tell Us Anything about Implicature in Non-co-operative Contexts?

So far, we have been concerned with cases involving the legal (and communicative) content of statutes and constitutional clauses, but I think the cautionary lesson may extend even further. Consider, for example, the case of *Bronston v United States*, in which the question was whether Samuel Bronston had correctly been found guilty of perjury, by virtue of having provided an 'unresponsive' reply to a question that in ordinary conversation would be taken to trigger a relevance implicature (or quantity implicature, depending on the analysis), the content of which would be false.[25] Bronston, who for a five-year period had a personal bank account in Switzerland, was asked the following question: 'Have you ever [had a bank account in Switzerland]?' His reply was this: 'The company had an account there for about six months.'

Now, had the 'conversation' between Bronston and the examining lawyer been governed by the norms of ordinary conversation, ie the norms governing the co-operative exchange of information, Bronston would have counted as having – via implication – incurred commitment to the false proposition that he himself had not had an account in Switzerland. The Supreme Court, however, unanimously held that Bronston should not have been convicted of perjury.

[22] See Philips (2014) 381.
[23] See Sampson (1819).
[24] Sainsbury (2014) 5.
[25] 409 US 352 (1973).

Some authors are tempted to see this 'fact about legal practice' as evidence that in the context of cross-examination, the conversational maxim of relevance (or quantity) does not apply:[26] the thought is that absence of perjury means absence of implicature, which in turn means that the relevant maxim is suspended/in abeyance. If that is correct, then the law provides an important context within which we can empirically verify predictions made by different pragmatic theories: insofar, for example, as one theory of implicature predicts the existence of an implicature in *Bronston* while another does not, it seems that legal practice would give us a reason to favour the latter over the former.

Now, on the assumption that a witness is – vis-à-vis perjury liability – committed to *p* if, and only if, she communicates that *p*, it makes sense to take *Bronston* to be about the presence or absence of a false implicature, and, thus, to view the Supreme Court's verdict from a linguistic perspective. (The jury instructions provided at the District Court trial also do a lot to bolster this view.[27]) It may – on this perspective – also seem natural to take the Supreme Court's decisions as telling us something about the legal content of the perjury statute, namely whether or not it extends to false implicatures.

As before, however, the linguistic perspective is too simple. Most significantly, as the court saw it, the issue in *Bronston* was not at all about the presence or absence of a false implicature, but – rather – the proper distribution of responsibility in an adversarial fact-finding process. 'If a witness evades,' the court said, 'it is the lawyer's responsibility to recognize the evasion and to … flush out the whole truth with the tools of adversary examination.'[28] Its verdict was that the perjury statute did not apply to literally true but unresponsive answers, even on the assumption that such responses were 'false by negative implication.'[29] It is entirely consistent, then, with the court's decision to reverse Bronston's conviction that an implicature was in fact present in the context of his cross-examination. As a result, facts about legal practice regarding the treatment of perjury cases do not seem able to adjudicate between rival pragmatic theories – at least not in the way envisaged. It is simply not the case that a witness is – vis-à-vis perjury liability – committed to *p* if, and only if, she communicates that *p*.

Further, once we give up the assumption that legal content is identical with, or constituted by, communicative content in favour of the Pro Tanto view, the court's decision also no longer tells us anything about whether the perjury statute extends to false implicatures. As we have seen, on the Pro Tanto view, the fact that a statute provides a jury/court with a *pro tanto* reason to convict does not necessarily make for the end of the matter – it still has to be determined whether any other legally relevant considerations defeat that reason. The trial court held that none did, while the Supreme Court found otherwise. So, on the Pro Tanto view, it is not inconsistent with the Court's decision that the perjury statute applies to false implicatures.

[26] See eg Levinson (1983) 121–22, Martinich (1984) 33 and Sinclair (1985) 384.
[27] 409 US 352 (1973) 355.
[28] ibid, 358–59.
[29] ibid, 352.

Now, whether this is the best analysis of the case is up for debate, of course, but that is not the issue here; rather, the point is simply that once we recognise the fairly complex relationship between language and law, it becomes clear that the decision in *Bronston* does not tell us very much about the presence or absence of implicatures in the context of cross-examination or about the legal content of the perjury statute.

BIBLIOGRAPHY

Alexander, L (1992) 'Proving the Law: Not Proven', *Northwestern University Law Review*, 86, 905.

—— (2010) 'Telepathic Law' 27 *Constitutional Commentary* 139.

Allott, N and Shaer, B (2018) 'The illocutionary force of laws', *Inquiry* 61, 351–69.

Asgeirsson, H (2016), 'Can Legal Practice Adjudicate Between Theories of Vagueness?' in R Poscher and G Keil (eds), *Vagueness and Law: Philosophical and Legal Perspectives*, 95–126 (Oxford, Oxford University Press).

Atlas, JD and Levinson, S (1981) 'It-clefts, informativeness and logical form' in P Cole (ed), *Radical Pragmatics* (New York, Academic Press) 1-62.

Audi, R (1973) 'Intending' *Journal of Philosophy* 70, 387–403.

Bach, K (1994) 'Conversational Impliciture' *Mind and Language* 9, 124–62.

—— (2002) 'Seemingly Semantic Intuitions' in J Keim Campbell, M O'Rourke and D Shier (eds), *Meaning and Truth* (New York, Seven Bridges Press) 21–33.

—— (2006) 'The Top 10 Misconceptions About Implicature' in BJ Birner and G Ward (eds) *Drawing the Boundaries of Meaning* (Amsterdam, John Benjamins) 21–30.

Bach, K and Harnish, RM (1979) *Linguistic Communication and Speech Acts* (Cambridge, Mass, MIT Press).

Bader, R (2016) 'Conditions, Modifiers and Holism' in E Lord and B Maguire (eds), *Weighing Reasons* (Oxford, Oxford University Press) 27–55.

Balkin, J (2007) 'Original Meaning and Constitutional Redemption' *Constitutional Commentary* 24, 427.

Bar-Hillel, M and Wagenaar, WA (1991) 'The Perception of Randomness' *Advances in Applied Mathematics* 12, 428–54.

Barak, A (2005) *Purposive Interpretation in Law* (Princeton, Princeton University Press).

Barnett, R (1999) 'An Originalism for Nonoriginalists' 45 *Loyola Law Review* 611.

Baude, W and Sachs, S (2017) 'The Law of Interpretation' 130 *Harvard Law Review* 1079.

Baum Levenbook, B (MS) *Beyond Legislative Intent* (Manuscript on file with author).

Bennion, F (1990) *Bennion on Statute Law* 3rd edn (Harlow, Longman).

Bishop, JP (1882) *Commentaries on the Written Laws and Their Interpretation* (Boston, Little, Brown).

Bix, B (1993) *Law, Language, and Legal Determinacy* (Oxford, Clarendon Press).

Boudreau, C, Lupia, A, McCubbins, M and Rodriguez, D (2007) 'What Statutes Mean: Interpretive Lessons from Positive Theories of Communication and Legislation' *San Diego Law Review* 44, 957–92.

Bratman, M (1981) 'Intention and Means-End Reasoning' *The Philosophical Review* 90, 252–65.

—— (1999) *Faces of Intention: Selected Essays on Intention and Agency* (Cambridge, Cambridge University Press).

Broome, J (1997) 'Is Incommensurability Vagueness?' in R Chang (ed), *Incommensurability, Incomparability, and Practical Reason* (Cambridge, Mass, Harvard University Press) 67–89.

Calfee, J and Craswell, R (1984) 'Some Effects of Uncertainty on Compliance with Legal Standards' *Virginia Law Review* 70, 965–1003.

—— (1986) 'Deterrence and Uncertain Legal Standards' *Journal of Law, Economics, & Organization* 2, 279.

Carston, R (2010) 'Explicit communication and "free" pragmatic enrichment' in B Soria and E Romero (eds), *Explicit Communication: Robyn Carston's Pragmatics* (Basingstoke, Palgrave Macmillan) 217–85.

Chang, R (1997) 'Introduction' in Chang (ed), *Incommensurability, Incomparability, and Practical Reasoning* (Cambridge, Mass, Harvard University Press) 1–34.
Chilovi, S (2018) 'Grounding Entails Supervenience' *Synthese* https://doi.org/10.1007/s11229-018-1723-x.
Coleman, J (2007) 'Beyond the Separability Thesis: Moral Semantics and the Methodology of Jurisprudence' *Oxford Journal of Legal Studies* 27, 581–608.
Craswell, R (1993) 'Property Rules and Liability Rules in Unconscionability and Related Doctrines' *University of Chicago Law Review* 60(1), 1–65.
Dan-Cohen, M (1984) 'Decision Rules and Conduct Rules: On Acoustic Separation in Criminal Law' *Harvard Law Review* 97, 625–77.
Dancy, J (2000) *Practical Reality* (New York, Oxford University Press).
—— (2004) *Ethics Without Principles* (Oxford, Oxford University Press).
Davis, W (1984) 'A Causal Theory of Intending' *American Philosophical Quarterly* 21(1), 43–54.
Dretske, F (1988) *Explaining Behavior: Reasons in a World of Causes* (Cambridge, Mass, MIT Press).
—— (1989) 'Reasons and Causes' *Philosophical Perspectives* 3, 1–15.
Duxbury, N (2008) *The Nature and Authority of Precedent* (Cambridge, Cambridge University Press).
Dworkin, R (1977) 'The Model of Rules II' in *Taking Rights Seriously* (Cambridge, Mass, Harvard University Press) 46–80.
—— (1986) *Law's Empire* (Cambridge, Mass, Harvard University Press).
Easterbrook, FH (1983) 'Statutes' Domain', *University of Chicago Law Review* 50, 533.
—— (1988) 'The Role of Original Intent in Statutory Construction' *Harvard Journal of Law and Public Policy* 11, 59.
—— (1990) 'What Does Legislative History Tell Us?' *Chicago-Kent Law Review* 66, 441.
—— (1999) 'The Case of the Speluncean Explorers: Revisited' *Harvard Law Review* 112, 1913.
Ekins R (2012) *The Nature of Legislative Intent* (Oxford, Oxford University Press).
Ekins, R and Goldsworth J (2014) 'The Reality and Indispensability of Legislative Intention' *Sydney Law Review* 36, 39–68.
Endicott, T (2000) *Vagueness in Law* (Oxford, Oxford University Press).
—— (2011) 'The Value of Vagueness' in A Marmor and S Soames (eds), *Philosophical Foundations of Language in the Law* (Oxford, Oxford University Press) 14–30.
Endicott, T and Spence, M (2005) 'Vagueness in the Scope of Copyright' 121 *Law Quarterly Review* 664.
Feldman, Y and Teichman, D (2009), 'Are All Legal Probabilities Created Equal?' *NYU Law Review* 84, 980–1022.
Finlay, S (2016) 'Ought: Out of Order' in N Charlow and M Chrisman (eds), *Deontic Modality* (New York, Oxford University Press) 169–99.
Fletcher, G (2000), *Rethinking Criminal Law* (Oxford, Oxford University Press).
Fodor, J (1991) 'You Can Fool Some of The People All of The Time, Everything Else Being Equal; Hedged Laws and Psychological Explanations' *Mind* 100, 19–34.
Geis, ML (1995) 'The Meaning of *Meaning* in the Law' *Washington University Law Quarterly* 73, 1125–44.
Gilovich, T, Vallone, R and Tversky, A (1985) 'The hot hand in basketball: On the misperception of random sequences' *Cognitive Psychology* 17, 295–314.
Goble, L (2013) 'Prima Facie Norms, Normative Conflicts, and Dilemmas' in D Gabbay et al (eds), Handbook of Deontic Logic and Normative Systems (Milton Keynes, College Publications) 241–352.
Goldsworthy, J (1994) 'Implications in Language, Law, and the Constitution' in G Lindell (ed), *Future Directions in Australian Constitutional Law* (Sydney, Federation Press) 150–84.
—— (2005) 'Moderate and Strong Intentionalism: Knapp and Michaels Revisited' *San Diego Law Review* 42, 669.
—— (2003) 'Raz on Constitutional Interpretation' *Law and Philosophy* 22, 167–93.
—— (2010) *Parliamentary Sovereignty: Contemporary Debates* (Cambridge, Cambridge University Press).
Greenawalt, K (2010) *Legal Interpretation: Perspectives From Other Disciplines and Private Text* (Oxford, Oxford University Press).

Greenberg, M (2004) 'How Facts Make Law' *Legal Theory* 10, 157–98.
—— (2010) 'The Communication Theory of Legal Interpretation and Objective Notions of Communicative Content' *UCLA School of Law Working Paper Series, Public Law & Legal Theory Working Paper* 10–35, available at SSRN: https://ssrn.com/abstract=1726524.
—— (2011a) 'The Standard Picture and Its Discontents' in L Green and B Leiter (eds), *Oxford Studies in Philosophy of Law* Vol 1 (Oxford, Oxford University Press) 39–106.
—— (2011b) 'Legislation as Communication? Legal Interpretation and the Study of Linguistic Communication' in A Marmor and S Soames (eds), *The Philosophical Foundations of Language in the Law* (New York, Oxford University Press) 217–56.
—— (2014) 'The Moral Impact Theory of Law' *Yale Law Journal* 123, 1288–1342.
Greenberg, M and Litman, H (1998) 'The Meaning of Original Meaning' 86 *Georgetown Law Review*.
Grice, HP (1971) 'Intention and Uncertainty' *Proceedings of the British Academy* 5, 263–79.
—— (1989) *Studies in the Way of Words* (Cambridge, Mass, Harvard University Press).
Griffin, J (1986) *Well-Being: Its Meaning, Measurement and Importance* (Oxford, Clarendon Press).
Guttel, E and Harel, A (2008) 'Uncertainty Revisited: Legal Prediction and Legal Postdiction' *Michigan Law Review* 107, 466–500.
Hadfield, G (1994a) 'Weighing the Value of Vagueness' *California Law Review* 82, 541.
—— (1994b) 'Judicial Competence and the Interpretation of Incomplete Contracts' *Journal of Legal Studies* 23:1, 159–84.
Hahn, U and Warren, PA (2009) 'Perceptions of Randomness: Why Three Heads Are Better Than Four' *Psychological Review* 116, 454–61.
Harman, G (1986) 'Willing and Intending' in RE Grandy and R Warner (eds), *Philosophical Grounds of Rationality* (Oxford, Oxford University Press) 363–80.
Harnish, R (2005) 'Commitments and Speech Acts' *Philosophica* 75, 11–41.
Hart, HLA (1994) *The Concept of Law* 2nd edn (Oxford, Clarendon Press).
—— (1958) 'Positivism and the Separation of Law and Morals' *Harvard Law Review* 71, 593–629.
Hart, HM and Sacks, AM (1994) in WN Eskridge, Jr and PP Frickey (eds), *The Legal Process: Basic Problems in the Making and Application of Law* (New York, Foundation Press).
Hawthorne, J (2004) *Knowledge and Lotteries* (Oxford, Oxford University Press).
Hershovitz, S (2015) 'The End of Jurisprudence' *Yale Law Journal* 124, 1160–1204.
Hilpinen, R and Føllesdal, D (1971) 'Deontic Logic: An Introduction' in Risto Hilpinen (ed), *Deontic Logic: Introductory and Systematic Readings* (Dordrecht, Reidel) 1–35.
Horty, J (2012) *Reasons as Defaults* (New York, Oxford University Press).
Hurd, HM (1990) 'Sovereignty in Silence' *Yale Law Journal* 945–1028.
Husak, D (2008) *Overcriminalization: The Limits of the Criminal Law* (Oxford, Oxford University Press).
Jackson, F (1998) *From Metaphysics to Ethics* (Oxford, Oxford University Press).
Kahneman, D and Tversky, A (1972) 'Subjective Probability: A judgment of representativeness' *Cognitive Psychology* 3, 430–54.
Katz, G, Portner, P and Rubinstein, A (2012) 'Ordering Combinations for Modal Comparison' in A Chereches, *Proceedings of SALT 22* (Ithaca, CLC Publications) 488–507.
Kerr, B (2012) 'Dissenting Judgments – Self-indulgence or Self-Sacrifice?' https://www.supremecourt.uk/docs/speech-121008.pdf.
Kim, J (1974) 'Noncausal Connections' *Noûs* 8(1), 41–52.
—— (1993) *Supervenience and Mind: Selected Philosophical Essays* (Cambridge, Cambridge University Press).
Kolodny, N (2018) 'Instrumental Reasons' in D Star (ed), *The Oxford Handbook of Reasons and Normativity* (Oxford, Oxford University Press).
—— (unpublished) 'Toward a Principle of Instrumental Transmission'.
Kratzer, A (2012) 'The Notional Category of Modality' in A Kratzer, *Modals and Conditionals* (Oxford, Oxford University Press) 27–69.
Lawson, G (1992) 'Proving the Law' *Northwestern University Law Review* 86, 859.

Levinson, S (1983) *Pragmatics* (Cambridge, Cambridge University Press).
Lewis, D (1973) *Counterfactuals* (Cambridge, Mass, Harvard University Press).
—— (1979) 'Scorekeeping in a Language Game' *Journal of Philosophical Logic* 8, 339–59.
Lord, E (2008) 'Dancy on Action for the Right Reason' *Journal of Ethics and Social Philosophy* 2(3), 1–6.
Lupia, A and McCubbins, M (1998) *The Democratic Dilemma: Can Citizens Learn What They Need to Know?* (Cambridge, Cambridge University Press).
MacCallum, G (1966) 'Legislative Intent', *Yale Law Journal* 75(5), 754–87.
Manning, JF (2001) 'Textualism and the Equity of the Statute' *Columbia Law Review* 101, 1–127.
—— (2003) 'The Absurdity Doctrine' *Harvard Law Review* 116(8), 2387–2486.
—— (2005) 'Textualism and Legislative Intent' *Virginia Law Review* 91, 419–50.
—— (2006) 'What Divides Textualists from Purposivists?' *Columbia Law Review* 106, 70–111.
Mantel, S (2015) 'Wordly Reasons: An Ontological Inquiry Into Motivating Considerations and Normative Reasons' *Pacific Philosophical Quarterly*.
Marmor, A (2001) *Positive Law and Objective Values* (Oxford, Oxford University Press).
—— (2005) *Interpretation and legal theory* 2nd edn (Oxford, Hart Publishing).
—— (2007) *Law in the Age of Pluralism* (Oxford, Oxford University Press).
—— (2008) 'The Pragmatics of Legal Language' *Ratio Juris* 21, 423–52.
—— (2011a) 'Can the law imply more than it says?' in A Marmor and S Soames (eds), *Philosophical Foundations of Language in the Law* (Oxford, Oxford University Press) 83–104.
—— (2011b) 'The Dilemma of Authority' *Jurisprudence* 2(1), 121–41.
—— (2011c) 'An Institutional Conception of Authority' *Philosophy & Public Affairs* 39(3), 238–61.
—— (2013) 'Truth in Law' in M Freeman and F Smith (eds), *Current Legal Issues: Law and Language* (Oxford, Oxford University Press) 45–61.
Martinich, A (1984) *Communication and Reference* (New York, De Gruyter).
McNamara, P (2014) 'Deontic Logic' in E Zalta (ed), *Stanford Encyclopedia of Philosophy* (Stanford, CA, Stanford University), http://plato.stanford.edu/archives/spr2014/entries/logic-deontic.
Moore, M (2009) *Causation and Responsibility* (Oxford, Oxford University Press).
Morganti, M and Tanyi, A (ms) 'Can Reasons Be Propositions?' (Manuscript on file with author).
Neale, S (2005) 'Pragmatism and Binding' in Z Szabó (ed), *Semantics versus Pragmatics* (Oxford, Oxford University Press) 165–285).
—— Neale, S (2007) 'On Location' in M O'Rourke and C Washington (eds), *Situating Semantics: Essays on the Philosophy of John Perry* (Cambridge, Mass, MIT Press) 251–393.
Ostertag, O (2018) 'Cruelty and kinds: Scalia and Dworkin on the Constitutionality of Capital Punishment' *Inquiry* 61, 422–43.
Perry, J (2011) 'Textualism and the discovery of rights' in A Marmor and S Soames (eds), *Philosophical Foundations of Language in the Law* (Oxford, Oxford University Press) 105–29.
Philips, I (2014) 'Cetacean Semantics' *Analysis* 74, 379–82.
Pietroski, P and Rey, G (1995) 'When Other Things Aren't Equal: Saving Ceteris Paribus Laws from Vacuity' *British Journal for the Philosophy of Science* 46, 81–110.
Plunkett, D (2019) 'Robust Normativity, Morality, and Legal Positivism' in D Plunkett, S Shapiro and K Toh) (eds), *Dimensions of Normativity: New Essays on Metaethics and Jurisprudence* (Oxford, Oxford University Press).
Plunkett, D and Sundell, T (2013) 'Disagreement and the Semantics of Normative and Evaluative Terms' *Philosopher's Imprint* 13(23) 1–37.
Pollock, JL and Cruz J (1999) *Contemporary Theories of Knowledge* (New York, Rowman and Littlefield).
Poscher, R (2012) 'Ambiguity and Vagueness in Legal Interpretation' in L Solan and P Tiersma (eds), *The Oxford Handbook of Language and Law* (Oxford, Oxford University Press) 128–44.
Prakken, H and Sartor G (1996) 'A Dialectical Model of Assessing Conflicting Arguments in Legal Reasoning' *Artificial Intelligence and Law* 4, 331–68.
Radbruch, G (1910) *Einführung in die Rechtswissenschaft* (Leipzig, Quelle & Meyer).
Radin, M (1930) 'Statutory Interpretation' *Harvard Law Review* 43, 863–85.
Raz, J (1972) 'Legal Principles and The Limits of Law' *Yale Law Journal* 81, 823–54.

—— (1975/1999) *Practical Reason and Norms* (Oxford, Oxford University Press).
—— (1979/2002) *The Authority of Law* (Oxford, Oxford University Press).
—— (1985) 'Authority, Law, and Morality' *The Monist* 68, 295–324.
—— (1986) *The Morality of Freedom* (Oxford, Oxford University Press).
—— (2001) 'Sorensen: Vagueness has no function in law' *Legal Theory* 7, 417–19.
Recanati, F (2002) 'Does Linguistic Communication Rest on Inference?' *Mind and Language* 17, 105–26.
—— (2004) *Literal Meaning* (Cambridge, Cambridge University Press).
—— (2012) 'Pragmatic Enrichment and Conversational Implicature' in D Graff Fara and G Russell (eds), *The Routledge Companion to Philosophy of Language* (London, Routledge).
Rodriguez, DB and Weingast, BR (2003) 'The Positive Political Theory of Legislative History: New Perspectives on the 1964 Civil Rights Act and Its Interpretation' *University of Pennsylvania Law Review* 151, 1417–1542.
—— (2007) 'The Paradox of Expansionist Statutory Interpretations' *Northwestern University Law Review* 101, 1207.
Ross, J (2009) 'How to be a Cognitivist about Practical Reason' *Oxford Studies in Metaethics* 4, 243–81.
Ross, J and Schroeder, M (2012) 'Belief, Credence, and Pragmatic Encroachment' *Philosophy and Phenomenological Research* 88, 259–88.
Ruger, TW, Kim, PT, Martin, AD and Quinn, KM (2004) 'The Supreme Court Forecasting Project: Legal and Political Science Approaches to Predicting Supreme Court Decisionmaking' *Columbia Law Review* 104, 1150.
Sainsbury, M (2014) 'Fishy business' *Analysis* 74, 3–5.
Sampson, W (1819) *Is a Whale a Fish? An Accurate Report of the Case of James Maurice against Samuel Judd* (New York, Van Winkle).
Scalia, A (1987) 'Address Before the Attorney General's Conference on Economic Liberties in Washington, D.C. (June 14, 1986)' in *Original Meaning Jurisprudence: A Sourcebook* 101 (US Dep't of Justice).
—— (1997) *A matter of interpretation: Federal courts and the law* (Princeton NJ, Princeton University Press).
Scalia, A (2005) 'Law and Language (review of Steven Smith, Law's Quandary)' *First Things*, November, 37–46.
Schauer, F (1987) 'Precedent' *Stanford Law Review* 39, 571.
—— (1991) *Playing by the Rules* (Oxford, Oxford University Press).
Schauer, F (2010) 'Is There a Psychology of Judging?' in DE Klein and G Mitchell (eds), *The Psychology of Judicial Decision Making* (Oxford, Oxford University Press).
Schiffer, S (1972) *Meaning* (Oxford, Oxford University Press).
Schroeder, M (2007) *Slaves of the Passions* (New York, Oxford University Press).
Schroeder, M (2011) 'Holism, Weight, and Undercutting' *Nous* 45, 328–44.
Searle, J (1976) 'A Classification of Illocutionary Acts' *Language in Society* 5, 1–23.
Shapiro, Scott J (2002) 'Authority' in J Coleman and S Shapiro (eds), *The Oxford Handbook of Jurisprudence and Philosophy of Law* (Oxford, Oxford University Press) 382–439.
—— (2006) 'What is the Internal Point of View?' *Fordham Law Review* 75, 1157.
Shepsle, K (1992) 'Congress is a "They," not an "It": Legislative intent as oxymoron' *International Review of Law and Economics* 12, 239–56.
Silk, A (2017) 'Modality, Weights and Inconsistent Premise Sets' *Journal of Semantics* 34, 683–707.
Silver, K (ms) 'Constitution and Exclusion: The Limits of Sharing' (Manuscript on file with author).
Sinclair, MBW (1985) 'Law and Language: The Role of Pragmatics in Statutory Interpretation' *University of Pittsburg Law Review* 46, 373.
Smith, D (ms) 'A Problem for the Equivalence Thesis' superseded by 'The Meaning of a Statute and the Content of the Law' (Manuscripts on file with author).
Soames, S (1999) *Understanding Truth* (New York, Oxford University Press).

—— (2008) 'Drawing the Line Between Meaning and Implicature – and Relating both to Assertion' *Nous* 42:3, 529–54.
—— (2009) 'The Possibility of Partial Definition' in *Philosophical Essays, Vol II* (Princeton, NJ, Princeton University Press) 362–81.
—— (2010) *Philosophy of Language* (Princeton, NJ, Princeton University Press).
—— (2011) 'What Vagueness and Inconsistency Tell Us About Interpretation' in A Marmor and S Soames (eds), *Philosophical Foundations of Language in the Law* (Oxford, Oxford University Press) 31–57.
—— (2012) 'Vagueness and the Law' in A Marmor (ed), *The Routledge Companion to Philosophy of Law* (New York, Routledge) 95–108.
Solum, L (2008) 'Semantic Originalism' *Illinois Public Law Research Paper No 07-24*, available at http://ssrn.com/abstract=1120244.
—— (2013a) 'Communicative Content and Legal Content' *Notre Dame Law Review* 89, 479–520.
—— (2013b) 'Construction and Constraint' *Jerusalem Review of Legal Studies* 7(1), 17–34.
Sorensen, R (2001a) 'Vagueness has no function in law' *Legal Theory* 7, 385–415.
—— (2001b) *Vagueness and Contradiction* (Oxford, Oxford University Press).
Sperber, D and Wilson, D (1995) *Relevance* 2nd edn (Oxford, Blackwell Publishers).
Stalnaker, R (1968) 'A Theory of Conditionals' *Studies in Logical Theory* (American Philosophical Quarterly Monograph Series 2) 98.
Stanley, J (2005) *Knowledge and Practical Interest* (Oxford, Oxford University Press).
Sunstein, C (1989) 'Interpreting Statutes in the Regulatory State' *Harvard Law Review* 103, 405–508.
Väyrynen, P (2009) 'A Theory of Hedged Moral Principles' *Oxford Studies in Metaethics* Vol 4, 91–132.
Vermeule, A (1998) 'Legislative History and the Limits of Judicial Competence: The Untold Story of Holy Trinity Church' *Stanford Law Review* 50, 1833–96.
Waldron, J (1994) 'Vagueness in Law and Language: Some Philosophical Issues' 82 *California Law Review* 509–40.
—— (1999) *Law and Disagreement* (Oxford, Oxford University Press).
—— (2011) 'Vagueness and the Guidance of Action' in A Marmor and S Soames (eds), *Philosophical Foundations of Language in the Law* (Oxford, Oxford University Press) 58–82.
—— (2012) 'How Law Protects Dignity' *Cambridge Law Journal* 71, 200–22.
Waldron, K (2013) 'Jurisprudence for Hedgehogs' *NYU School of Law, Public Law Research Paper No. 13-45*, available via SSRN, http://papers.ssrn.com/sol3/papers.cfm?abstract_id=2290309.
Whittington, K (2004) 'The New Originalism' 2 *Georgetown Journal of Law & Public Policy* 599.
Williamson, T (1994) *Vagueness* (London, Routledge).
—— (2002) *Knowledge and its Limits* (Oxford, Oxford University Press).
Wodak, D (2018) 'What Does "Legal Obligation" Mean?' *Pacific Philosophical Quarterly* 99, 790–816.
Yaffe, G (2009) 'A Procedural Rationale for the Necessity Defense' *Journal of Value Inquiry* 43(3), 369–90.
Zimmerman, D (2002) 'The Constitution of Persons by Bodies' *Philosophical Topics* 30, 295–338.

INDEX

www.ingramcontent.com/pod-product-compliance
Ingram Content Group UK Ltd.
Pitfield, Milton Keynes, MK11 3LW, UK
UKHW020816290926
15470UKWH00003B/1189

9 781849 466066